STORIES I'D TELL IN BARS

JEN LANCASTER

Altgeld Shrugged, Inc.

❁ Created with Vellum

Contents

Stories I'd Tell In Bars

BY JEN LANCASTER

Other Titles

—————

BY NYT BESTSELLING AUTHOR JEN LANCASTER

Author's Note

MANY KNOW ME AS "THAT AUTHOR WITH THE FOOTNOTES." (I DIDN'T INVENT THEM, I JUST MADE THEM A *THING*.) HOWEVER, INCLUDING FOOTNOTES CAN BE A CRAPSHOOT IN AN EBOOK SITUATION FOR A VARIETY OF BORING, TECHNICAL, STACK-OVERFLOW REASONS. FOR THE PAPERBACK EDITION, I WORRIED FOOTNOTES MIGHT BLEED OFF THE PAGE IF I DIDN'T PROPERLY CALCULATE THE PRINTING SPECS.

SO, WHAT WOULD HAVE BEEN FOOTNOTED MATERIAL WILL NOW BE BRACKETED AND ITALICIZED WITHIN THE TEXT ITSELF. I PROMISE THIS WILL FEEL THE SAME. *[SWEARSIES.]*

ONE

Back In Black

"OLD AGE and treachery will always beat youth and exuberance."

\- David Mamet

I WAS HAVING A *MOMENT*.

A meltdown, if you will. I was at the intersection of bitch-panic and rage-stroke. Wasn't sure which path I'd follow, as both roads appeared equally rocky. The problem was I felt like the only analog girl in a digital world. Except no one would accuse me of being a "girl," as I was pushing fifty and everyone around me was twenty.

Not hyperbole, either.

The other Young Adult authors on the dais at the book convention that day had barely been out of their teens. Wide-eyed and fresh-faced, they were so young, so exuberant, yet to be worn down by a cynical world. And there I was in the middle of them, easily twenty-five years their senior, like Grandma Goddamned Moses. All I was missing was a Jitterbug phone and walk-in bathtub.

[What's more distressing is that I secretly covet both products.]

After I arrived home, I viewed tweeted photos of the discussion panel. In some respects, these pictures weren't as bad as I'd feared. I came across less "crone" and more "coach of a champion high school cheerleading squad."

Perched there in my sassy jean jacket with the collar flipped, highlight powder on point, lobbed haircut flat-ironed just-so, trying desperately to blend, any convention passerby would have thought, "She's not like a regular mom; she's a *cool* mom!"

You know what? Didn't make me feel any better.

While fifty might be the new forty, and given enough med spa budget, I can work it like it's thirty-five, the reality remains. The natural state will always be that the upcoming generation shoves the previous one out of its way. The only possible exception to this rule applies to those of us in Generation X, where the outnumbering Boomers refused to be budged. (Yeah, thanks for that.)

Anyway, a woman on the panel *[or girl?] [or gal?] [what is the acceptable nomenclature for a person of the female variety who is twentyish, I truly do not know]* was a debut author and her book hadn't yet been released.

Small and blonde, she seemed delicate, almost break-able, her movements birdlike. The poor thing was so nervous. This was her first live event. I wanted to knit her a sweater and cook her some soup. I hoped she had the fuzziest of jam-jams back at her hotel, and someone there to tuck her in, to kiss her forehead, and to tell her it was all going to be okay.

Then she said she'd gotten started writing on Wattpad

four years ago–literally *when she was a teenager*–and was up to ninety million views. Or likes. Or hearts. Or something. The audience went wild, having recognized her user name from the app, while I was still trying to work out, "A what-pad, now?"

Again, analog girl in a digital world.

After the panel ended, I continued to ruminate. *[Note: I wasn't mad at the author, she was darling.]* Regardless of how many memoirs and novels I'd written or the effort I'd devoted to my career, twenty-year-olds were becoming instant publishing superstars, despite *having never sold an actual book.*

Yeah, that felt *awesome.*

When I told my husband Fletch about this, he made the point, "Isn't that exactly what all you bloggers did to the old guard fifteen years ago?"

"No!" I barked. But, maybe?

"Are you jealous?" he asked. He was making himself a ham sandwich as we talked. Our brindle pit bull's soulful brown eyes traced his every movement, from the care with which he spread the mayonnaise to his precision in slicing tomatoes. Libby would do a better job convincing us she was starving if her muffin top didn't spill over both sides of her thighs when seated.

I replied, "*Please.* I am peanut butter *and* jelly at this point. What kills me is that publishers are dying to put out Millennials' books and if I want to keep working, I've got to cater to them, appeal to them. I have no idea how to do that! We speak entirely different languages. But I could learn theirs. I picked up Italian, right?"

He replied, "Yeah, but you forgot it immediately."

He selected the greenest, most crisp piece of lettuce from the bunch of romaine, rinsing the leaf carefully before blotting it dry with a paper towel, while Libby did her best to look like one of those despondent, wet pit bulls you always see shivering in a drainage pipe in the ASPCA commercials.

[If those ads don't make you send a check, or at least dive for the remote, then congratulations on having no soul.]

"I forgot how to speak Italian because I stopped taking lessons. That teacher was a con artist." *[This can't be said enough; the twelve dollar Italian lesson is a lie.]* I continued. "My point is, Millennials give zero fucks about learning *our* language. No one's running seminars in the office on 'How to Work with Generation X.' If today's any indication, people that age think I'm dinosaur. I'd be better off trying to write books for dogs."

Fletch tossed a piece of ham to Libby. She snapped it up with great delight, dancing and wagging before realizing she'd broken character. I could practically see her internal monologue: *"Okay, Libs, you're cold, you're damp, you're living in a big pipe. Go!"*

"People love books about dogs."

"I meant books for dogs to read to themselves."

He asked, "Is that why you're filling your McDonalds cup with wine?"

It was. I'd dumped my Coke, rinsed off the ice, and swapped it out for some of Italy's best screw-top *vino*.

See? I still knew one word.

I told him, "I hate feeling too old to matter. Advertisers are falling all over themselves to find ways to sway the Millennials. Yet in a great twist of irony, they are the least materialistic generation out there. They DGAF, which I had to look up the first time I heard it because I thought it had something to do with the Air Force. They don't want to accumulate, they don't want to acquire, they want experiences, they want to put good back into the world. Hey, pitch to *me*, marketers! Woo *me*! I *love* stuff!"

He laughed. "You had my sympathy... and then you lost it."

I was crabby and felt like sulking, so I said, "I'm taking my dog and my McGrigio to go watch the big TV."

[Many Millennials don't even have a big TV, if they own one at all. This, I'll never understand. How do they watch Game of Thrones *on an iPhone screen? Author George R. R. Martin put a lot of love into all that raping and murdering and pillaging and I feel these images should be viewed on no fewer than sixty inches of high definition.]*

I stuffed my pocket with a handful of treats to convince Libby I was the better bet than Fletch and his sandwich. We headed up the stairs.

Had Fletch understood how demoralized I was, he'd have been more sympathetic. Honestly, I felt like a former Kentucky Derby thoroughbred with a lame ankle and modicum of self-awareness, all, "Nah, don't bother with the pasture, bro, just send me to the glue factory already."

Normally, I have much more chill about the whole aging thing, to the point that I volunteer my birthdate even when no one's asked. "I was born in nineteen sixty-seven," I'll say.

"O-kay," the barista will reply. "Venti almond latte, then?"

I know I'm not over the hill, far from it. This is the healthiest I've been in years. I'm more fit now than I was at thirty. I look better, I live better, and I can run a mile without stopping. Not so impressive, except I couldn't do that when I was twenty. The world is still wide open to me and I'm just getting started in so many ways. It's my theory that you start to decline, that you truly begin to "age" when you decide, "That's it, it's over, there's no turning back now, this is my slow, steady descent."

That day, I worried I was rapidly approaching that point.

I swore to God, if I had to learn, say, one more new TV remote, I'd cross the Rubicon. No exaggeration, we have twelve of them and they're all the same exact size and shade of black and I can't read a button on any of them. I tell them apart by touch. The sticky one (from the time I had more spare ribs than napkins) switches it from satellite mode to PC; that's key if I want to watch anything other than what's on the Dish. If someone in this house ever invests in a box of Clorox wipes, I'm screwed.

[I would buy the shit out of a Jitterbug remote, just so you know.]

For a while, I thought texting was going to be my personal Waterloo. To be clear, this is not a technology thing. I understand texting just fine; I simply don't like it so I won't use it, except to tell someone I'm running late. In my opinion—which no one shares—texting is for, "Do you want me to pick up lunch, yes or no?"

I hate texts.

Texts are not for evergreen conversations, especially those better served by punctuation.

A text says, *"Whatever you're concentrating on is less important than what I'm about to say so immediately stop and indulge me, me, me, now, now, now."*

Unless you're on fire and you require my bucket of water, no.

Send me an email.

Text me an evergreen conversation and I'll get back to you when I'm good and goddamned ready, which might be two weeks from now. If your text is nothing but emojis–

if you expect me to decipher your message like I'm Howard Carter reading the hieroglyphics on the walls of King Tut's tomb–then I will get back to you never.

[I'm aware that everyone else on the planet prefers to text, even grandparents, if adorable BuzzFeed listicles are any indication, so it's a lost battle. But this is my windmill and I'll tilt at it all I want.]

Anyway, that day, I wasn't my usual *Almost Fifty, Fuck Yeah!* self. The event sent me into a shame spiral. Were all my skills suddenly useless? Was I on the verge of extinction? Had I mastered what no one needed anymore, having become adept at all the wrong things? I was great at driving a stick shift car. I could pen a letter in cursive like no one's business. I could dial a rotary phone lickety-split. I crushed it on the word processor. I could program a VCR-wait; I could never actually do that.

What's sad is that I felt far too young to have to fight to remain relevant. I hated worrying that I'd be written off because I'm not covered under warranty anymore, even with all these miles left, even though I still have some *[metaphorical]* new car smell left.

I was also a bit blue having come to a professional fork in the road. While interesting things were happening in Hollywood, I was struggling with traditional publishing. Editors said no one wanted my brand of humor anymore; levity and fun were out of style, like so many pairs of harem pants. Readers sought a deep emotional dive now. They wanted *capital-I Issues*. In my head, I was all, *"Have women stopped taking beach vacations? Are pedicures illegal? Have wine-and-book clubs been disbanded?"*

One editor told my agent, "You're showing me vintage Jen Lancaster; unfortunately, I want new Jen Lancaster."

As a memoirist, the stories and the person are one and

the same; they're co-mingled. Hearing I couldn't be *me* anymore if I wanted to write was a bite in the ass. *[P.S., if I could please be completely different and appeal to Millennials? Even better.]*

Seemed to me the whole universe was chasing after that which was shiny and new and *[in my opinion]* still unformed, that people like me, people my age, we were being forgotten, that our experience was no longer valued.

I groused to Libby, "Why not just put us in warehouses or something for the next forty years or so until we die, get us out of the way, you know, off the roads and all? Ooh, even better, they could do a *Logan's Run* with us!"

She kissed my nose. At seven, we're about the same age in dog years. She knows how I feel. I gave her a treat, which she chewed with great gusto.

I wondered, was I obligated to apologize for being on the cusp of fifty? Did I need to seek permission for still taking up my square foot of space? For even considering anything I had to say to be of relevance?

Then I thought, "Fuck. That. Noise."

Wine in hand, emotional support pit bull at my side, I reached for the stickiest remote and settled in to binge watch. I was a few seasons behind on *Younger*, a show where Liza Miller (Sutton Foster), a forty-year-old divorcé, pretends to be twenty-six to get a foothold again in the publishing industry, having previously left to raise her daughter. Lying about her age was the only way she could be hired.

This show was exactly what the doctor ordered.

A few points to make here: first, one would think that in an industry predicated on words, not image, age wouldn't matter, but *one would be wrong*. Liza absolutely must maintain the lie to keep her job. Shame on you and your ageism, Empirical Publishing. Nora Ephron would not be your friend right now.

Second, this is the only television program I've ever seen that's based on a book that I haven't read. Shame on me.

[Get on that, self.]

Third, do me a proper and watch this, please. The show is so well-written and acted. Sutton Foster's comedic timing is a thing of beauty, but Diana, the VP of Marketing, played by Miriam Shor, may well be my spirit animal. In real life, most of her publishing peers are being "rightsized," which is a fancy way of saying "being replaced with someone younger and less expensive, experience be damned."

What I particularly loved is how they demonstrate the situations in which Gen Xers feel cast aside and underappreciated for having paved the way.

Ahem.

[Wait, what is it I'm expecting here? A cookie? A hug? Additional wood for my cross?]

However, I didn't anticipate getting a sense of how tough it is for Millennial women right now. Things aren't all fixies and tats for them, either. There's this enormous mantle of expectation on them and they're literally never, ever going to be done paying student loans. Some of these kids are taking jobs in big cities making thirty bills a year *[that means one thousand, yes?]* and they're forced to share a single bedroom with three other people and eat canned tuna every day because they have six figures' worth of debt from an Ivy League education that got them a job where they make thirty bills a year.

Also? Bedbugs.

I guess it's not easy out there for anyone, at any age.

Viewing the show altered my mood so much that my fog of depression lifted. I packed away my self-pity. I realized I'm not such an old dog; I'm a middle-dog, if that. My best tricks are yet to come.

Younger was an object lesson in opting for the unconventional path. Had Liza not taken a leap of faith, had she done what everyone else told her to do, she'd be selling ties at Neiman Marcus, not helping Kelsey launch the Millennial imprint. She followed her gut and her reward was everything she wanted, including a smokin' hot twenty-six-year-old boyfriend. *[More thoughts on this in Chapter Two.]*

The show reminded me that I've never faltered when I've just been me, when I've been true to myself, when I've set my own course, instead of trying to follow what others have dictated.

A while back, I ran across this great line on, of all places, TotalFratMove.com. It read something like, *"Yeah, history repeats itself; it's called tradition."* I thought about that quote as the credits rolled at the end of season three.

I realized I *liked* vintage Jen Lancaster.

And I wasn't alone here.

I had a moment of great clarity... and then I decided I was done. I was done twisting myself into knots to satisfy the trend du jour, done trying to be all things to all people instead of just taking control and publishing the kind of stories I wanted to write on my own.

Real stories.

Stories I'd tell you if we sat down across a table from each other, connected face-to-face. We'd have no middleman there, no third party with an agenda jumping in, trying to change the direction of the narrative to better fit the theme to match some graphic the art department picked, or more appropriately align with the points in the publicity team's media pitch. We'd just be people, having a genuine conversation, talking and laughing.

Telling stories in bars.

The way it should be.

TWO

Happy Wife, Happy Life

"IT IS NOT LACK of love, but lack of friendship that makes unhappy marriages."

- Friedrich Nietzsche

SOMETIMES I JOKE with Fletch that if anything ever happened to him, I'd head straight to Cougar Town. I said this a lot in my *Twilight* Team Jacob days, I won't lie. However, nothing could be further from the truth now. In fact, the only part of *Younger* that bothered me was when forty-year-old Liza continued to date twenty-six-year-old Josh after the initial (acrobatic and enthusiastic) hook-up.

A *twenty-six-year-old* boyfriend?

Good Lord, that sounds exhausting. Thank you, no. The roommates. The pizza boxes. The futons. The hair pomade. The hair pomade alone could have its own spinoff.

Liza and Josh are perpetually falling into bed each

episode. On a visceral level, I get it. Plus, Darren Star created the show. He's the *Sex and the City* guy, so he's obligated to make for spicy viewing. But at some point, these two characters are going to take a cross-country road trip. If all they have to discuss while they're trapped in a front seat together is their acrobatic and enthusiastic hook-ups, that's going to get real boring, real fast. If she doesn't flat-out lose it because of the jug-band music he insists on playing, I'm betting they run out of shit to say once they get past Ohio.

Wait, I'm being generous.

More like Pennsylvania.

Personally, an age gap like that would be far too daunting for me. I couldn't be with someone who didn't get a Milli Vanilli reference, especially if I used it as a verb, i.e. "Wow, she really Milli Vanilli'd that Super Bowl half-time performance, amirite?"

I train with a guy who's twenty-six. He's the only person I know that age. On the plus side, he's the nicest young man ever. So polite, so well-mannered. He rarely makes me do rope slams because he knows how much I hate them; I appreciate that. Sometimes when I make meatloaf or oatmeal chocolate chip cookies, I bring him the extras in a Tupperware container. I fret over him if I think he looks too pale, which is always, because he wears SPF 100.

[Millennials are way into sunscreen, which, good for them. Their skin won't be like a football when they're my age. The whole no-cancer thing is a bonus, too.]

However, for all my trainer's fine qualities, I cannot imagine wanting to date him or anyone in his peer group. I'd much rather have margaritas with his parents so I could tell them what a great kid they raised.

Anyway, as I plowed through the second and third seasons of *Younger*, I was delighted when Liza started crushing on her more-age appropriate boss, who sleeps not on a sweaty futon in a fetid apartment with roommates and scads of empty pizza boxes (and a bathroom I don't even want to imagine), but in a sweet Manhattan town-house, on what I'd guess are Frette sheets. He also has a second home in the Hamptons, an added bonus.

I haven't yet started the fourth season, but I have high hopes for Not Josh.

What I'm saying is the only trip I'd take to Cougar Town would be literal. In lieu of having to date a twenty-six-year-old boy, I would find a town where they rescue wild cougars and then I would adopt a whole bunch of them and I'd take them home. The only swiping would be that of the big cats with their massive paws and razor-sharp talons when they eventually maul me to death.

Again, this sounds like a better alternative than Tinder.

Fortunately, Fletch and I are solid. I'd like to hope I won't be alone, and subsequently eaten by my pets, for many years to come. We aren't happy by accident. This is a conscious choice, one that takes daily action. If *you* would like a happy marriage, I have tons of sage advice that I'd love to share. For example, why don't you cook your husband a nice brisket once in a while?

[Feminist manifesto; you're writing it wrong.]

Lemme back it up for a sec; I'm not a marriage profes-sional. I want to make that clear. I have no formal therapy training, no state-sanctioned credentials, nothing like that. Should you want a list of step-by-step strategies to improve your spousal relationship by someone with advanced degrees/a lot of student loan debt, go elsewhere.

My advice trends less academic and more along the lines of, *"Don't laugh when he complains that the dry cleaner shrunk all his pants after multiple Brisket Nights."* True story.

My only claim is that I'm a skilled amateur at the whole "staying married" business. My expertise stems from being a difficult person successfully coupled for the better half of her life to an equally difficult person during particularly trying times.

When life's effortless, when everyone's young and trim and healthy and rolling in stock options, when there are no hills to climb or detours caused by roadblocks, it's easy to stay together. Throw in some conflict? Then not so much.

Like steel, marriages are tempered and proofed by flame, and, baby, we've been lit AF. Fletch and I have endured more than our fair share of bullshit in the past few decades, losing employment, cars, apartments, pets, peace of mind, tempers, safety and security, and, in Fletch's case, no fewer than five iPhones.

Who loses *five* iPhones? Those things ain't free, you know, even with insurance. One is tempted to string his phone through the sleeve of his coat, like a pair of children's mittens.

Phones notwithstanding, we've triumphed over the issues that send lesser mortals–and their separate vinyl collections–retreating to the safety of everyone's parents' basements.

Full disclosure: many of the problems we've faced have been our own damn fault. And sometimes, we've caused them even when we thought we were doing the right thing.

For example, Fletch quit his job to manage my career when we moved to the suburbs. For three years, I was the primary breadwinner and chief decision-maker.

Maybe I was living the feminist dream during that period, but the arrangement threw off the balance of power in the household. It didn't work for us. We learned we're happier when our lives are more egalitarian and decisions are made together. When we share the burden of resolution, we half the efforts and double the results.

So, credential-wise? We have a doctorate in *still liking each other*, even when we get it wrong. We seek each other out and we talk. *A lot.* We're like two Talmudic scholars, only instead of dissecting Jewish law, we're sharing a post-mortem on *90 Day Fiancé*. We don't agree here, as I am Team Mohamed and he is Team Seriously, Everyone on This Show Sucks, Why Are We Watching and Should We Do the Next One Now, I Think So, Yes.

Our world is a veritable barrage of words, of never-ending persiflage, with comments and phrases and opinions and observations hanging as dense in the air as cumulus clouds. When marriages fail–as half do–the culprit is often a lack of communication.

Couples simply stop talking.

As we're perpetually, eternally in conversation, we have a solid idea of who the other person is and on rare occasions when we're not sure what the other needs, we clarify.

For example, when one of us is upset about something, the other asks, "Do you want me to help you solve this problem or do you want me to commiserate?"

[Had I needed more than a good sulk on McGrigio Day, I'd have told him and we'd have talked it out.]

I mention this advice in every memoir because it's such a relationship saver, whether it's when you're communicating with a spouse, a friend, a coworker, etc. That's because unsolicited advice can be the match to the accelerant when all the other person needs is a hug.

[*Maybe you want to assess the situation before you automatically default to grappling your coworkers. Laws and all.*]

Also, before this goes too saccharine and turns into a sappy love letter, I'll be frank. There are times when my beloved is chewing his dinner too enthusiastically. [*I call these "weekdays."*] Even though his manners are excellent, the sound of his chewing is amplified because of a sinus surgery he had ten years ago. The procedure turned the inside of his skull into an echo chamber. Said surgery also rendered him–or so he claims–unable to blow his nose, so he constantly snuffles during allergy season. In Illinois, this runs all spring, most of summer, the entire fall, and the better part of winter.

As for the snuffle, it's more of a *hork*.

Hork. Hork, hork.

However annoying you may imagine this sound, I assure you, it's worse in person, thus making pork chops into *hork* chops.

Between the occasional *hork*, he's concurrently providing an in-depth summary of all the things that might have gone awry when he rewired the spark plugs on his project SUV while he flips through nine thousand channels on the kitchen TV, never landing on one for more than a millisecond. When faced with all these stimuli at once, I'll briefly fantasize about placing a throw pillow over his augmented blowhole.

I never want him to stop breathing... I just want him to shut up for a second. I'm always interested in what he's saying, but sometimes there's so many words to process that my brain needs to buffer to catch up.

When this happens, when Fletch notes the vaguely

murder-y set of my shoulders or my Kung-fu grip on the utensils, he'll end his soliloquy on All Things Pep Boys. He'll ask, "Should I put on *Tiny House Hunters* or sleep with one eye open?" and then we're fine again.

That is, until I commit the Cardinal Sin of letting the dogs lick empty cat food cans or I eat *[detonate]* a croissant in his car or I begin my PhD defense yet again on *Humidity, Its Impact on Color Treated Hair, and Whether I Should Cut My Bangs* or I tap into his secret stash of good paint-brushes and then it's *he* who wields the steak knife.

The key is not to be a person who doesn't suck because that's impossible. The key is to be a part of a couple who takes turns sucking *equally*.

In marriage, and, truly, in life, someone must have the last word. Think about it; how often is the last word the hill on which we'll die? We've all had times in our lives when the conflict's finally been resolved and everyone's about to retreat to a neutral corner and then someone can't help themselves, saying one more thing, and then, *bam!*

World War III.

The last word sets the stage for whatever comes next.

The last word is *everything*.

So, in the upcoming Fletch-centric stories, I'm ceding the last word to him. Because, really? I love tag-teaming our tales together. He's the only reason I would put on pants and go to a bar. He makes everything more fun. And after twenty-four years together, that's significant.

Each essay will end with his take on whatever I've written, thus allowing him the final say. He wasn't convinced about this until I pointed out that Chris Kyle and his wife did the same thing in the *American Sniper* book. *[Fletch was a huge fan of Kyle and his beard.]*

Fletch is delighted because whomever has the last

word is generally considered the victor. I'm pleased because this means he's obligated to finally read at least part of my memoirs.

Everyone wins. But mostly me.

And now, let's start at our beginning.

"THE ARMY CERTIFIED me to administer piss tests."

When Fletch dropped this gem into one of our earliest conversations, my initial reaction was not, "Oh, Imma *marry* him."

He and I had been speaking over the course of the week, but this is the first line I can recall from a time back when we were "him" and "me" and not yet "us."

I remember letting out a bark of laughter. *"That's* your home-run swing?"

In November of 1994, he and I were hanging out at the Wabash Yacht Club, a long-since-extinct Purdue bar. We'd just worked a weekend shift together at the new restaurant where we'd met. A fresh pitcher of Molson Ice sat between us, slowly leeching condensation onto the scarred wooden table. I gestured at him with my pint glass. "Your best line is telling me about watching guys peeing? I'm supposed to react... how? What's your expectation?"

I was giving him shit because that's what I did with people I dug; I messed with them. I liked that he was older than most of the guys on campus. Because of his prior military service, he was twenty-six, eleven months younger than me. My rule was that I'd only date those within a year's range of my own age. Older was creepy and younger was annoying. The year's span was the sweet spot.

He topped off my beer, all matter of fact. "Not a line. You asked me about what I did in the Army and I answered you."

He wasn't a smarmy suck-up. I gave him points for that, too. He could have said a bunch of stuff that made him sound heroic or badass. Instead, he went with quirky. Bold choice.

"Did you literally spend three years watching dudes whiz in cups or did you do anything else?"

He nodded. "Did plenty of stuff, but nothing else was as funny."

"Fair enough," I replied. "I'm curious; why did you learn that skill? Did you want to cheat the urine screens? Game the system?"

This wasn't an idle conversation; it was a fact-finding mission. If he was into weed, I needed to know. While not a big deal, and we could be friends, I didn't want to date a Doobie Brother. My personality aligned more with drinkers than pot smokers. No judgment, just preference. For me, it was like the difference between being a Dog Person and a Cat Person. Dog People should be with Dog People and vice versa. If you're into chasing cars, it's hard to relate to someone who compulsively bats yarn.

"Nah, that what the Army assigned. Who would pick that on purpose? Drugs aren't my thing. I go the other way." He raised his Molson Ice. "Thanks to Nancy Reagan, I learned to *just say no*."

He was joking, but this was a legitimate campaign in the early 1980s. Just saying no was how the First Lady suggested the youth of America avoid the whole scourge of recreational drugs.

Personally, I didn't need Mrs. Gipper telling me what to say; my own disinterest was sufficient. You see, I'd carefully constructed a narrative for myself back then. Even though my feet were planted in the middle of Huntington County, Indiana, my heart was in Martha's Vineyard. Narcotics were the purview of those who didn't flip their collars or layer their Izods, in my *[uptight, simplistic, naïve]* opinion.

Looking back, my abstinence was less a function of convictions and more because I was too much of a dork to be invited to parties. One doesn't stumble into many dens of iniquity on the way to a speech meet. Let's be real here. I'd have snorted rails off a hooker's ass if a preppy guy named Kip or Trip or Chip handed me the straw.

The first time I was offered drugs in college, I did say no... mainly because I couldn't figure out how to work a water pipe. The whole process gave me flashbacks to my failed attempts at learning to play the flute in sixth grade, what with all the coordination, awkward finger-place-ment, and breath control.

College did dispel some fictions of drug usage, though, like that anyone who smoked pot was lazy or dumb. My fraternity friends who partook–many of them Dean's List, and one a concert violinist–showed both initiative and commitment to the art of getting high. They could make bongs out of anything. I'm talking milk cartons, soda cans, cereal boxes, pineapples, lawn gnomes, saxophones, etc. Denis Leary provided the best summary in his show *No Cure for Cancer:*

"They say marijuana leads to other drugs. No, it leads to fucking carpentry."

I decided to finally just say yes at an apartment party second semester of my freshman year because I was anxious to fit in. The preppy thing wasn't the slam-dunk

I'd envisioned. Also? I was tired of being called "Nancy Reagan."

The off-campus scene was far different from that of Greek life, mysterious and unknown. Collars didn't instinctively defy gravity, nor loafers automatically call out for pennies. Some people didn't even *wear* loafers; I was intrigued. I wanted everyone to like me, to look past my crisp, pinstriped oxford and wool sweater tied *just so* around my shoulders, and see my sense of adventure.

I wanted to finally be cool.

Partygoers sat in a circle, perched on worn shag carpeting or rump-sprung Naugahyde couches, discards from a family's rumpus room, circa 1973. *"Okay,"* I thought. *"Let the high times roll."*

I valiantly tried to inhale whenever the ceramic pipe made it to me. Having committed to breaking the law, I was less concerned about possible arrest and more dismayed about all the germs on the mouthpiece. Trying to appear nonchalant, I'd take the pipe with my shirt-sleeve-covered fingertips. Was starched cotton an effective prophylactic against cold sores or lip herpes? I hoped so. No amount of Clinique Rose Gold gloss could cover that up, I was sure.

When it was my turn, I'd pull in a deep breath of smoke. I tasted notes of black tea leaves and wet dog fur and charbroiled ass. I'd hold my breath in my lungs as long as I could until I was overcome with the urge to cough.

Generally, this lasted two-tenths of a second.

Having now taken this dramatic step, having crossed the event horizon, I waited for the earth to adjust on its axis. I looked for all the secrets of the universe to be revealed, to be equally blessed and cursed with a swell of knowledge, to receive the kind of divine inspiration that prompted Samuel Taylor Coleridge to pen *Kubla Khan*.

How would I best use this altered state of consciousness?

What might I build or create or imagine, having freed a previously shackled portion of my mind?

What would my stately pleasure dome decree?

"Let's explode eggs in the microwave!" I exclaimed.

With rapt attention, my squad watched those matte white orbs rolling from side to side as they spun on the carousel, trembling slightly before detonating in a hail of yolk and shell, with surprisingly resonant and satisfying pops.

The host quickly caught on to what we were doing and forbade us to discharge any more of his breakfast foods. A gimlet eye on us, he retrieved his cat and locked it in his bedroom.

Please, we were idiots, not sociopaths.

Eggless, we had to dig deep into our collective well of creativity. My gay best friend mustered up a solution by way of neon glow stick. He ripped off the top with his teeth, as though activating a grenade in the heat of battle. He whipped that stick around the room, spraying every wall and dated furnishing and guest with stray bits of luminescence. Then he cut the lights for the full planetarium experience. We were splattered with thousands of tiny, incandescent stars, each of us part of a celestial canopy, heavenly constellations twinkling all around us.

We had become our own fabulous universe.

He had replicated the wonders of the cosmos, the magic and the majesty of the midnight sky, right there in that shitty West Lafayette apartment. The room was thrown into hyperspace and the stationary stars began to whip past in streaks of light. I felt like I was in the front seat of the Millennium Falcon, hurtling through space and time in a galaxy far, far away.

Everything surrounding me was beauty and truth and life.

Until it wasn't.

Sweat began to pour off me and the contents of my stomach–soft serve ice cream, peach schnapps, and a handful of wax potpourri I'd earlier mistaken for Gummi bears–roiled in an unholy stew. The smell of poached eggs was overwhelming. Without benefit of loafers or coat, I ran outside to vomit in a snowbank. All I could think the entire time was, *"Nancy Reagan was right."*

After that, I just said no to smoking pot, and, for quite a while, poaching eggs.

Over the next few years, I did experiment, yet found I was happiest with longneck Miller Lites or Solo cups full of trashcan punch, safely ensconced in the confines of a familiar frat house or bar. My few forays into illegal substances are much like my brief dalliance with eschewing loafers for Birkenstocks, a footnote on the permanent record that is my life.

An aberration, at best.

By the time Ronnie and Nancy rode off into the sunset at the end of his final term, NyQuil was the most rock-and-roll drug in my medicine cabinet. That's why I was pleased to hear Fletch was of the school of saying no, too.

I told him, "I don't smoke pot, either. The only time I tried weed was 1986. I threw up peach schnapps and potpourri in a snowbank after losing my shoes."

"Nice visual," he said.

"That's *my* home-run swing," I replied.

From that night on, we stopped being a "him" and a "me" and we became an "us."

———

FLETCH'S LAST WORD:

Reader, I married her.

I knew a lot of guys who did cool shit in the military. I am immensely proud of the eight years I spent in the Army Infantry, although I never transcended the level of "Garden Variety Grunt." I say that with all the due respect to my brothers that were harder than woodpecker lips and never wore a set of wings, beret, or other insignia that set them apart.

I've been fortunate to know and train with Army Rangers, Green Berets, and Navy SEALs, and the Army did send me to some advanced schools that would have been more impressive than the forty-hour Urinalysis Collection Observer course. Did I mention that qualified me to be a Company Prevention Leader? No, because I don't like to brag.

I was starting to think that Jen and I were meant to be. And I had learned in my communications classes that "self-disclosure" should be "appropriate and well-timed." No shit, that was my major. So, of course now was the appropriate time to disclose that, "The Army sent me to school to watch dudes pee in cups. Not just send them into a stall with an empty and trust the product is legit, but to visibly observe the 'sample leave the source and deposit in the receptacle.'"

The story was never intended to be impressive (obviously.) I figured if it creeped her out then it wasn't meant to be; but if she helped me finish that pitcher of Molson Ice, we probably had a future.

THREE

The Long Con

"IT IS the fool who thinks he cannot be fooled."

- Joey Skaggs

I AM NOT A VICTIM.

I mean, I'll never be one to give bank routing information to a Nigerian prince. I can't be scammed into wiring cash to a "friend" stranded in "Europe," no matter how legit the email may seem.

Because I'm paranoid, I refuse to share secure information on the phone, even when it's me who called the credit card company in the first place. I browbeat every single person holding a clipboard near my house because that's what robbers always carry to blend into the background.

Yeah, little girl, you *look* like a Girl Scout, but how can I be sure?

[Fortunately, those little tin foil hats flatter my coloring.]

The reason I see conspiracies everywhere is because

I'm the one-two punch of wary and observant. I'm your neighborhood Gladys Kravitz, peering out from behind her curtain sheers. Never forget, Mr. Kravitz called her paranoid, too, but Mrs. K. was the only one who figured out that something untoward was happening in Samantha Stephens' house.

Who knew what being witch-adjacent might do to property values?

Old Gladys was the patron saint of her block in my book.

Being called distrustful is compliment, as that means people know I'm paying attention. Sure, it's impossible to plan a surprise party for me, but I don't even celebrate birthdays now so it doesn't matter.

Anyway, I *used* to be all these things.

Because, despite my Constant Vigilance™, I never saw the long con coming when I signed up for an Italian class a few years ago. Originally, I'd planned on learning via the pricey Rosetta Stone discs, but then I found the deal of a lifetime.

"Only one hundred and twenty bucks for ten sessions? Taught by a native Italian speaker and not some grad student from Ireland like in college? Why, I'd be stupid not to take advantage of this opportunity!" I thought to my naïve self.

To backtrack, I'd started writing a bucket list book in 2013. Learning a foreign language was one of my goals. I decided on Italian because I loved my college 101 course, despite it having been taught by a genuine leprechaun. At a university famous for churning out astronauts and engineers, Purdue's Liberal Arts department used to be a bit of an also-ran.

[Full disclosure: I'd never be admitted to Purdue now, Little Miss SAT Score That Didn't Have a Comma in It.]

No one thought it odd to have an Irish citizen teach a bunch of American undergrads a romance language. Our entire course was conducted in Italian, not because this was more enriching, but because we couldn't decipher the TA's brogue when he spoke English. Remember how Bono used to sound in the early '80s, all *Soondah, Bluddah Soondah*? Charming on college radio, but kind of a bitch when figuring out which workbook pages to complete.

Luckily, I already had an ear for the language. When I was a kid, my maternal grandparents traded terms of endearment in Italian. Eventually I learned that when Grampa said, *"Tua nonna e la puttana del diavolo,"* the literal translation was, *"Your grandmother is the whore of the devil,"* which is less endearing. Still, should you need to insult someone, Italian's the most lyrical way to do so. Italian's neither too self-important like French nor too phlegmy like German. And, unlike Spanish, there's no impetus to roll the rs like a complete frigging douchebag.

[Confidential to the random dude in line ahead of me; it's Chipotle. *You shame everyone when you order a burrrrrrrito.]*

I was all about Italian class. One of the first things I learned (outside of the fact that I was the only person who completed assignments) was that Donatella, my instructor, led tour groups to Italy.

I was intrigued.

I planned to visit Italy as part of my book project. I wanted to figure out the whole travel thing on my own. However, the notion of heading overseas was daunting, especially since my last passport expired in 1989.

Perhaps the path of least resistance would be to sign up for one of these tours? Lots of other students had traveled with Donatella previously and the walls of her classroom were covered with shots of joyful travelers in front of picturesque places.

If I weren't already sold, then her subtle but constant pitching would have brought me on board. With the benefit of hindsight, I realize we never discussed class topics that didn't dovetail into something magical students might experience while on tour. At no point did I comprehend that the super-affordable language class was basically a time-share presentation.

Hearing fanciful tales of luxurious villas in Sorrento, I desperately wanted to join the Amalfi Coast tour, but the dates overlapped with a paperback release. I eventually pulled the trigger on a trip to Rome with Fletch in the summer of 2014. Turned out to be the vacation of a lifetime... but that's a whole different story.

With a happy ending.

The siren song of Italy was almost impossible for me to ignore after I'd been there. I'd find myself lingering in the international aisle at Mariano's Supermarket, quietly reading the labels on their few Italian products as a sort of mantra.

When Donatella announced a brand new, all-inclusive tour to her hometown in Southern Italy, with equal time allotted to the east and west coast, I had to find a way to get there. I mean, eating unlimited fresh pasta and swimming in foreign seas. What was not to love?

I ran the tour idea past my girls. I didn't pressure them, knowing how difficult it might be to schedule time away from their various responsibilities. In the end, the itinerary sold itself. Who wouldn't want to take a sail on the Adriatic? Or sample farm-to-table cuisine in the Italian countryside? Or visit a vineyard for a wine and Spumante tasting? Plus, the trip was all-inclusive at an incredibly fair price. Really? The whole thing seemed almost too good to be true.

[Spoiler alert: nothing is ever too good to be true.]

Our flight to Italy was glorious. Due to weather delays in other cities, the plane was practically empty. Everyone claimed her own row and we arrived in Rome rested and refreshed.

My friends Alyson, Julia, Alex, and Joanna, and I made up part of the tour group. The other half were three sets of couples from Northern Illinois and Southern Wisconsin, as well as my teacher and her husband. We noticed that all the couples indulged in the free beer and wine offered on international flights, whereas none of us drank to avoid jet lag.

After landing in Rome, we were to take a luxury coach to the Puglia region of Italy–the spur on the heel of the boot–where we'd spend four days relaxing in a quaint, family-owned beachfront hotel, with ample time to swim each morning before our excursions began.

The first sign of trouble was when the "luxury coach" turned out to be more of a modified "rape van." Since there was no cargo-hold, all the luggage was stacked precariously in the rear seats, causing Mt. Samsonite to avalanche whenever we'd hit a bump.

Longing for the comfort of an airport shuttle or perhaps a school bus, we crammed into seats best suited to kindergartners.

Donatella promised we'd have Wi-Fi in our rape van, which was important because our beach hotel wasn't wired. Except when we asked for the password, Donatella replied the Wi-Fi was in a different, four-days-from-now ride, not this one. Disappointing, but certainly not a harbinger of impending doom. I was sure I could find something to look at other than YouTubes of goats who yelled like people.

After hitting the road, we quickly deduced that thirteen passengers and twenty-six assorted bags put far too much strain on poor L'il Rapey's engine, so we found ourselves traveling at seventeen kilometers per hour.

Not an exaggeration. I could see the speedometer from my tiny seat.

Also, our driver had never driven a stick shift before, so we all tried to coach him through his learning curve. Upshifting from second to fifth was his signature move.

We played the game of noting what went faster than us on the road, but quickly tired of pointing out *everything*, including bicycles piloted by the elderly and infirm. Once the driver stopped concurrently blasting the air conditioner and the heat, our speed increased to an impressive twenty-five kilometers. The good news is that at no point did our chauffeur stop taking phone calls for his sport-book business while we crawled across the country. If you need to place a bet in Puglia, I know a guy.

Five hours into the journey that was supposed to take three, we stopped for lunch.

At a gas station.

Let me just say this; I've enjoyed many Amoco egg salad sandwiches in my day. I'm all about grazing from the cooler. Hell, half the reason I love road trips is because of gas station snacks, like those Hostess cupcakes with the orange frosting? My God, those give me life. But, when we've paid for an all-inclusive "luxury tour" of the greatest food country on earth, it's reasonable to expect an actual lunch, and not microwaved burritos eaten while sitting next to a pyramid of windshield washer solvent.

[Wait, I mean burrrrrrrritos.]

The gas station boasted a hot food bar in the corner next to the restrooms. The only items I recognized were oddly-topped pizzas and wizened old hot dogs, wrapped in antique French fries. Honestly, that combination would have appealed enormously, had they not been sitting under the heat lamp since Berlusconi's first bunga-bunga party. Also, I'd just observed the chef exit a toilet stall, bypassing that whole pesky hand-washing step entirely.

I bought a bottled water and sat at a picnic table next to the windshield washer solvent, across from Julia. She looked at my purchase and said, "You're not eating?"

I replied, "I don't eat in Italian gas stations."

She shrugged and took a bite of her zucchini and... paperclip? bumblebee? covered pizza slice. She chewed thoughtfully for a few moments before spitting out the pizza in a rather violent manner. I handed her my water. She rinsed her mouth and wiped her tongue with a stack of napkins, then stated, "I guess I don't eat in Italian gas stations, either."

Before we re-boarded, our faction asked Donatella what the deal was with the driver. She replied with what has since become a trigger mechanism for me. Said gesture is a shrug that includes a slight shoulder raise. There's also a turning over of the wrists and a splaying of the hands while the forearms spread. The mouth opens as if it means to say something, but then stops itself, as if having thought better. Occasionally, a small, "Eh," may first escape before the lips are pressed back together as the shoulders relax.

This, I have come to realize, is the universal *Pretending to Give a Fuck Whilst Giving Zero Fucks* motion.

She told us, "My contact did not send the right kind of bus." No, "I'm sorry, I'll make it up to you," or, "Crazy, right?" or, "Do you want to put fifteen bucks on Tampa Bay?"

"How long until we get there?" I asked.

"Soon," she replied, with great confidence.

This was the first of so very many untruths to come.

Thing is, no one from the Team Couple part of the group was complaining, largely because they spent the whole ride passed out due to the free airplane booze.

Three additional claustrophobic hours later, we arrived at our destination.

When Donatella described the hotel, she mentioned it wasn't going to be quite as plush as where we'd stay during later legs of the trip. She said her friend owned this place and it was located on a beautiful beach, so she was sure we'd love it.

I'd envisioned a Hampton Inn, clean and comfortable and nice, but not overly heavy on the amenities. Like, maybe there wouldn't be a minibar or free HBO.

Also, when Fletch and I had been to Italy, I learned how to not be an Ugly American. We tried to be Zen, extra chill, all Mr. and Mrs. Citizen of the World, ready to get down with whatever Rome had to throw at us. We accepted that American standards simply don't coincide with the European way of life. We learned we could have charm/history or we could have ice. Pick one. I wasn't expecting the Ritz.

However, given what we'd pre-paid per night, and that we'd traveled off-season, I had some expectations regarding cleanliness, comfort, and condition. History was optional.

Turns out our hotel had a bit of a past. In the 1960s, the building had once housed... wait for it... a gas station.

Decorated in a style best described as "Former

Communist Bloc Chic," my room boasted four twin beds, jutting from the walls at random angles best described as "snaggletoothed," all of which had to be navigated around to reach the broken TV, the disconnected phone, and the one functional light fixture out of five.

My room faced the beach, but I didn't have "windows" overlooking the water. Or, even a window. Instead, I had one small, gloomy security door draped in swaths of stained fabric, leading out to a balcony made of balsa wood and chewing gum.

With a single glance, I knew the structure wouldn't support the tiniest Italian, let alone my generous American ass, so I never went out there. The great irony is that although I was fifty feet from the water, I'd still have to listen to my ocean sounds app to fall asleep because, no window.

Anyway, after our arrival, we hit the showers. As I hosed off in the salt water [the only bonus, my hair looked like I'd used sea spray] I noticed a couple of bumps on my legs. However, I was distracted when I realized that the shower drain didn't perform this one crucial job and I'd caused a great flood. I used the bathmat to sop up what I could before meeting Joanna downstairs.

The hotel's website boasted striped umbrellas dotting a white sand beach, buffeted by a blue-green sea, which looked exactly like I'd imagine the South of France. I'm now convinced the photo was from the South of France, because our beach was nothing but gray sand, covered in empty Fanta bottles and Croatian medical waste, overrun by packs of stray dogs.

[In retrospect, I wish I'd taken photographs but I didn't realize that I might eventually need them for Plaintiff's Exhibit A.]

The hotel's owner knew I was an author, so he gave me a paperback about this place. Said book had a sandcastle on the front, making the town of Torre Mileto look twee and rustic. I thought this was a sweet gesture and I pledged to improve my attitude. More chill, less pill.

Later, I realized the shot wasn't a sandcastle at all; it was an old, broken paddleboat. So, we flew halfway around the world to stay somewhere that's filthy to the extent they were obligated to place garbage on the promotional material. Swimming was out, largely because none of us wanted Hep C. I never laid so much as a toe on the beach.

To keep from turning into a complete Ugly American, I began expressing my frustration by emitting heavy sighs, instead of, you know, cutting a motherfucker.

Sigh.

I tried to temper my disappointment over dinner. The wine helped. After we ate, we returned upstairs to barter with one another. I traded one of my non-blood-stained pillows to Joanna for an extra lamp and Julia swapped Alyson an adapter in exchange for actual shampoo instead of the dishwashing liquid packets placed in our showers.

I wanted to cry as I prepared for bed in my dismal room, noting that the bathroom in the Baptist summer camp I attended in junior high was far more opulent than this. The cracked white walls were gray with age and the drain was clearly just a suggestion, like one of those black holes Wile E. Coyote would paint on a wall to trick the Road Runner. The yellowed shower curtain clung tenuously to the rail on its three yet-untorn loops of plastic. Everything was covered with a fine sheen of rust or mildew. I imagine no one wanted to scrub the moldy parts of the tile too hard, as this was likely load-bearing penicillin.

Still, I pledged to wake up less Ugly American and more Citizen of the World, because when would I ever be in Italy with friends again? After washing my face in salty water, I conducted my first major transaction in the bathroom since arriving in Italy.

That's when I discovered that the toilet had stopped flushing.

I put on a bra and marched downstairs, because, non-functional phone.

In English and panicked Italian, I explained how the flush button on the wall wasn't working. Donatella's friend, the owner, offered me the Shrug, then told me I was probably trying to flush wrong.

Sigh.

I pleaded for his help, explaining again that the issue was the button itself and not my ability to apply pressure to it. Reluctantly, he followed me upstairs.

For modesty's sake, I'd closed the lid of the odd, square, taupe-colored toilet that had once been white, back during the promise of the Kennedy administration. And even though the non-functional flusher had nothing to do with my deposit, the owner insisted on looking anyway, prompting me to shriek, "No! No! It's the button, not the bowl!"

Then, because our waiter from dinner heard me, he came upstairs. He, too, decided to peek, despite my protests. That made for awkward meal service for the rest of the trip.

The men took turns using closed fists to punch the small metal disc on the wall, wailing on it as though they were our van driver's enforcers, trying to collect on a welched bet. After twenty-five wall-rattling blows apiece, the toilet finally, mercifully flushed.

"See?" the owner said, like somehow I was the problem. "Is fine."

We had to go through this exercise every time I wanted the toilet to flush, which is why I started to pee in the bidet.

I did not feel like a Citizen of the World.

At this point, I was ready to go home. I needed something to feel familiar or comforting. All I wanted was to watch *The League*, but Netflix didn't work in Italy. Or at least it hadn't worked while I was on Wi-Fi in Rome. Desperate, I tried anyway. Success! I found a solid signal on my iPad!

I laughed at how I had gamed the system. See, I didn't want to spend three bucks per episode on iTunes *like a sucker* when I knew I could watch a stream for free. Genius!

The next morning, I received a text from AT&T about being *two hundred and ten dollars* over the international data plan I'd purchased. I spoke to a customer service rep who told me that just because I *could* watch Netflix in Italy didn't mean I *should*.

Sigh.

Before breakfast, Joanna and I took a walk to see if the surroundings were less grim as we got farther away from the gas station, I mean, hotel. We discovered the only points of interest were yet another pack of stray dogs, *[they do become significant later, put a pin in that]* a camp of Romany caravans that had popped up across the street in the night, and a vacant lot where the world's biggest butternut squash was growing, amid rotting figs and a vibrant yellow-jacket population. Every single guest at breakfast mentioned the squash, largely because it had been the high point of the tour thus far. I wish I were kidding.

That's when I had my first epiphany. The thing about Americans is we seek out exotic destinations. In our heads, we're all secretly Anthony Bourdain. As a people, there's almost no place on earth we won't visit. That our group was only the second set of Americans to ever set foot in this town told me that we *weren't anywhere any American would ever be dumb enough to go.*

When I looked again at the book about Torre Mileto, I learned that this area is also considered *un paradisio per i serpenti,* which directly translates to "a paradise for snakes," particularly asps.

So, snakes *and* garbage in the marketing material. Noted.

After breakfast, we gathered for our first excursion. We didn't want to drag our electronics around, so we asked Donatella where we could store our valuables. Like many European hotels, we were required to leave our keys on the counter where anyone, including the new across-the-street-Romany neighbors, could retrieve them. Surely there was some system in place to keep guests' laptops or passports secure.

Shrug.

With a Best Buy full of products in our bags and everything else of value tucked in our money belts, we headed off to the museum, five minutes away in the picturesque village where Donatella grew up.

We boarded the new and slightly improved rape van driven by another of Donatella's friends, an Italian version of Matthew Modine. Five minutes later, plus forty, we arrived.

The museum was owned by yet another friend of Donatella's. The place wasn't a "museum" so much as a random collection of items that her pal found in a flea market and put on display. You know, I go to flea markets all the time to buy old shit. Apparently, I'm a curator, too.

Some exhibits featured old female department store mannequins with their thick '60s eyeliner and heavy lashes, only they were dressed in male soldiers' uniforms. The whole thing had a distinctively *RuPaul's Drag Race* feel to it.

I loved that part.

Donatella's docent friend–who, credit due, was so enthusiastic–would give lengthy, ostensibly educational Italian explanations about what we were seeing. Donatella would extrapolate these great swaths of information into a sentence, such as, "They were farmers."

I did not love that part.

The folks in Team Couple were hungover, so they were quiet at the museum, save for their leader, who was named Manny. He didn't speak Italian. Instead, he labored under the assumption that if he spoke rudimentary Spanish loudly enough, the Italians would understand. *[I bet the Germans have a snarky word for this, like shoutenassen-holen.]* Also, the faux-seum was the greatest thing he'd ever seen, which leads me to believe that Manny's home-town of Racine leaves much to be desired.

Next up, a visit to Donatella's family's chapel. I envisioned something windswept and romantic, a place where George Clooney might tie the knot. Instead, it was a single, windowless twelve by twelve room that smelled like centuries of fungus and toadstools, and contained a large statue of what I believed to be Jesus wearing gardening gloves.

I began to suspect we were there seeing the Blessed Father of Beets and String Beans not to connect with history, but because this was a free activity.

I was sensing a theme.

After all this excitement, which was almost too much for Manny, Donatella's aunt magnanimously decided to open her store especially for us. This was noteworthy because literally every single shop in the village was closed due to the Sabbath. We couldn't even buy water.

Her aunt's shop? She sold shoes. Slightly *used* shoes.

I had my second epiphany then – I realized we weren't in this town because it was beautiful or culturally significant, at least in any appreciable way. I realized that we were here because my teacher was looking for us to fund her trip back to see her friends and family.

Long con.

Long fucking con.

Back at the hotel for lunch, we watched Team Couple chug as much free wine as possible. None of us partook because the rape van didn't have a bathroom.

Conversation was impossible as Manny dominated the discussion. Neither Joanna, Alyson, nor I were Catholic, so we didn't know what a pilgrimage site was and Donatella didn't care to explain. Thankfully, Manny was there to share his profound thoughts and feelings on the concept of pilgrimage. We learned he was partial to cranberries, but didn't care for stuffing. His favorite part was the football afterward.

We boarded the van to get to the site. An hour into what should have been a forty-five-minute ride, I noticed that Julia's legs were dotted with the same kind of bites I had. The five of us did side-by-side comparisons. We were all chewed up, every one of us. That's when we discovered that the back of the van was completely infested with fleas. I guess you can't live around that many stray dogs without consequences.

Donatella's response?

The Shrug.

Our infestation problems were forgotten when we noticed how high up in the mountains we'd traveled. Plus, we were driving way too fast in a top-heavy rape van on terrifying two-lane switchbacks. One would imagine that Italian Matthew Modine might want to stop texting and pay attention, or at the very least not pass other cars on blind turns while doing so, but *one would be wrong.*

They say travel broadens you and teaches you about yourself. What I learned about myself is that I'm afraid of heights. When I relayed this story to a friend, she corrected me, saying what I was afraid of was toppling over the minuscule guardrail and bouncing four thousand meters down to my death.

Because we were in the wilds of the Italian mountains, no one bothers with fences so we also experienced the thrill of stopping short to avoid hitting free-range ponies.

The only thing that kept me from losing it was imagining that maybe if I died a spectacular death on an Italian mountainside, my passing would be mentioned on the news and I'd somehow become a cult favorite for dying too soon, too young, with too much unfulfilled promise, thus posthumously making my dream come true of hitting number one on the *New York Times* bestseller list.

But I probably wouldn't. I would likely just be dead and all my few mourners would discuss is how one person could have so damn many flea bites.

Two hours later, we arrived at the pilgrimage site. Was it a carnival? Was it a crematorium? We still didn't know.

Italian Matthew Modine launched into a lengthy explanation. As he spoke, I swore I smelled wine on his breath. Figured I was imagining, as what kind of professional would have drinks before transporting thirteen souls through harrowing mountain paths?

Donatella summed up his explanation as, "It's a pilgrimage site."

Fortunately, we had Manny there to explain the concept to us in *Shoutenassenholen*. Also, because Team Couple was too busy swilling wine at lunch, we hadn't left on time. We arrived too late to visit the Lombardian Gate, which is the one reason we'd come.

Shrug. Sigh.

We told Donatella that the ride terrified us and asked if there was an alternate way home, as Joanna had already consulted and found a solution on Google maps.

Donatella said that, yes, the highway route was shorter, but wasn't as scenic. This is what she did; she took whatever problem we pointed out and tried to spin it as a selling point, saying how Americans had never traveled her route. To me, that no American had this experience before wasn't so much a benefit as it was a warning.

I assumed I was the only person who was upset because... I'm not low maintenance. I'm often the center of my own small universe. And I have a PhD in complaining. (Hell, *I* tune me out most of the time.) That's why I figured my opinion was skewed.

To this point, though, we'd not downloaded with each other. Donatella's husband kept hovering around us whenever it looked like we might be bitching, so we didn't have a chance to talk until then.

Consensus?

Not only was this trip miserable and uncomfortable

and in no way as advertised, but also dangerous and terri-fying. We'd each privately thought ourselves jerks for being unhappy, but it wasn't until we came together that we realized this shit wasn't right, regardless of how much everything delighted Manny. [*I believe my exact words were, "Manny would fuck a ham sandwich and call it a Merry Christmas," so his opinion was to be discounted.*]

Now, it'd be one thing if we were friends with Donatella and all came to her hometown to hang out with all her people. But to have paid a whole bunch of money and been sold a bill of goods?

Long con.

On the three-hour-plus trip home–in the dark, in the rain, on mountain roads also inhabited by free-range cattle–we learned that our expedition to the organic farm-house had been cancelled, as had our boat trip around the Adriatic. All the other excursions involved more treks through the mountains with a driver I later did witness drinking while in our employ. When Joanna suggested that consuming vino on the job was cultural, I asked her how that worked out for Princess Diana.

[*I know. Still too soon. Doesn't invalidate my point.*]

Essentially, we'd be stuck on Syphilis Beach for the next three days without a single damn thing to do that wasn't terrifying or dangerous. Donatella had proven to be a fraud, as everything thus far had been grossly exagger-ated at best or a lie. Stood to reason that nothing would improve.

With Donatella's husband desperately trying to eaves-drop, we whispered about a possible mutiny, while furi-ously scratching our flea bites.

Our decision to abandon the tour wasn't set until we returned to the hotel. We were promised a night of entertainment, which turned out to be thirty local eight-year-olds dancing the Tarantella for three hours.

I'm not sure if you buy into the whole afterlife business. I do. I believe our actions here on earth translate to what happens to us post-mortem. I believe in Heaven, which I imagine looks different from person to person. Like, for Joanna? No dogs. For me? All the dogs! Now, if there's a Hell–and my actions are predicated in anticipation of this–my version, my eternal punishment includes thirty local eight-year-olds dancing the Tarantella.

Stick a fork in us, we were *done*.

We didn't formally decide to bail until after our "wine and Spumante tasting" which included no actual tastes of wine or Spumante. Instead, we received a sales pitch from one of Donatella's husband's buddies in the basement of a storage facility in the middle of some random city.

We did get to see the wine processing plant, though, upon Manny's request. That was scenic, if you like industrial parks and mounds of rotting produce. My favorite part was afterward when Italian Matthew Modine kept swerving off the road because he'd been drinking at lunch.

As we parsed out every broken promise and unmet expectation with Donatella, she listened intently, nodding as Julia laid out our case. We decided to leave the tour and head back to Rome five days early because at least we'd have something to do there that didn't involve flea-ridden rape vans, Manny, or a swift and imminent death.

At the end of our conversation, Donatella agreed it was best for us to go since we were unhappy. She smiled kindly and then told us there were no refunds. Although she was sorry, we wouldn't see a penny of the ten thousand dollars' worth of food, lodging, and tours still due to us collectively.

Then she shrugged.

There's no happy ending here. Yes, we took off for Rome, but not before encountering more stray dogs in the train station. Our first Airbnb apartment was so filthy and roach-filled that we abandoned it, so there's a whole second and third part of this story, too.

By the time we landed somewhere safe and decent, we were sick of Italy and had exhausted all our spending money in providing our own room and board for a second and then third time. At that point, we legitimately could have sent one of those, "Help me, I'm broke in Europe!" emails.

The lesson here is twofold: first, the twelve dollar Italian lesson is a lie, and, second, a Rosetta Stone disc will never give you fleas.

FOUR

Love Is

"THOSE WHO CANNOT LEARN from history are doomed to repeat it."

- George Santayana

"THIS IS A NIGHTMARE."

Those words raced through my head as Fletch and I stood face to face, holding hands in front of the minister on that balmy Las Vegas day in September, 2002.

"My worst nightmare."

No, I wasn't having cold feet, balking at the idea of coupling up legally and permanently. We'd known we should be together since shortly after we'd met eight years earlier. Yet ours was not a love at first sight scenario. In my opinion, this phenomenon is a myth. Love at first sight is only *a thing* regarding dogs or designer purses.

Instead, Fletch and I bonded over having so many esoteric commonalities. For example, I'd never met another Midwesterner who adored the state of New Jersey as much as I did.

[*Why is New Jersey a perpetual punchline? My God, they pump your gas for you!*]

I suspected he was a keeper when, while flipping channels on a lazy Sunday afternoon, we both squealed at the opening yodel in the movie *Raising Arizona*. (This was before everyone realized the genius of the Coen brothers.) After our mutual, spontaneous outbursts, we turned and looked at each other like, "Hold up, you like this, too?"

He and I were older than most undergrads on campus, Fletch because he'd served in the Army, and me because math is hard. We were both take-your-time kind of people. Neither of us were dying to dash up the stage at graduation and then directly down the aisle, like so many of our peers. In our minds, marriage was a lot like flossing after each meal; outstanding in theory, impractical in reality.

As for our differences, we figured out how to work around them. For example, early in our courtship, I asked Fletch to help me hang shelves in my studio apartment. When he arrived, I dragged the boards and brackets over to where I planned to position them above my desk. Then I fished in the drawer for some of the free-range nails I had rolling around in there.

"Gonna clear off your desk first?" he asked.

"No, why?" I replied, puzzled.

"The plaster dust will fall when we hammer in the nails."

"Like you'd be able to tell in here," I replied, referring to the unkempt state of the rest of the room, where shoes, magazines, waitressing aprons, hair ties, and cat toys arranged themselves into what I called "a nest."

He said nothing, instead pressing his lips together.

I liked how tidy he kept his own bedroom. I attributed his penchant for neatness to the military. I was quietly thrilled that his comforter matched the freshly laundered sheets. All his shoes were lined up on his closet floor *just so*. His bulletin board was a paean to right angles and neatly clipped edges, each concert ticket and photograph and bumper sticker posted equidistance apart.

Fletch's room was an oasis in the chaos of the rest of the apartment. He lived with a group of his fraternity brothers, where the shared living space reeked of musty gym bags and too much Polo cologne. An oversized, always-on television was proudly displayed atop of a stack of cinderblocks and two-by-fours. The space contained multitudes of dirty plates and an impressive array of empty bottles of booze *[the trophies awarded for binge drinking]* displayed the same way big game hunters exhibited carcasses of those animals they'd bested.

A surly iguana named Jimmy lived in a too-small tank on the dining room table, hissing and spitting at anyone who dared meet his eye, his only view that of squalor. The roommates had written a jingle for Jimmy that went: *"Who's the iguana that loves you? Jimmy the lizard, that's who!"*

However, the constant, drunken serenades did not improve his perpetually foul reptilian mood; it's possible the song caused it.

My own messy apartment made Fletch twitchy. He was far too polite to say as much, at least directly. Fletch has always been a Jedi master, so he eventually used this power to help me discover on my own that I'd prefer *not* living in a pigpen.

Good call.

However, these were the salad days and we hadn't gotten there yet.

"Shall we start?" I asked, gesturing towards the wall.

He was mute, assessing my strategy. I licked my finger and touched the wall in the approximate places where I'd planned to attach the metal slats.

"What are you doing?" he queried.

"Marking the spots where I'll place the brackets," I replied.

"No measuring?" he asked.

I pointed to the two wet spots. "I just did."

"With what?"

"These." I pointed to my eyes.

He pressed his lips even more firmly together, a gesture I'd eventually name Muppet Mouth. He purses so hard on occasion that it's like his head's a Jim Henson creation, where the whole bottom half can fold into itself.

"Okay," I instructed, handing him a slat. "You hold this here while I bash." I grabbed my loafer and placed a couple of nails in my mouth.

"You want me to *hold this here while you bash*?" he asked slowly and deliberately, his lip curling ever so slightly. "With your *loafer*? You're going to drive these nails with a shoe, and not, say, *a hammer*? That's your plan?"

I spat out the nails to answer. "Uh huh, why?"

"That's not how you hang shelves," he said.

"Sure it is," I replied. My family tackled home repairs like that all the time.

He simply said, "No."

"No?"

More emphatically, he replied, *"No."*

I said, "You have a better way?"

In fact, he did. He sat down at the chipped Formica

table in the kitchen alcove, gently displacing the cats who were napping in the fruit bowl. Then he made a supply list (a list!) before hustling me into his truck. He drove us to a strange and magical place called a "hardware store."

Having grown up in a household where the sole tool box contained a rusty set of Vice Grips and a paint-splattered butter knife, I hadn't a clue there was a better solution. He loaded up our cart with items like "electric drills" and "anchors" and "stud finders," the whole time explaining a job wasn't worth doing if it wasn't worth doing *right*.

Huh.

I was less in awe two decades later when it took him *six solid weeks* to repair and repaint an old dresser.

[Spoiler alert: YouTubing clips of Phil Hartman's old Anal Retentive Carpenter *skits on* SNL *did not motivate him to work faster.]*

Anyway, marriage had been on Fletch's list for years, but we'd never quite gotten around to it, even though we eventually saw the light about flossing.

Neither of us wanted children so that's one reason I wasn't in a huge hurry. The other reason was I didn't have much invested in the idea of being a bride. I didn't throw pretend weddings when I was little. While make-believe was a huge part of my childhood, "imaginary wife" was the last thing on my mind. I was far too occupied filling my bed with all my stuffed animals, navigating Jen's Ark through forty days and nights of torrential rains.

[Sure, those basic bitches out there could get hitched if they wanted, but some of us were busy saving every creature who ever roamed the earth, bro.]

I'd also spend my time practicing karate moves in my bell-bottoms and buffalo sandals, running drills so I could join Charlie's Angels the second Bosley started recruiting eight year olds.

When not engaged in feats of strength/heroics, I'd conduct interviews with myself in the bathroom mirror, clutching the microphone (hairbrush) and prepping for my close-up.

So, pretending to wear some fluffy dress?

That seemed like a lame goal in comparison. *Everyone* got married, even my weird evangelical cousin who fixed her teeth herself without having braces.

[FYI, she pushed on her canines with her thumbs all day for, like, six years, and that seemed to do the trick.]

Bottom line? I was far too busy for a mock wedding. I mean, I was enlightening and enriching Johnny Carson's viewing audience. I was kicking ass for *America*. Participating in pretend nuptials was beneath my creative endeavors.

I wonder if I'd have been more enthused about bridal games if my parents' marriage had been a better template. Their relationship was nothing I aspired to emulate. While my folks never split up, I can't remember them having much fun together; they didn't seem like *friends*. They weren't on the same team.

My parents weren't big talkers, at least to each other. However, my mom would spend hours on the phone with her sisters, running up the long-distance charges, complaining about my dad between other bits of family gossip. Then my dad would be furious when the bill arrived and my mother would throw a fit because she felt like not being able to talk however long she wanted was tantamount to being silenced.

So much of what was wrong could have been resolved if those two had calmly discussed these issues. My mom was lonely because my dad traveled all the time and she lived far away from her people. My dad was perpetually exhausted from extensive, high-stakes business travel. Sometimes he was stuck at a table representing Management, faced off against Teamster leaders, for six weeks at a time. That stress must have been unimaginable. The last thing he wanted when he got home was conflict or superfluous chatter.

I was only eight years old and I could see this; why couldn't they?

They were equally at fault for their lack of communication, my dad because his entire job was to stay steadfast and never give in, and my mom, for perpetually going from zero to hysterics in a split-second. Neither one ever acknowledged each other's needs or tried to operate within the other's parameters.

As early as grade school, I knew that if I wanted my dad on board for something, say, buying me some Gloria Vanderbilt jeans, I had to present the facts in a rational manner. He might not say yes, but he'd take my ideas under consideration, were he presented with a logical pitch. If I required my mother's buy-in, I'd make an emotional argument. She was always on the side of anything that appealed to her pride or sense of adventure, regardless of logic or feasibility.

My parents were always fighting, as neither one would meet the other halfway, never tailoring his or her approach to the other. While every other kid lived in fear of their parents' divorce, I started to wish they *would* end it already. I was nothing if not pragmatic. Two Christmases, two birthdays, two bedrooms, maybe even two dogs?

Sign me *up*.

Fletch had a similar experience with his family. Early

on in our relationship, we made the conscious decision to not replicate what we'd seen that didn't work. For example, we both respond better to logic, so when we're angry, the quickest route to resolution is rational conversation, not yelling. We're not always successful—and I'd be lying if I claimed to have never thrown a plate—but we try.

Despite years together, building our dispute resolution skills, confident that we'd found the right person, we were reticent. Less about marriage, per se, but weddings. Weddings were a shit-ton of work and we weren't up for the challenge; we didn't have the bandwidth.

Our attention spans?

Not so broad.

[Right now, as we sit outside and I read him a draft of this chapter, Fletch keeps commenting on a bird squawking in a tree across the yard. That's his sole input on what I've written so far. Endless fascination about a small, loud bird. You can feel *me rolling my eyes right now, yes?]*

Anyway, as we were newly-minted executives, we believed our ceremony should reflect our station in life. We wanted to get married dot-com millionaire style, even though we were barely dot-com thousandaires. Plus, all our friends already had weddings and because we were hyper-competitive and self-important, we intended our big day to crush everyone else's into a fine paste; that would take planning.

We'd started seriously discussing marriage in 2001, figuring it was finally time. While no one had bought a ring or joined a gym yet, we were headed in that direction. Essentially we'd planned to plan. However, I was downsized that fall due to corporate cutbacks after 9/11 and I channeled all my energies into a fruitless job search. Wedding plans were put on hold as I was far too spent trolling Monster.com postings to dither about fish forks.

A few months into my layoff, I lost my health insurance because I couldn't pay the premiums. I'd assumed I'd be working soon and had spent accordingly. Fletch had to fake allergies so he could fill my Claritin script. That worked for a while.

However, after an entire year being unemployed, I needed a new strategy. Suddenly our discussion was less about prime rib or salmon and more about how we'd continue to pay rent. We had to be pragmatic.

We could solve our problems if we were to get married. While I wanted to spend the rest of my life with him, I decided our forever should start ASAP because: (A) Claritin, and, (B) the receipt of enough wedding cash and prizes to dig ourselves out of the financial hole unemployment had created. We abandoned our plans for a huge, someday, impress-everyone 'do at the Drake on Michigan Ave on our own dime, instead opting for a modest, informal ceremony in Las Vegas at the end of the summer, financed by my parents.

[My mother made the offer because she thought if she had to wait for us to get around to writing checks, she wouldn't see a wedding in her lifetime.]

Taking the non-traditional route of a hotel/casino wedding was a huge relief. I didn't have to obsess over seating charts or florists, which had never interested me in the first place. I was especially happy to not have to pick bridesmaids.

"You don't want a wedding party?" Fletch asked.

I replied, "My friends are either in grad school or have little kids. No one can afford to throw us a shower and it's not fair to ask. Why, do you want groomsmen?"

"I've been in so many weddings, I feel like we have to, like a *quid pro quo*," he replied.

"Would you rather be a groomsman or just be a guest who can have fun, no strings, no obligations?"

He thought about this for a minute. "I choose fun."

I said, "Exactly my point. Wedding attendants are for people in their twenties. Once you hit your thirties, you lose your window to force your friends into identical strapless gowns and dyed-to-match shoes. No one has time for that."

We decided to stand in front of the minister alone. We wanted people to enjoy the day, hard stop. We didn't want to turn the whole thing into an obligation or a popularity contest. The ceremony would last fifteen minutes, so the officiant couldn't sneak in a sermon, either. Plus, with such an abbreviated timeline, we'd bypass the worst of the nuptial traditions, the reading of that awful *Love Is* verse that has vexed me since childhood.

While the message contained in First Corinthians is touching and heartfelt, I still hate it.

HATE.

The blame lies in its association with the creepy circa-1970 *Love Is* comic strip. Do you recall those? In each cartoon, the saucer-eyed lovers would be engaged in some thoughtful activity together, like, maybe he's helping her tidy up the house or she's by his side while he's in the hospital, and the caption would read, *"Love is... being there for each other."*

Sounds nice, right?

The kicker was these two lovers were: (A) children, and, (B) naked.

On occasion, one of them might be wearing a gardening hat or pair of running shoes, but that's it. Otherwise, they were nude, nude, nude, all day, all night. What the hell was happening in our country back then that no one else was weirded out by a cartoon about *two naked children*?

Was this because of Watergate?

Were high gas prices that distracting?

Was I the only person who had questions and concerns?

And where were their parents?

Wasn't anyone else all, *"Say, aren't you two a tad young for so much full frontal?"*

And why were they always baking bread and decorating cupcakes and scooping ice cream in the buff? I didn't care how much those kids loved each other, they still needed to *put on some goddamn pants if they were going to be in the kitchen.*

Speaking of naked people, our wedding hotel was the site of the 2002 Adult Film Awards that weekend. We discovered this fun fact at check-in when we found ourselves in the middle of wall-to-wall porn stars and producers. So many aviator sunglasses. So much chest hair.

This discovery sent my mother into a tremendous emotional tailspin. She was furious that the hotel was more concerned about the satisfaction of thousands of adult film industry guests with the hundreds of private events they'd booked over the week than my fifteen-minute ceremony and dinner for a handful of cousins.

[Fletcher is still talking about the bird. He's still talking about the bird. I'm reliving the day we pledged ourselves to each other for eternity and he's all, "That's quite a bird we've got there."]

While a blown-out wedding was something my mother

had been fantasizing about ever since I was in diapers, my father thought ceremonies were wasteful. So, instead of starting a wedding savings account to fund my mother's dream, he funneled all his extra cash into retirement accounts. No one would argue that wasn't the wiser choice. However, when the time came to pay for everything, he balked and, with no other choice, my mother charged everything on her credit card. This put them at odds once we got to the hotel.

Here's the thing… I was *thirty-four*. At some point in the *thirty-four years* leading up to the day of the wedding, they probably should have come to some consensus on how they might handle said expenses.

That's why when my parents walked me down the aisle, my mother decided to remain at my side. Seriously, she refused to have a seat. She'd decided if she were footing the bill, she was electing herself my maid of honor. Having no clue as to what was happening, my father remained standing as well. Fletch kept looking at me as if to say, "What the hell?" and I could only shrug.

We'd met the minister briefly before the ceremony and he explained how everything would shake out. The pianist would play a couple of songs while (most) people sat down, he'd give us our vows, we'd repeat them, we'd exchange rings, we'd kiss, then he'd introduce us as the married couple before we exited to one more piano song.

Easy enough.

By that time, we were both so stressed out by my mother's obsessing, my father's complaining, and my brother's passive-aggression that we couldn't wait for the wedding part to be over.

We gave our vows and exchanged rings. Fletch and I smiled at each other, thrilled to be at the finish line, ready to be pronounced husband and wife after so many years. Then the minister uttered the ten most devastating words in the English language:

"I'd now like to read to you from First Corinthians."

We gasped in unison, much like we did at the credits of *Raising Arizona*, only this time there was a dearth of joy, the absence of delight. I'd never discussed my contempt for First Corinthians so I had no clue that he despised it, too. As the minister launched into *Love Is*, Fletch and I locked eyes and we began to squeeze all the blood out of each other's hands.

"A goddamned nightmare," said my internal monologue.

I noticed the clench of Fletch's jaw and the pinch of his lips and he could see me screaming internally.

Then we both smiled.

At that moment, we knew that we were truly, *finally* one, suffering the same burdens and it was all worth it. We could already tell that whatever life had in store for us, whatever was to come next, whatever storms we might encounter along the way, we'd be okay if we stuck together.

While love is patient, love is kind, and love never fails, sometimes love is hating the exact same thing at the exact same time.

———

FLETCH'S LAST WORD:

"Do you see that crazy-ass bird? That's the craziest lookin' bird I've ever seen!"

Except for immediate family, I don't generally describe things as "crazy" because it's just too vague; however, in this case it was the only adjective that worked. Like a pair of Vise Grip pliers, it's rarely the right tool for the job, but when it is, it's the only tool for the job.

Our yard is generally populated with robins, cardinals, and blue jays. Their songs become repetitive to the point of familiar, even the blue jays with their loud jeering that reminds one of a hawk. So, when I heard what sounded like a crying baby stuck in the top of a forty-foot tree while floating around our pool on our two-person inflatable rubber ducky, it caught my attention.

I looked skyward, thinking, "If that's a baby, it's in trouble because I don't have a ladder tall enough to reach it. And I'm not climbing a tree to save a baby." Fortunately for all involved, there were no babies or other ground-dwelling mammals dangling from the forest canopy. But there was the strangest—no, craziest–looking bird I have ever seen.

For a moment, I thought it might be a small griffin. It had the proper eagle's head, but the body that should have been lion-esque was covered in feathers, had two bird feet, and was about ninety-five percent smaller than a lion. In retrospect, the body was more like a small owl, but the head was definitely from an eagle. Except for the beak, which resembled an anteater.

And then it opened its mighty beak like a strange, feathered caiman that could live treetops instead of jungle rivers, and let out a cacophonous, "Yeeeahhhoulll!" It reminded me of Howard Dean in that legendary campaign speech, and I wasn't the only one. I swear all the robins, cardinals, and blue jays fell awkwardly silent, and looked at each other all side-eye and muttered, "What the fuck did he just say?"

About that time, Jen wandered out to the patio, yammering something about our wedding, and all I could manage was "Do you see that crazy-ass bird? That's the craziest lookin' bird I've ever seen!"

FIVE

Lose To Win

———————————

I'M NOT sure how healthy bacon is in general, but I know it's incredibly delicious."

- Gwyneth Paltrow

"NO BEANS, no cheese, no corn salsa, dressing on the side, please," I instruct the waiter. I hand over my menu with a smile, taking a sip of my sparkling water. Look at me, a paragon of clean living! The adage about, "Nothing tastes as good as being thin feels," is wrong. Really, it's more like, "Nothing tastes as good as smug self-satisfaction feels."

Joanna and I are here at our ritual pre-opera dinner. Instead of ordering what looks good (the filet mignon medallions with blue cheese and veal demi-glace, with optional side of macaroni and cheese) and eating a reasonable portion, I'm having a blackened chicken salad with every bit of joy, flavor, and frivolity removed, or served on the side.

Joanna's a registered dietitian, so she helped me select the healthiest item on the menu. I'm trying to cut calories because I've started my gym's Lose to Win program and I want to put up a good first number to start off 2015 right.

I've been working out hard this week as my official beginning weight's already been logged. Oddly enough, I was disappointed when I found out we'd step on the scale in private. I figured nothing would motivate me more than being cheered on by the rest of my team as I stepped on the scale.

[Never thought I would speak such blasphemy.]

What's so ironic is that I've lost fifty pounds without restricting calories or doing formal workouts so I should be able to crush it now that I've joined an actual program.

A year ago, I'd challenged myself to lose twenty pounds for a chapter in *I Regret Nothing*, a memoir I'd recently finished writing. I thought if I approached weight loss from a wellness perspective–meaning if I addressed not only the physical aspects, but also the spiritual, emotional, social, intellectual, etc.–that I'd see more success.

[For those unfamiliar, my first memoir to hit the New York Times *bestseller list was* Such a Pretty Fat, *a weight loss book in which I did not get any less fat. In fact, over the past few years, I'd become bigger than I was when I'd started.]*

Turns out my wellness theory was right. Instead of sweating it out on the treadmill, I spent the year in introspection, looking at my habits, figuring out my triggers, finding ways to fill the gaps in my life without defaulting to treats. I met with an emotional eating therapist and started taking responsibility for my own choices and actions.

Ultimately, my being overweight was no one's fault but my own. Yet the paradox was in knowing that I was good enough, that I was a quality person, that I could accomplish anything, that I had value, regardless of my pant size. While I think it's easier to initially lose weight via self-loathing, the way to see lasting results are through self-admiration and self-care.

[Self-love is a creepy term and I avoid using it.]

Training myself to ask, "Are you hungry or are you bored?" was a game-changer. I denied myself nothing. If I wanted a burger, I'd have one. Not huge, and not all the time. I left every option on the table. If I wanted mayo on my sandwich, I'd add mayo. Not shitty diet mayo, but the best kind, I'm talking Duke's if I'd remembered to order it from Amazon, or Kewpie if I'd recently been by the Japanese market. How about cream in my coffee? No probs. Again, real cream, none of that powdery NASA bullshit.

I figured having some of exactly what I wanted would be more satisfying than endless helpings of "healthier" foods that didn't excite me. My parents used to buy these disgusting plastic tubs of yellow bread spread so artificial it couldn't even be called margarine. The difference in fat and calories between it and real butter was negligible, especially for what tasted like bathtub caulk.

What worked for me is taking the emotional element out of eating. There was no good food, no bad food, just food. However, I did watch my sugar intake. I told myself I could have dessert if I wanted and I kept a jar of Italian Nutella on hand for whenever I needed a bite of something sweet. *[Supposedly the same recipe as the US jars, but the*

European version is better. Trust me.] I tried to save dessert proper for special occasions.

One night, Fletch and I were out for a celebratory dinner and I was taking forever to decide between the carrot cake and key lime pie, both perennial favorites.

"I'm just not sure which memory I'd rather store in the ol' dessert spank bank," I told him.

A woman at a neighboring table choked on her wine.

"You might want to think about how that sounds before you say it out loud again," he'd replied.

I picked the carrot cake à la mode. Worth it.

The whole restriction-and-denial thing at tonight's dinner? This is new. But I've been killing it in the gym this week, so I might be okay with it. Every muscle is sore, but a good kind of sore, a Yeah, Girl, You Got This ache. In the car on the way to the train, I kept crowing to Fletch about how tight my quads were, how my hammies were humming. He told me I probably wasn't warming up or cooling down properly, and should use his foam roller when I got home.

The waiter delivers Joanna's glass of cabernet. Hmm. I do like the looks of that. So red, so velvety. So not a frigging glass of Perrier.

Going to the opera stone sober is new, too. Usually, we both meet up, having taken the train in to the city from our respective suburbs. Then we split a bottle of wine at dinner and quaff festive champagne cocktails between acts, which gives every performance a hazy, dreamlike quality, where the music envelopes us.

When our meals are served, I eat my stupid, boring, dry food, but spend the whole time watching Joanna's plate. She ordered the braised short rib with gnocchi.

Oh, I bet that pairs nicely with the wine.

"Would you like some?" she offers.

"No, I would not like some, I would like *all*, but I'm never going to accomplish anything if I quit and eat gnocchi on my very first test of will," I say.

After dinner and more wine (for one of us,) we head across the street to the opera. We're seeing *Madam Butterfly*, which is a Puccini opera. I normally love Puccini, but there's something about this production that's off, maybe because it's so minimalist and stripped down, but more likely because I don't have my beef and champagne buffer.

Champagne makes everything better. Fact.

There's one scene where the protagonist Cho-Cho-San is scanning the horizon for her beloved Lt. Pinkerton's ship. Her angst is almost palpable as she waits, but he never comes. She literally stares out from her perch for what feels like a lifetime. The stage rotates ever so slightly, revolving around in a giant arc that takes about the same amount of time as it does our earth to circle this sun. There's no singing. Just spinning at a snail's pace. Beside me, Joanna gently dozes off, wafting away on a raft made of gnocchi, bobbing in a cabernet sea.

I am wide awake, hungry, and bored to death.

This is why Lyric Opera House has ten bars set up in the lobby alone. They should print warnings on the tickets, like they do on prescription drug bottles. CAUTION: *Production may cause extreme drowsiness. Show must be consumed with no fewer than three alcoholic beverages.*

Finally, blessedly, the opera ends and Joanna and I part ways. Because the opera wasn't just painfully dull, it was long, I have to take the train line that goes to the east side of my town, instead of my usual that goes to the west side.

When I exit the train, Fletch is waiting on the opposite

side of the tracks, as neither of us are familiar with this station. I figure I can cut across and get to him faster than he can go all the way around, so I motion for him to wait and I begin to cross the tracks.

The snow on the rails is level with the platform, so I step out on the area where I'm supposed to cross between the two shelters. Except this is not the area where I'm supposed to cross and I can't tell because an overhead light has burned out. When I step, expecting to connect with platform, or at least a hard crust of packed snow, I immediately sink into fluffy snow down to my knee. My boot heel strikes the rail and I feel the impact all the way up to my spine because my calf is so tight from not having stretched. I lose my balance, landing face first onto the tracks, but there's so much fresh powder that my fall's broken.

Of course the one time I take a header like this, I'm completely sober. As this was the last train of the night, I'm completely safe in this spot for the next five hours, so I lay there for a second, laughing at the absurdity of the situation.

There are two teenage boys behind me on the platform, freaking the fuck out. They think I'm having a psychotic break because of the laughter. They hustle over to me, assuming I'm trying to commit suicide.

Their reaction stops my mirth right quick.

I feel terrible that I've made them panic. You see, Lake Forest has the unfortunate honor of being the train-suicide-death capital of the world. Too many of their class-mates have chosen this as a way out when academic pres-sure gets to be too much and that is tragic.

I assure the kids I'm fine and I get up, nothing damaged but my pride and maybe my ankle. I shake the snow out of my hair and brush it off my coat. I'm so glad this didn't happen when there were any commuters out here, I'd have been mortified.

I hobble to the car, where Fletch is waiting.

"I'm totally sober," I say by way of greeting. I have to angle/hop into the car sideways because my left ankle isn't cooperating. I sprained it once in college and have twisted it every couple of years since then, so I'm not surprised.

"Your fall scared me," he says. "You okay?"

"I'm fine, just my stupid ankle again." I explained how I misjudged the step, what with the lights having been so dim. I'm sure they're already kept at an ambient glow, as to not create light pollution in the downtown area, so it was extra-dark.

"Does it hurt?"

"Eh, not so bad. My muscles are still more sore than anything."

I can't seem to flex my foot, but it's probably just swelling.

I'm sure it will be fine.

———

THE ORTHOPEDIC SURGEON IS INCREDULOUS. "I'm sorry, how long ago did this happen?"

"Lemme think. Um, I did my weigh-in yesterday, down seven pounds, thank you very much, that would be Sunday, so... two weeks. Two weeks as of Saturday."

I've been hitting the gym in a foot brace as this thing isn't healing very quickly. I went to Acute Care the day after I fell and they said it was probably a sprain. My motion's somewhat limited but I can still ride the exercise bike. I also go to water aerobics and have been doing upper body workouts. My team coach would like to see more weight loss from me, but I think I'm doing well, considering.

Yesterday I was on the recumbent bike next to this loud-mouthed guy who was grousing about how many extra people were in the gym, due to participation in the Lose to Win program. He was all, "If you're fat, you should just put a piece of tape over your mouth."

The only thing that kept me from speculating aloud about his package size was that if I were to become a gym regular, I'd run into him all the time. I figured that I could be all sarcastic in the moment, or I could shame him by showing him my newfound healthy living every day. [*For once, I take the higher road. Never observed the view from up here before; I can see rooftops and everything!*]

The doctor shakes his head in disbelief. "You've been walking around on a ruptured Achilles for two weeks."

"What does that mean, exactly?" I ask.

"That means you are either the toughest person I ever met or the dumbest."

Suspect I do not want to know the answer to this question.

———

"HOW'S IT GOING IN THERE?" Fletch asks from the other side of the bathroom door. He sounds scared.

"Everything's fine," I say. I'm woozy from the morphine, but otherwise fine. Wait, not entirely true. My whole left side is numb. I don't like that, but that doctor assured me I would prefer this to the alternative. He said I'd get feeling back in a few days.

Fletch and I have just returned home from the hospital for my Achilles surgery. Can you believe this isn't even an overnighter? The doctor made me come in for repair today, after diagnosing yesterday. He said I couldn't hobble around on it a second longer. Luckily, having twenty-four hours' notice gave me enough time to order one-day shipping on crutches, a walker, and a knee scooter.

As I completed my one last workout on the bike last night, I cried, knowing that I wouldn't be able to exercise for a while, maybe a long while.

Ain't that something?

I spend my whole life hating the idea of movement, doing everything I can to avoid it, and then I finally figure out, "Hey, I'm sort of into this," and now, it's all taken away. The timeline for full recovery is unbelievable. I'd have been better off breaking a bone. I won't even be able to stand on this leg for months. I'm going to have to learn to walk again.

Let that sink in, won't you?

I won't know how to *walk*.

I'm not sure the full impact of what I've done to myself has hit me yet.

Fletch is still on the other side of the door. "When you say everything's fine, you mean..." he trails off.

"I mean that everything is fine."

I finish using the bathroom. I hoist myself up with the walker as I balance myself on my right leg. He's waiting for me in the doorway but I wave him off. I make it over to the bed myself.

Watching me, he says, "Thank God."

"For what?"

"When you were in there, I thought, '*I would take a bullet for her. I would lay down my life for her. I would kill for her. But if she needs me to, like, clean her, she's gonna have to go ahead and die in there, because I can't. I cannot.'"*

I am still half-anesthetized and slow from the opioids, but I muster up the strength to be appalled. "What would you do if I couldn't wipe my own ass? And you know I'm only wrapped from the knee down. I'm not sure how you think ladies use the toilet, but feet are not involved, they are not a part of the process. A lot of the magic between us is keeping the bathroom portion a mystery, but you're aware of basic biology, right? So, I'm curious, what was your plan?"

"I was going to call Joanna."

"You were going to call Joanna. To drive an hour. Each way. To wipe my ass."

"Yes."

"That is good information to have," I say. "Please double check the long-term care portion of our health coverage."

"Done and done."

"Hey, Fletch?"

"Yeah?"

"It's a good thing I can only kick with one leg right now."

———

I SLEEP until the next day. When I wake up, Fletch is setting up a brand-new, plug-and-play TV in the little sitting room where I'm stationed. He uses Velcro to attach the remote to the nightstand so I can't lose it. He doesn't want me to get bored or lonely and is afraid I'll hurt my neck staring at my iPad.

He also delivers flowers from an author friend who I

didn't even realize had my home address [*Amy Hatvany, you are a class act.*] Later, he serves a hot meal from my friend Gina who drove two hours round trip in rush hour without even telling us she'd been here, because she knew I wouldn't want to be seen with dirty hair. More flowers arrive, as do fruit bouquets. My phone and my email are blowing up with well-wishes right now.

Every couple of hours, Fletch comes in and trades out the dogs, so everyone has a chance to visit. Maybe I can't walk right now, but it's good to know there are those in my life who'll carry me if I need it.

———

THUS FAR, I haven't been in tremendous post-op pain. In fact, I stop taking the meds about three days after the surgery. Turns out, I hate opioids. Did not see that coming.

After the initial endorphin rush of learning who's on my personal Nice List, I've experienced a bit of post-op malaise. I've been depressed and I haven't wanted to do anything. I've spent a week without putting in my contacts, styling my hair, or applying makeup.

While I've bathed daily, some days, it's all I have the energy to do and that makes me sad. I had no idea surgery would take so much out of me. I hate to complain because I'm the best-case scenario right now. I mean, I don't have obligations that can't be fulfilled from home. I rescheduled some professional engagements, but no big deal. I can't be fired; I work for myself. I have good insurance, a helpful husband/coterie of concerned friends, very little pain, and, because I ruptured my left tendon, the ability to drive. Even that's extra-lucky. Had I stepped with my right foot, I'd be off-road for eight weeks' time minimum. I'd be housebound.

Until I lost use of the cable that supports half my body, I took for granted simple tasks, like feeding the dogs or pulling an item off a high shelf or carrying a cup of coffee. I certainly had no clue how Herculean daily chores such as bathing could be.

I spent the last week giving myself ear infections by rinsing my hair in dirty tub water, my own personal Ganges, until I figured out how to angle my knee-scooter in such a way that I could navigate over the six-inch entry threshold to the shower. That was a serious victory, enough so that I started to feel the first stirrings of vanity again.

After my successful shower, I catch a glimpse of myself in the big wall mirror behind the tub. I'm still naked, drying off with one knee perched on my scooter, jubilant in the newfound freedom to rinse in unpolluted water. As I take in the scene and all my reflected glory, I think, "This is a really specific type of fetish porn."

I finally sit in front of my magnifying mirror, and sweet Jesus, without daily Tweezer Time, all the stray hairs on my face have encroached. They're reclaimed lost ground like the jungle would an abandoned road.

People talk about having one person in their life that they can count on to clear their browser history if they should die an untimely death. I don't need that. While I peruse a lot of shameful things, i.e. chickens wearing hand-knit sweaters, I don't seek out anything truly mortifying or in any way illegal.

Instead, Imma need that porn buddy to promise to be my tweezer pal.

So, if nothing else, I am acquiring gratitude, patience, and humility, one wiry hair at a time.

———

I'M LEARNING to be clever, finding new ways to resume daily life activities. Because reaching anything on the floor is a crapshoot, I now carry silicone-tipped barbecue tongs; I store them in my knee scooter's attached wire basket.

Shameful, but useful.

For the first week, I avoided the stairs. I realized I'd eventually need to access my office (and wanted to watch the big TV) so I perfected the move I call Baby Army Crawl up the stairs, not to be confused with The Upright Crab Scuttle I execute on the way down. As these moves require both hands, I've taken to stuffing anything I need to carry in my clothes.

Fletch patently refuses to remove the iPad from the back of my underpants, no matter how many times I explain that I'll fall off my crutches if I try to do it myself.

What's unfortunate is the only pants I can wear over my protective CAM boot are my wide leg-yoga dealies. Thing is, I bought them all sixty pounds ago, so they're too big and if I carry anything heavier than a water bottle in my pocket, they slip down when I'm on the crutches I use upstairs. Most nights, I find myself in a race with the devil to get to the couch before I finish pantsing myself.

While I do haul up stuff with messenger bags, I keep forgetting them in my office. There are literally four of them piled up in there, which is why I had to carry my box of spinach salad tucked under my chin and the fork in my bra.

Every day I'm discovering what else I can do. On Saturday, I figured out how to vacuum the house via scooter and before that, I roasted a chicken Thomas Keller-style. Poor Fletch had to hear me gloat about making a magnificent dinner with, "One foot tied behind my back!" the whole night, but I believe it was worth it. Suspect it was less obnoxious than the string of great meals I made a few years ago when I kept exclaiming, "I am the Babe Ruth of making dinner!"

Losing my fitness trajectory has bothered me most. The first couple of weeks, I tried doing these sit-and-be-fit videos for seniors, but the music was a serious buzzkill. I am more Eazy-E and less *Swingtime with the Oldies!* Plus, I felt awful being bested by arthritic eighty-year-olds.

[Not metaphorically, literally.]

Then I found a series of videos from LiveExercise Launchpad. A trainer would demonstrate seated exercises for those with limited mobility and the morbidly obese. She'd work out with a bigger man named Rob. His size matched his enthusiasm. He was so keen on being in these videos. Oh, such gusto and passion he had, repeating every one of the trainer's commands.

What I'm saying is motherfucker could not shut up.

I hated him.

I was so weak, so tired, but I was not about to let this peppy loudmouth lap me. Couldn't have it. My competitive nature kicked in and drove me to last five minutes, then ten, then fifteen. I worked harder because of him. He's why I've been given the okay to get back in the pool for aqua fitness, provided I'm wearing my special protective boot. The orthopedic surgeon said, "You can't hurt yourself in the water." I chose not to mention how I'd hurt myself on the way home from the opera because I didn't want him to change his mind.

After my first water aerobics session, I'm still terribly weak and every senior in the class outlasts me.

[BTW, the golden gals don't mess around. Those ladies ain't playing.]

Part of my performance problems stem from not using the right equipment. I have a boot cover that is supposed to be "suitable for swimming" yet it actually "sucks for swimming."

Technically, my boot stays watertight under the cover, but I have so much air trapped that I cannot keep my leg submerged for the life of me. Every thirty seconds my damn foot bursts up out of the water like the splashdown of the Apollo 15 command module Endeavor. Very frustrating on all counts, especially because I'm wiped out two days following the session.

It's a problem.

That I will somehow solve.

———

I SPEND all week trying to figure out how to befriend Kobe Bryant. I saw a documentary about his Achilles rupture and we've gone through so many of the same things. (Maybe to slightly different degrees.) He even inspires me to find a high-tech Achilles boot like his. This may be the first time a sports celebrity has influenced my choice in footwear.

Now I'm determined that he and I would be besties because we have so much in common.

He's an athlete, I'm an athlete.

It's like we were separated at birth.

I wonder how he feels about yoga pants?

———

WHEN I RETURN to aqua aerobics today, I have an additional week's worth of rest under my belt, as well as a VACOcast with optional waterproof cover, and a pump to remove excess air, thanks to Kobe.

Point of clarification, Kobe didn't send this to me. After I saw a picture of him wearing one of these at a gala [because I was Google-stalking him], I tried to place an order on the manufacturer's website, but they were sold out in my size.

Fortunately, I found a used boot for sale on Craigslist. Fletch and I met up at a Dunkin' Donuts with a twenty-something guy who was selling his, having just graduated back into wearing shoes after four months. His friends were with him and they were so sweet, talking about how the kid had struggled with this injury, too.

Unfortunately, I decided to pick up a dozen chocolate glazed and jelly-filled, in addition to my new DME.

Baby steps.

Going forward, I won't take fitness for granted again, I'm sure of it.

While learning to live with a temporary disability, I've come to appreciate the simple activities of daily life, like running to the door to sign for a package, carrying a cup of tea up the stairs, or delivering a well-deserved round-house kick when I learn too late that a certain spouse subbed regular aspirin for the chewable kind I'd requested without first informing me.

On these sub-zero February days, when I use my knee-scooter to get to the garage, slide down the two steps on my butt, crutch the car, drive to the gym, crutch to the car's hatch, take out my second scooter while standing on one leg, scoot to the locker room, shrug into my swimsuit while trying to not topple over, scoot down the wet tile hallway to the pool, crawl into the water for aqua aerobics, and then do the whole thing in reverse while my wet hair freezes as I stuff my scooter back into the car, I have to wonder how much easier exercise will be when I can do it without a whole Walgreen's worth of durable medical equipment.

Considerably, I suspect.

After class, I chat in the locker room with some of the nice ladies on my Lose to Win team. *[Yes, I'm still tracking my diet and counting my aqua aerobics sessions for the competition. My participation counts and I think I'm losing. I can't tell because I can't stand still enough on the scale with one leg.]* I'd normally join my teammates in the hot tub, but I fear that in the new rubber casing, I'll cook my foot *sous vide*.

Anyway, I make the point that the biggest challenge thus far has been trying to maintain my dignity. I tell her about how a couple of nights ago, I made these gorgeous chocolate-dipped strawberries for Valentine's Day, thinking said dish seemed "romantic."

Fletch came into the kitchen while I was eating one of the gorgeous, romantic berries. He found me leaning over the sink to catch the crumbs I couldn't retrieve, on my scooter with my barbecue tongs in the basket and a diet iced tea in my pocket, pants flying at half-mast.

I realized then the dignity ship has long since sailed.

———

EVEN THOUGH I spend five months in a boot (even while

sleeping) and six months in physical therapy, the Achilles rupture ends up being the best thing to ever happen to me. Fletch posits this is because with the temporary handicapped sticker, I got the best parking spots. Also, everyone moved out of my way when they saw me coming on my scooter. Essentially, this is everything I ever wanted out of life. But I think it's so much more than that.

Without having lost my capability to walk, I would have never appreciated the miracle that is the functional human body. Maybe I would have kept up my healthier habits, but maybe I wouldn't.

Now I'm sure I will.

At this point, I'm down about eighty pounds. Having never lost significant amounts of weight, I didn't know I'd have to replace all my underwear. Who would have guessed your skivvies don't just shrink along with you?

The day I realize I need to order more, I'm sitting in my office. I need to go smaller, but I can't recall what size I've been in for so long. So I simply drop *trou* at my computer because that's the most expedient way to check the tag.

Poor Fletch.

There's always something unexpected going on when he steps into my office, like the time I was doing research for a book and he was all, "Are you... watching Pantera videos?" As I'm bent over, I don't *see* him when he walks into my office and encounters my bare, full moon. I only hear him scuttling away, saying, "Nope, nope, nope, don't tell me, don't want to know."

I know I've lost weight during the Achilles debacle, but I don't realize how much until I'm trying to get dressed for an event and every item I own is huge.

Hand to God, I didn't know clothes could get bigger.

That's why after twenty-three years of having to shop

exclusively in plus, I get to walk *[hobble]* into the regular-sized department at Lord & Taylor for the first time. I'm so ready to step into a fitting room with sizes that might finally slide over my shoulders and past my hips.

Of course, the only thing I see are ponchos. There are frigging ponchos everywhere. While I love ponchos, I want to punch a mannequin because, damn it, I could fit into a blanket with a hole cut in the neck a hundred pounds ago.

Then, once I find regular-people sized things that are not ponchos, I panic that snotty saleswomen won't let me shop, à la Julia Roberts in *Pretty Woman*. This triggers every fear, every anxiety I thought long since dormant.

They'll know I don't belong. They'll smell it on me.

I worry they'll direct me back past the area where snow tires are sold, which no one realizes Lord & Taylor even *carries*, returning to the plus department where I belong, if for no reason than I've been there for two and a half decades.

When I finally do run across a clerk, I notice she's wearing black opaque tights and a pair of silver sparkle Toms and I finally grasp that I have nothing to fear here.

I try on several items.

Ultimately, I buy a poncho.

This time, because I want to.

SIX

Color Wars, A Timeline

"STYLE ISN'T JUST about what you wear, it's about how you live."

- Lilly Pulitzer

OCTOBER 1980

The Preppy Handbook is published. I'm twelve years old and unfamiliar with the concept of satire. I take everything Lisa Birnbach writes as moral imperative. When she says Lilly Pulitzer is "key," I interpret this as gospel truth.

Again, because I'm twelve and a product of a sub-par public school system.

I pledge to find me some Lilly but I quickly discover I've neither the funds nor access here in North Central Indiana. Yet there are half a dozen spots locally where I might procure a Carhartt protective work jacket.

In my nascent opinion, this sums up everything wrong with where I live.

I content myself with argyle socks and alligator shirts [*yes, I realize it's technically a crocodile, I told you I went to a shitty middle school*] procured at the neighborhood golf course pro shop. Am deeply disappointed that I can't acquire any Lilly and even more so that my friends won't call me "Muffy," no matter how much I plead.

Make long-term plans to find better friends.

Years later, I'll hear Lisa Birnbach speak at a lunch. Within the first thirty seconds, she alienates half the audience—myself included—in a hateful political rant, apropos of nothing.

Never meet your idols, you'll only be disappointed.

June 1990

I spend the summer living in Boston. For the first time, I witness people wearing Lilly togs. Is glorious! Now I finally have access to shop Lilly, but no cash to buy her as I'm saving for tuition.

I concentrate on an achievable sartorial goal. I make daily jaunts to the Jordan Marsh department store, demanding to know when they're getting the Kelly-green, boat-shoe-soled Keds I saw in a magazine. The sneakers arrive the day before I return to Indiana. All's right in the world.

Mid 1990s

Yeah, still at college. Grunge is on trend and I wear Birkenstocks, which would clash audibly with the shift dresses I can't afford anyway. I forget about Lilly.

For now.

Late 1990s

I'm hired by an insurance company to call on physicians on the North Shore of Chicago. I visit Lake Forest for the first time. I recall this place being "key," per Birnbach. I spot much free-range Lilly on the street. I'm ever-so-charmed by the cacophony of pinks, greens, and yellows. Yet it's still too expensive; is like Lilly and I are destined to be apart forever.

Early to mid 2000s

A bunch of stupid shit happens, most of it terrible, unless you enjoy reading riches-to-rags memoirs, in which case, do I have some stories for you! Acquiring Lilly takes a backseat to trying to pay the gas bill with a voucher from the CoinStar.

August 2009

I visit the Hamptons for the first time. Twenty-nine years and a few bestselling books later, I can finally afford Lilly.

Except now I'm too fat for her clothes.

P.S., Lilly fabric is sold only in one-yard strips. Per crafty friends, it would be "a total fucking nightmare" to align prints and sew me a shift dress. At this point, Lilly and I are the would-be lovers in a romantic comedy. The audience knows we'd be so perfect together, truly happy, except we're perpetually just missing each other at the corner coffee shop or catching the other's eye as we travel on trains going in the opposite directions.

Really, it's a goddamned tragedy.

August 2009 to January 2015

I do the plus-size walk of shame through the Lilly department to ogle the goods. I'm on guard for the sales-clerks who'll ask me if I'm shopping for a gift, or perhaps a daughter, because... Bitches never complete their sentences, yet their meaningful silences speak volumes, as in *No Pulitzer for you, Porky*.

Whenever left to browse without judgment, I buy an accessory. Of course the scarves' bold colors and patterns seem custom-made for my skin tone.

Of course they do.

January 2015

Target announces a partnership with Lilly Pulitzer, which is set to include plus-size. I scream with so much joy that I lose my voice.

Social media explodes with the news. Over-privileged sorority girls and plus-size bloggers alike are appalled, for very different reasons. The bloggers are pissed because the plus items will be sold only on line, which is yet another insult as Target seems to consider bigger women and pregnant women to be one and the same.

[Spoiler alert: they aren't.]

The Millennial sorority girls are furious because now they're going to look like the poors who shop at big box retailers, and then how will everyone know that *they* have the kind of indulgent mommies and daddies who pay for their college educations AND delightful shift dresses?

To the bloggers, I say, "I feel you, and, yet..."

To the sorority girls, I say, "Definitely boycott. More for me."

January 2015

I undergo Achilles rupture repair surgery. While this has nothing to do with expensive cotton dresses directly, put a pin here, this part becomes relevant soon.

March 2015

The Lilly + Target Look Book is released and I immediately favorite sixty-six items, including the dresses I've wanted so badly for the lion's share of my life. I pay off one of my credit cards and then shove it in a desk drawer so that I won't be tempted to use it.

When the time comes to claim my Lilly, I'll be ready.

Early April 2015

I cross off days in my Lilly planner. April 19th can't come fast enough.

Mid-April 2015

I am now down significant pounds and I make my first non-accessory-based Lilly purchase. Who knew she offered XL? The dress is too tight, but hopefully not for long, as I've been deeply committed to getting healthier/smaller. In the interim, I look forward to wearing the shit out of Target + Lilly, especially for the price point.

April 18th, 2015

Morning

I make a paper list, prioritizing everything I want. My plan is to start at the top of my list and keep going until Visa calls about potential fraud.

[American Express did the same thing once when I was buying sneakers. Given my charge history—unhealthy dinners, fancy accessories, and Lane Bryant—they didn't believe I'd shop in a running store.]

Anyway, I cannot believe I'll finally have something Lilly that I can wear right-freaking-now other than a shoe, a bag, or a scarf. I scour the web for tips on how to score the most merch and set up my Target.com profile accordingly. I learn that even if I place an item in my cart, it's not mine until I pay. Someone could snatch it away if I'm not speedy enough with my typing, which is why I preregister. I don't want to lose out on a thirty-five-year quest because I've fat-fingered my address in an adrenaline surge.

I'm so excited I can't even stand it!

One thing tempers my joy after perusing Target's Facebook page, though. I run across a comment from a teenage girl's mother. Her plus-sized preppy daughter has been waiting her whole life to buy some Lilly *[RIGHT?!]* and she's just now seeing that the items are offered only online. The daughter's devastated. She longed for the experience of finally trying on clothes with her thinner friends and now she can't.

This breaks my heart.

I'm so disappointed for this stranger's kid. As an adult, I know what it's like when fit friends shop the cute stores, and I'm all, *"Come find me at Cinnabon when you're done."* To go through this experience as a teen when everything feels a million times worse? I can't.

Yet this is not my circus, these are not my monkeys. I'm not involved, I'm not the world's hall monitor.

So, do I want a swimsuit?

Yes. I want all the – goddamn it, I'm still on this kid thing.

I read that the daughter's been squirreling away her birthday cash for months in anticipation. She has the funds to buy a few pieces, but the family doesn't have a credit card she can use. She might have to miss the whole goddamned sale if her mom can't figure something out. And the girl is so sweet that she tries to tell her mom that she'll be okay whatever happens.

No. NO. Stop.

Stop thinking about this.

This is what happens when I'm nosy. I find out things I don't want to know and then I'm stuck carrying them around with me. It's my own fault for being snoopy.

Let it go.

Instead, I'll just check out the pretty rickrack fringe on the scarf and-

The mother isn't asking for anything in her post, no special favors, no accommodations; she's just venting her frustration, articulating how and why this business decision impacts real people.

I think about my stupid credit card waiting for me in my desk and I'm overwrought with guilt. I have such empathy for this family, even though nothing in this situation has anything to do with me.

"Universe, please let this kid get what she wants. Please give her a win," I ask in silent prayer. I'm glad she has a family who cares so much, a mom who's so invested in her happiness that she prioritizes her daughter's needs over her own. But I wonder if when she sees all her pals in the Fan Dance dress she wanted, that unconditional love will feel like it matters at all.

Maybe I should step away from the computer for a while.

April 18th, 2015

Afternoon

I web-chat with a Target.com rep to find out what time the items will be available online after never being able to connect with anyone on their (800) number. I don't understand why Target.com won't let me pre-order, or why I can't transfer my Look Book favorites to my cart, but, whatever.

I have faith in Target.

A few years ago, I had dinner with their book-buying reps and I learned how the company operates. That is, when I wasn't having a heated argument with them over whether Don Knotts was gay, not that it mattered either way.

[Who knew this was such a hot-button issue?]

The process is, each buyer spends a rotation purchasing for a different region of the store. Those doing reading material now might oversee housewares or electronics on the next round; it's all widgets as far as Target's concerned. That's because their inventory-management systems are sophisticated to the point they can predict the success of a product based on a single item in a single store in an hour's time. Their algorithms are *freaking amazing*.

Yet this explains why there have been so few decent extended sizes in the stores when their plus selection used to be plentiful and adorable. Though baggy now, I still have the darling Target tan-and-pink argyle sweater with the white oxford collar that I bought in the early 2000s.

I imagine a thin female buyer (or maybe a young man) who didn't know how plus clothes should fit was cycled into the rotation. I imagine his or her picks didn't sell. This is likely because the buyer wasn't aware he/she should opt for sturdier, more flattering fabrics which drape better, or for tops that cover the hips.

[Newsflash: most bigger girls don't love belly-shirts. And for the love of all that is holy, no one wants pants sheer enough to show cellulite.]

While I advocate for being comfortable with yourself at any size, this tends to be easier in clothes that draw attention to assets, not liabilities. So, when consumers didn't snap up the flimsier, silk-type fabrics and hip-skimming garb, that told Target that women of size didn't shop there, so they carried less. We subsequently bought less, to the point that this department morphed into two sad racks of basics, often accidentally mixed with maternity-wear.

Because this can't be stated enough, plus and maternity are *not the same thing*.

April 18th, 2015
Late afternoon
I wonder how that kid and her mom are doing.
April 18th, 2015

11:39 p.m.

"You going to bed?" Fletch asks.

"No," I reply. "I'm going to sit here until I can place my order online when the site goes live."

"Ha, what are you going to do, stay up all night?"

"Of course not! I'm going to set my alarm to wake up and check every hour until dawn. I mean, what am I, a college student pulling an all-nighter because she never read her Bio textbook?"

11:59 p.m.

Fletch comes into my office to say, "Hey, I just saw something interesting on a new family tree leaf. Looks like I'm descended from-"

I cut him off, screeching, *"The site might go live any second, no talking, I need to concentrate!"*

April 19th, 2015

12:05 a.m.

Social media reports that the site won't go live until 12:00 a.m. PST. I consider hitting the sheets, but who am I kidding? No kid can sleep on Christmas Eve, especially if it's possible that Santa might appear early with a sack full of appropriately-sized shift dresses.

Also, it's already abundantly clear that I *am* a college student about to pull an all-nighter because I never read my Bio textbook.

Like it would be the first time.

12:06 a.m.

I have refreshed the web page twenty times in the past minute, with my iPad and phone at hand, just in case. The model who looks exactly like Tracee Ellis Ross remains ever vigilant on the Look Book page.

12:07 a.m.

Reports indicate that some links are coming online, but

I can't access them, no matter how quickly I refresh. *Tracee Ellis Ross's doppelgänger, why must you taunt me?*

12:08 a.m.

I start clicking the posted Twitter links, willing to chance that this is a scam. I'm able to grab three shift dresses and the one weird satin romper-type piece that I don't even like solely because I've been whipped into a thirty-five-year-brewing kind of frenzy.

Aieeee, this is the best night of my life!

I don't even look at accessories because I am not going to content myself with the fat-girl consolation prizes of scarves and bags, okay?

Not. Happening.

I want a shift dress that fits me right now. While I begin the checkout process, everything but the shoes and the weird piece disappear because I wasn't fast enough, damn it!

12:09 a.m.

I click again and again, trying to check out as I load new items in my cart. I keep getting the Target dog with the bull's-eye, which is basically the new Fail Whale. Hate this dog so much. Also, hate Tracee Ellis Ross by osmosis. That's it. Am taking *Blackish* off my DVR as soon as this nightmare is over.

12:10 a.m.

The links suddenly show items as unavailable. Pieces are already selling out and the site's not even technically live yet. What in the actual fuck? Is the demand truly this great? In my head, I knew it would be the event to end all events. In the real world, I imagined it wouldn't be so popular. Wouldn't Target have anticipated demand and planned accordingly? How can this be? The Twitter-verse begins to lose its collective mind as #LillyforTarget trends.

12:11 a.m.

Almost every tweet in my timeline is either the fortunate few who've placed orders or the bulk of everyone else who hasn't. The panic is palpable. Mentally, I congratulate Target's PR team because this is an unmitigated success with all the brand-awareness. At the same time, I curse the IT team.

Agony!

Ecstasy!

Prints!

12:12 a.m.

Thousands of women just like me are going through the exact same rollercoaster of emotions right now. One of the big draws of blogging back in the day was the appeal of "finding one's tribe." If the trending #LillyforTarget is any indication, with their jokes about this being the preppy women's Hunger Games, I've stumbled onto mine. I try not to let my mind wander to thoughts of that girl because it bums me out.

She'll be fine, right?

12:13 a.m.

I discover tweets from my new best friend, Jason Goldberger. He's the president of Target.com. He assures everyone that the links shouldn't have been leaked and that online buying has been halted. He confirms that we can shop at 2:00 a.m. and the full inventory will be available. YAY!! The sensible person would try to get some sleep now.

I am not sensible.

12:14 a.m.

I have a moment of perspective. My life won't end if I don't get what I want, despite impeccable planning and budgeting. Also? I live in a world where hunger, poverty, homelessness, war, and melting polar ice caps are legitimate concerns, where nice teen girls can't catch a break, and where the true disaster of Lindsay Lohan playing Liz Taylor exists, so I try to keep my freak out to a minimum.

I am wholly unsuccessful.

12:15 a.m. to 1:59 a.m.

Obsessively refreshing Target.com and dying over the hilarious hashtagged tweets, where users are begging Jesus to take the wheel at Target.com.

OMG, *these people should be my friends!*

Suddenly, bonding over terrible sports teams makes sense.

At this point, I notice I'm trying to buy Lilly without wearing my pearls (even though I'm wearing my jammies) and I immediately right the situation.

Clearly, I need my talisman.

Pearls are my signature item, my good luck charm, my calling card, if you will, because they add an air of elegance to anything. A string of pearls and a pair of Ray Bans transforms every woman into Audrey Hepburn. Fact.

I became obsessed with pearls when I was fifteen and received a strand while we were staying at my great aunt Arabella's house in Boston. My mother took her own prized necklace and gave it to me in a tiny red silk bag on the morning of my birthday. I'd been coveting this particular piece of jewelry for years and was over the moon at the largess of this gift. I wore them for the family event that night and felt like a movie star, the heady combination of Diane Lane with her girl-next-door appeal and Phoebe Cates and her exotic charm. I'd never received such a meaningful present. Pearls made me feel confident and worthy, an external validation of what I hoped to cultivate internally.

When we returned to Indiana, my mother took the pearls back without explanation or apology. Honestly, I believe she was so wrapped up in the bliss of having been in back east for a big family event that her joy manifested itself in her being more generous than intended. She had giver's regrets. Instead of living with her decision, she simply rescinded. I'd still sneak wearing them whenever she wasn't around... weren't they technically mine?

As an adult, I discovered freshwater pearls. I like them just as much as their more sophisticated, expensive older sisters. Plus, I can buy freshies on Amazon.com for less than fifty bucks! Now I have them in a handful of lengths and sizes and I always carry a spare in my purse. That's just in case I ever forget to put them on before I leave the house. I feel naked without their familiar weight around my neck.

[Honest to God, I'd rather forget to wear deodorant.]

Pearls on, I'm still panicking, despite my earlier dose of perspective.

While I have faith in Target's abilities, a part of me worries the site will crash the minute everyone logs on. I tweet to Jason Goldberger that this had best work or he's going to experience the wrath of angry, preppy, fat women wielding pitchforks in Minneapolis.

He does not respond. I give him a pass, assuming he's a tad busy. I appreciate his transparency, so there's that. TargetStyle's twitter feed assures me *[by me, I mean everyone]* that all is well and the wait will be worth it.

2:00 a.m.
Site is not live.
2:01 a.m.
Site is not live.
2:02 a.m.

Site is not live and now my coming completely and utterly unhinged has frightened poor little Libby. She thumps her tail anxiously as she watches me from her spot on the bed.

2:03 a.m.

Ahhhh!!! I'm in!!! Let's do this.

I click on a few items at a time, grabbing the pieces I want most, knowing the smartest way to go is to check out after every few items.

From what I understand, online buyers are able to purchase only five items of the same style to keep people from sweeping up everything and then selling the whole lot on eBay.

Well, *good.* I'm glad because hoarding is horseshit. Sure, it's capitalism, but it's also super-douchey and terrible karma. The whole point of this exercise is to get something awesome at the discount price-point.

Happy with the few shift dresses and the Nosey Posey shirt, I click to check out. And all the contents of my cart go poof.

Gone.

Into the ether.

2:04 a.m.

I simultaneously try to shop on my phone, iPad, and desktop using two browsers. Poof! Poof! Poof, poof! Everything's vanishing! Now the light blue dress is legit sold out! *Target, why is this happening?* Did your marketing department even TALK to the IT guys? Give 'em a head's up? Didn't anyone prepare for this at Target corporate?

This already feels as dumb as the time the stores covered all the big red protective safety spheres with fabric that made them look like beach balls. Said covers only lasted a day, at least at the Target on Elston in the city, because they were practically begging to be kicked, only for the kicker to discover they were solid cement.

[FYI, I know where to buy a fine protective CAM boot, in case it ever happens again. In fact, I'm wearing mine right now.]

2:05 a.m.

The website has crashed.

Where's my pitchfork, Jason Goldberger?

Target won't say the website has crashed; they use Orwellian doublespeak to say they're "optimizing the experience." Newsflash: *my experience is the opposite of optimal right now, you filthy sons of bitches.*

If they know how much Tide to buy for the whole company based on one shelf in Lima, Ohio, why are they so grossly unprepared for this? Their reaction is like those folks who are perpetually surprised that it's Christmas already. Does no one own a calendar?

2:06 to 2:31 a.m.

Make it work. Pleeeeeease. Jason Goldberger, I implore you, make it work. I do not tweet *"I am Googling where you live and sharpening my pitchfork, Goldberger!"* because, crazy. That doesn't stop me from thinking it.

Seriously, Jason Goldberger; I thought you were cool.

I refresh the page every three seconds. Nothing. I should go to bed and cut my losses, leaving early for the store tomorrow. Maybe I can get XLs in the store and they'll eventually fit?

Or I could just buy shoes and scarves and bags, like always.

Like fucking always.

2:32 a.m.

Aha! In again! I grab a few of the key items and check out before the whole thing goes down again like so many over-privileged Millennial sorority girls. Listen up, sisters: for all your grousing, for all your posturing, for all your, "It's not REAL Lilly quality," and, "I would never buy tampons and dresses in the same place," *I know you're here, too, or else the damn website wouldn't have crashed.*

Wait, I'm finally able to execute a small purchase!! Success!

2:33 a.m.

Or is it a success? How come I'm not getting a confirmation email?

2:34 a.m.

Seriously, where's my email?

2:35 a.m.

What if I don't even like how shift dresses look on me?

2:36 a.m.

And why is the site down again? *Argh.*

2:37 a.m.

Do I just go to bed? Like I could sleep with all this adrenaline coursing through me. Or am I committed and I should soldier on? I really did want some scarves and bags, not in lieu of the clothes, but in addition. I've seen the Dog of Despair so many times that Spuds McKenzie-type bull terriers will forever be a trigger for me.

And, you, Tracee Ellis Ross? You're on notice.

2:38 a.m.

Fill cart, cart disappears. Dog of Despair.

2:45 a.m.

Fill cart, cart disappears. Dog of Despair.

2:59 a.m.

Fill cart, cart disappears. Dog of Despair.

3:01 a.m.

Confirmation email appears and my own dog hides again when I begin yelping.

Then the site goes down.

3:10 a.m.

TargetStyle blames the snafu on "overwhelming excitement." I can't imagine they didn't see this coming. Again, they are a master class in predicting their customers' behavior. How'd they so miss the mark here? The plan couldn't have been to hype everyone up, release a tiny amount of product, then let customers twist in the wind... right?

3:11 a.m.

Again, I am sorry, polar bears, for being more worried about festive prints and affordable pricing than the environment. Ditto for Syria. Tomorrow, I will be a good person, concerned for and engaged in the world around me. But tonight, I will be a deranged, pajama-wearing, pearl-clad lunatic who is incapable of any thought, save for, "Refresh! Refresh! Refresh! I hate you, Tracee Ellis Ross!"

3:12 a.m.

I hope that kid isn't going through this, too. I want her to get her dresses.

Maybe even more than I want me to get them.

3:17 a.m.

Ha! Back up, back in, and I complete one final transaction for clothes. Okay. I can live with this. Didn't pick up everything I wanted, but that just means there's more for all the other late-nighters. I'm not (that) greedy. I'd planned on going to Target in the morning but now I revise my plan, seeing the frenzy. I shall leave at first light, so I'll try to catch a couple of hours of sleep.

3:18 a.m.

I get in bed with *The Royal We*, by the Fug Girls. They

are the opposite of Target right now, as they've under-promised and over-delivered. I love this book.

I can't sleep. Too keyed up.

3:35 a.m.

Wide awake.

3:45 a.m.

Wide awake.

4:00 a.m.

Wide awake. I should probably see if I could buy some plates, as I'm up.

4:01 a.m.

Wide awake, 500-server error. Not even a dog this time.

4:30 a.m.

Wide awake, 500-server error. Scream the screen, "Take my money, goddamn it! Why won't you take my money?"

5:00 a.m.

Wide awake, back up, but items keep disappearing from my cart. I want to kick the Target dog every time he tells me my cart is empty. I want to kick him HARD. I want to "take him to a farm" where he can "live with a nice family."

As for Jason Goldberger?

Vanished from social media like so many pineapple serving bowls.

5:30 a.m.

Site is back and fully operational... and sold out of EVERYTHING.

Screw it, I'm having breakfast and getting dressed.

6:35 a.m.

Arrive at Target in Vernon Hills. I'd planned on hitting the Target a little farther away in Mundelein, but I don't know the layout of that store, so I figured I'd lose valuable time trying to find stuff.

I'm not the first person in line.

6:35 a.m. to 7:58 a.m.

Everyone talks and makes friends, all of us sharing what we love about Lilly. One woman tells us she had a quilt made from all her daughter's old Lilly dresses and she could look at every scrap of fabric and remember her daughter at that age. She even got a shot of the quilt to Lilly herself before she passed on last year. Suspect her daughter is not one of the spoiled assholes from Twitter.

The mood is light and convivial, likely because we're at the head of the line and have confidence we'll at least end up with something, as that seems less and less likely for most.

Is worth noting that the blonde to brunette ratio here is ten to one. And every car in the lot is a newish SUV.

7:59 a.m.

We take position at the front door, much to the employees' amusement and the confusion of a couple of old guys making an early run for foot powder, orange juice, and Tums. There are easily one hundred women in line behind me.

8:00 a.m.

Speaking of running, the doors open and everyone runs.

She runs.

He runs.

You run.

We all run.

I run.

I run?

I forget for a minute that I'm wearing an Achilles CAM boot. Shit, *why am I running?* I should not run. Running is really, really dumb. My physical therapist is going to murder me. I had surgery three months ago. I just got done walking with crutches *last week*. And yet, the crowd crushes in behind me and I realize that if I want anything, and if I don't care to be trampled under so many Wellies and ballet flats, I need to pick up the pace.

I dash to accessories and nab two purses and one overnight bag, and with that, the whole display is cleared. How are there only one of each of these items? Shouldn't there be, like, so many more?

8:01 a.m.

The accessories area is decimated, as is the clothing rack. Wait, there's only a single rack of adult dresses? For this many people?

8:02 a.m.

Is this how everyone on the Titanic felt when they counted the lifeboats?

8:03 a.m.

I grab the last set of glasses from the now-empty housewares display.

8:04 a.m.

Gone. It's all gone.

I check out, having picked up the green straw purse, the blue and gold overnight bag, and the green and white scarf/sarong with little pink balls on the border. I gave a Lake Forest woman one of the purses and she swapped me the two lounge chairs. I don't find out until later that neither chair accommodates more than one hundred and sixty-five pounds, so even though I'm thinner, *I'm still too fat for this furniture.*

Still, I consider myself lucky.

Most people didn't get anything.

Outside of the running into the store, I didn't see any terrible behavior, any shoving or elbows being thrown, or any single person sweeping everything into her cart to list on eBay later. Really, no one could have. The inventory didn't exist. What I saw was a bunch of Lilly devotees, thrilled at the opportunity to score a less expensive slice of the pink and green pie.

8:44 a.m.

I'm home and ready to get into bed, reflecting on how badly the last nine hours went, what a tremendous waste of time and resources it all was. I feel awful for the bulk of the shoppers who were walking around shell-shocked, with nothing in their carts. They came to stock up, they stood in line before opening, and they left empty-handed. I know life isn't fair, and it can be argued that since I had a few items, and not just one, I was part of the problem.

However, I don't understand not making the hype and the inventory commensurate. I grasp how limited supplies build buzz, but couldn't Target have doubled or tripled the stock and still gotten the same results? Or were the Lilly products considered a loss leader and the whole thing rolled out exactly to plan?

I send out my final tweet on the debacle, speculating on the above. I fall asleep not having any idea if the orders I placed will be fulfilled, or, if I'll even like anything. I didn't have a chance to feel any of the material, or even see the garments in person. I haven't a clue as to the fit, either. I can almost guarantee that whatever I receive won't measure up to thirty-five years of anticipation and nine straight hours of pure focus.

Nothing could.

April 20th

My last tweet on this debacle is featured on *USA Today*, *CNN*, and the *Today* show online. My Facebook post about it gets more than ten thousand likes, reaching an audience of five hundred thousand eyeballs. Oh, the irony of spending months trying to promote my books, only to land national coverage by freaking out over #Lilly-forTarget.

The news reports on how the website "almost crashed" which makes me think Target's definition of "almost" differs greatly from my own.

BTW, it's been radio silent on both TargetStyle's twitter and Jason Goldberger's. The only apology they've offered is that of being sorry that we were frustrated. The "I'm sorry you feel that way" nonsense is worse than no apology at all.

Despite the backlash, despite the pitchfork-wielding women who just wanted to pick up something pretty, despite the collective, utter waste of time and effort, the Target execs knew exactly what they were doing because they couldn't buy this kind of publicity.

Target's happy.

Lilly Pulitzer's parent company's stock skyrocketed today. The folks at Lilly corporate are happy. The eBay re-sellers? Well, they're *really* happy selling items at a higher price than they'd get for Lilly proper.

The only losers are the devoted consumers, especially those of us who are plus-sized, or on a budget.

And I'm worried about the kid.

Did she get *anything?*

I hate how I lost perspective—and my mind—during this endeavor. I mean, I'm a fan of Lilly's clothes, no denying that. I've wanted her dresses for a long time. But these are not the zenith of my existence. I'm mad that I allowed myself to be swept up in the whole fiasco. I'm sure there are weeks, nay, months, that I don't think about Lilly.

[This time is called "winter."]

I became obsessed and it's my own damn fault.

Something good needs to come of this fiasco, all this stupid angst can't be for naught.

I click back to that mother's Facebook comment on Target's page but I can't locate it. However, after I'd read her post, I'd tracked down the woman's personal page so I knew her name. I had been curious [read: was the nosiest Posey] and I wanted to see who this lady was. What prompted her to leave that kind of post?

What I'd found was a single mom who ran her ass off for the benefit of her family. Her posts were infrequent, but every one of them was a love letter to her kids. I feel like she should be recognized for caring, for having rallied on her daughter's behalf.

I return to the mom's personal Facebook page to see if she's posted any status updates. She hasn't. That's troubling. I can't tell if her daughter had any success and I'm worried. I can't enjoy mine until I confirm she has hers.

Then I realize I've been waiting for Target to make this right when that's not the solution at all. So I type out a private message on Facebook. And then I wait.

April 23rd

With that mother's blessing, I pack up all my best clothing that no longer fits to send to the daughter. Lots of pieces still have tags on them, too. I'd been storing a handful of special garments for years, like my favorite cashmere sweaters and the bejeweled skater dress I bought in London but never wore. While I do a charity purge twice yearly, I'd never been able to part with these few garments because I was waiting for the right time. Now I know that this is it. I'm so happy that someone will finally have the chance to love this stuff as much as I do.

In my Facebook message, I tell the mom to consign

what she and her daughter don't like, but she insists they'll donate instead. They both want to pay it forward, too.

Right before I tape closed the boxes, I toss in one last thing—a strand of freshwater pearls. Every girl deserves to wear a piece of jewelry that makes her feel like anything's possible.

I think of something Lilly once said as I seal it all up:

"If you haven't any charity in your heart, you have the worst kind of heart trouble."

SEVEN

High Times II, The Electric Boogaloo

"FOR WHAT DO we live but to make sport for our neighbors and laugh at them in our turn?"

- Jane Austen

SEVEN YEARS AGO, Fletch and I went from renting the best house in a bad city neighborhood to owning the worst house on a pretty suburban street. Honestly, we didn't care because we loved our place and the term "worst" is relative in a town like Lake Forest, about which F. Scott Fitzgerald said, "Once I thought Lake Forest was the most glamorous place in the world. Maybe it was."

[Kingdom Come Farm, the storied estate belonging to the woman on whom he based his character Daisy Buchanan, and who inspired him to pen The Great Gatsby, *has since fallen into disrepair. The property is about to be razed and divided thirty ways to make way for single-story ranch houses. My feelings on this are mixed.]*

What we learned owning the least desirable property in one square mile is that no one comes to greet you. We'd heard about suburban neighbors showing up at the door with cookies and baskets of wine to welcome the new folks, but that wasn't our experience. In fact, we went years without meeting anyone.

Years.

That was fine. I wanted to live somewhere quiet with lots of room for our dogs, and if I had to drive back to the city to see friends, so be it.

Almost five years into our tenure here, I heard strange voices coming from my driveway. I stalked out of the kitchen, ready to yell at the trespassers–and threaten them with a shovel, if needed–because I clearly don't have enough to do when I'm not on deadline.

Instead of a pack of marauding bandits, I found some neighbors. The couple had chased Argo, their errant Golden Lab, into the dense woods surrounding our front yard and couldn't get him back.

Argo was close enough to see, but thanks to the all the undergrowth that had yet to be cleared, he wasn't close enough to grab. They were trying everything in their power to coax him out–funny voices, little dances, threats and recriminations, followed immediately by heartfelt apologies–but to no avail.

I grabbed some treats from the house and, through teamwork, we convinced Argo to join us. The dog seemed sort of swanky and was immediately taken by our off-brand of dog cookie, full of beaks and assholes. I bet Argo ate nothing but organic at home. We had a pleasant conversation and I was glad to have fought my initial instinct to shout at the nice people.

Their names were Brad and Angie Smith. *[Fake names to*

keep from painting them with my eventual stupidity, because, inevitable.] While somewhat younger than us, they were cool, they were hip, and the best part was that they didn't have kids.

Finding another childfree couple in the suburbs is like stumbling across a unicorn in the wild. You throw a chain around that shit and *lock it down.*

That's why when Fletch and I discovered a heavy piece of monogrammed card-stock in our mailbox, inviting us for dinner, I insisted we go. He was surprised as I'm usually the one looking for any excuse to not have to put on pants.

His skepticism was palpable.

"Why do they want to meet us?" he asked.

"Probably because we live in the same neighborhood?" I replied.

"We had such a good streak going," he said. "Five years with zero interaction with anyone."

"You realize that's a strange goal, right?" I asked.

"Yet it's worked for us so far."

Despite my overwhelming desire to fit in, that's never quite happened here, largely because we're childfree in a family-orientated community.

Our bigger stumbling block, though, is that we're do-it-yourselfers in a town where everyone else simply "calls a guy." For the first few years here, we tried to be "call the guy" people, too, but it just wasn't us. On any given Sunday, the fine folks of Lake Forest have seen us doing everything from re-grading the gravel on our driveway to tuck-pointing the bluestone on the front porch. Fletch is running the show, with me assisting, unless it's a gardening project and then roles are reversed. That's why Fletch was ready to despise Mr. and Mrs. Smith on principle.

They were "call the guy" people, he just knew it.

"I bet the husband doesn't even *own* chainsaw pants," Fletch huffed as we made our way to their house, carrying the only non-screw-top bottle of wine we had in our collection.

"They're dogs-not-kids people," I argued. They were on *our* team.

"A Lab is barely a dog. A Lab is a stuffed animal that shits outdoors."

"Oh, yeah, I hate pets you don't have to do up Hannibal Lecter-style just to take on a walk," I said, referring to the multi-leash protocol I employ when walking Hambone.

[When Loki, our thousand-year-old, Shepherd-Husky-Let's-Not-Kid-Ourselves-He's-a-Wolf decided he was done being the Alpha, that created a power vacuum that neither of our idiot pit bulls knew how to fill. The girls, Libby and Hambone, scuffled and now they're afraid of each other, so we're working with a vet behaviorist to repair the relationship. We're all Elsa and Anna up here as we move them separately from room to room and we take a lot of extra precautions that look, well, sort of crazy from the outside. My main strategy is to run the naughty out of them. While Hambone's a superstar on-leash, better behaved than every dog in this 'hood, I keep her extra-restrained, just in case.]

Then I told him, "If you don't like the couple, if you're not into them, tell them you have a migraine and we can excuse ourselves early."

Surprisingly, we both fell profoundly in love with the Smiths during dinner, and at no point was Argo's head not in Fletch's lap. Brad and Angie were entertained by our antics, rather than horrified. They even seemed charmed at having to walk us home, Fletch because he was hammered and me because I fell over a doggie gate and sprained my ankle.

At least I didn't barf in a snowbank. Progress!

Reflecting on our evening the next day, my foot wrapped in an ace bandage and propped on a pillow, I told Fletch, "This is why we can't go to nice places."

Still, the super-cool Smiths weren't scared off. They seemed intrigued by us! Over dinner, we discovered that they'd already made half a dozen pals in our area and we slowly came around to the idea of being friendly with other adults in our own zip code, maybe even the ones who'd procreated.

Everything was perfect.

Almost.

Another downside of having the worst house in the neighborhood is that everyone's place is nicer than ours on the inside, too. When we entered Casa Smith and saw rugs that had never been besmirched by a pit bull with a delicate bladder and no sense of shame, or couches upon which no feline claws were ever sharpened, we were mortified by the damage our pets had wrought. Team Well-Trained Golden Lab was looking pretty good. We always found ways to party at their place instead.

Six months into our relationship, Angie asked, "Are you *ever* going to invite us over?" We couldn't put off the inevitable; if we wanted to stay friends, we had to reciprocate.

We spent weeks getting the homestead in shape. We didn't just vacuum or dust or steam carpets, oh, no. We literally repainted, stripping wallpaper in the laundry room. *[Not just due to the Smiths. The upgrades were needed.]* We turned our boring beige living room into a showplace with Confederate Red walls and fresh white trim. Fletch painstakingly removed the old finish from the fireplace, taking hours to clear each tiny, detailed portion of the dentil molding, armed with nothing but an awl, a heat gun, and a *Serial* podcast. I painted the wood paneling surrounding the hearth the color of green that copper turns when it's oxidized.

Finally, we had a room worthy enough to host our new friends.

The plan was to invite them here for appetizers, then we'd go to a nice restaurant in town. Having spent so much time cleaning, I couldn't manage cooking, too. They arrived, and with the lights turned down, the air cinnamon-scented, my signature cheeseboard loaded and staged, our horrible dogs stashed away in various bedrooms, we *almost* looked like had our shit together.

Close enough for me.

We took an Uber to the restaurant. Conversation flowed as easily as the wine. I compared us to the other diners, most of them the kind of aged preppies that Lisa Birnbach once detailed; Fletch and I were keeping pace.

We were witty. We were urbane. We were the best version of ourselves.

We were bound to screw it up.

When the tequila shots arrived after dinner, the night began to devolve. I forgot to be Best Behavior Jen, morphing instead into my natural state of Hold My Beer Jen.

I dropped the illusion of being someone who was above sharing a Fudgesicle with a dog. I was just myself, for better or worse. On the other side of the table, Fletch turned into G.I. Joe with a soupçon of redneck, white trash, hee-haw-hoedown thrown in for good measure. He spoke of grunts and weapons and his glory days, monitoring cups of whiz for 'Merica.

Meanwhile, I was spouting off about my deep and abiding love for classic hip-hop when our young waiter passed by our table. "Wait, are you talking about *Rick Ross*?" he asked, incredulous. "Here? In the back dining room, where nothing interesting happens *ever*?"

I offered up a line from Ross's *Hustlin'*, detailing how I cut my lines wide and fat and deep. Everyone in the room was impressed with my sick flow, especially the older gal with the walker and the oxygen tank.

Oh, yes. MC RSVP, right here.

At this point, I demanded he take my iPad and play all the Tupac in my music library, "Before something bad happens." He complied and Angie and I were soon shouting the lyrics to *California Love*.

I made her rap.

I made the VP Mergers and Acquisitions *rap*.

In the meantime, Fletch had dragged Brad to the bar and was forcing shots of whiskey down his throat. That's the thing with Fletch and me; we don't rise to other people's levels. *We bring them down to ours.* The restaurant cleared out quickly after that.

Soon, the four of us found ourselves in the backseat of our waiter's mom's minivan. Let me just say that again. *Our waiter's mom picked us up in her minivan.* I have no idea how this came to pass, or why no one else in the party thought Uber to be the preferable alternative.

We went to the waiter's house to drop off his mother, and then he commenced driving us home. Fletch and I tag-teamed, both insisting we head to the Smith's house, knowing that if we went back to our place, we couldn't maintain the elegant façade we'd created earlier. We feared we might accidentally show them where our anxious dog Hambone had shredded the carpet all the way down to the subfloor and eaten through part of the wall, all, *"Check this shit out!"*

[We wanted them in our life, but we didn't want them to know how we lived.]

I grilled our server with questions and I learned that he'd graduated college with honors, but couldn't find a professional job. That's why he was temporarily living at home and serving. He explained he wasn't thrilled about this turn of events, but what can you do?

I was suddenly and profoundly aware of how hard a road the Millennials had and I was sorry.

"So..." the waiter began as we cruised west. "Anyone want weed?"

Why his question shocked me, I'm not sure. Maybe getting high with his patrons was his way of making do. I knew on many levels that the world had changed since 1986, particularly when it came to marijuana. Were I in college now, smoking pot would be the new normal. As usage becomes more and more decriminalized, students consider weed an attractive alternative to drinking to excess. Hell, the *Denver Post* appointed a Cannabis Editor to the paper. We're living in new times, in high times, if you will.

I had to make a choice. At that point, two roads diverged in the yellow woods *[metaphorically.]* Between the woods and the frozen lake, the darkest night of the year, I... I took the road less traveled by.

Unlike the rest of those losers in the van, I just said yes to drugs.

Fletch cracked up at my decision. "This is my wife, Snoop Dog," he announced to no one in particular. I ignored him. If he chose not to be *cool*, to be hip, to be *au courant*, that was on him.

With the kind of enthusiasm only a person full of wine, cheese, and far too much Patron can exhibit, I grabbed the damp joint and inhaled, filling my lungs with the vaguely familiar flavors of wet dog fur and black tea leaves and charbroiled ass. I'm sure I looked incredibly in the know, terribly young and urbane and trendy... for the entire two-tenths of a second it took before I erupted in a massive coughing fit.

"Chicks cannot hold they smoke, that's what it is," Fletch said, quoting Michael Anthony Hall's iconic *Breakfast Club* line.

"Shut up," was the snappiest retort I could muster.

I'd heard the hybrids now are much stronger than the ditch-weed we used to have, but honestly, I didn't feel it. I tried again. Nope, unremarkable.

The universe didn't open and no great truths were revealed. I felt even more sorry for college kids today. I wish they could have been around in my time, when frats hosted keg parties for the whole campus and no one worried about landing a job after graduation. Halloween costumes made everyone happy, not angry. Sure, we had less stuff to watch on TV back then, but we were so busy speaking to each other face to face that we didn't notice.

At this point, we'd arrived at the Smith's home and Angie opened more wine because *that's* what we needed. Argo eyed us warily from his crate, all, "What's with the kid with the apron?"

I took a few more hits, feeling nothing. I figured I was too old and too tubby for pot to have any effect, but I was so pleased with myself for having a sense of adventure!

Our waiter left rather abruptly after he singed off his

bangs, trying to light another joint on the six-burner Viking range. Years ago when Fletch smoked Marlboro Lights, he'd done the same thing. That happened on Thanksgiving when everyone was upstairs in the TV room, playing Wii Bowling. Fletch tried to be all nonchalant when he entered the room, hoping we were too involved in the game to notice, but the whiff of burnt hair and the missing eyebrow were hard to miss.

We wished our waiter well and bade him a goodnight, the smell of carcinogens lingering in his wake, like so many yet to be fulfilled dreams.

Eventually, Angie drifted off to bed and Brad and Argo had to walk both of us home again because we are the kind of people you can't take anywhere, any time.

At least he didn't call a guy to do it.

Fletch immediately crashed on the couch while I tended to our dogs, reflecting on the evening. At least we didn't set our faces on fire; I reveled in that small victory.

I thought back to me at eighteen, tossing my cookies in that snowbank outside of the anonymous apartment party. I'd come a long way since then. Older and wiser, beholden to no preconceived notions. I'd given the Smiths a glimpse of who I was behind the façade and they didn't find me wanting.

I mean, no, I still wasn't about to let them go poking around the TV room upstairs, yet I was quietly content in having made a decent impression. While smoking didn't reveal a new universe, it helped me see I was happy in my little corner of the world.

"P.S.," I said to myself, "today's weed is lamesauce."

At least that's what I though until I woke up at 6:00 a.m. on the bathroom floor, my skirt up around my waist and my underpants at my ankles, having passed out while sitting on the toilet.

Let's milk that, shall we?

I passed out while sitting on the toilet.

Once I came to my senses, I threw up wine and cheese and brisket and Patron, which was far more unpleasant than ice cream and peach liqueur and potpourri. I laid back on the cool tile, realizing that every part of me ached in some way, from head to toe and especially my lungs, which felt like I'd been inhaling mustard gas. I shan't elaborate on how I smelled.

I was way too old for this shit.

I showered and tended to the dogs again and then crawled back into bed until mid-afternoon.

"Hey, Woody Harrelson, how was your night? Enjoy yourself?" Fletch smirked when I finally made an appearance in the great room. He looked none the worse for wear. He was camped out in front of *This Old House*, Libby on his lap and Loki at his side. "Do I need to get us tickets for Coachella now? Want to watch *Pineapple Express*? Wanna make a road trip to Burning Man? Are we moving to Colorado? Shall we subscribe to *High Times* first, then get you that medical marijuana card, or vice-versa?"

My response was obvious.

I just said no.

FLETCH'S LAST WORD:

There were no tequila shots for the men, because clear liquor is for people who have no soul. Brad and I were drinking all the Japanese whiskey. I know whiskey, but I didn't even know

Japanese whiskey was a thing. For the uninitiated, it is a thing, and it is excellent.

We all got busy after that. I think Jen had a new book coming out. We didn't see Brad and Angie for a while. It was maybe six months later until we met up for dinner again. I suggested we order a couple of bottles of wine for the table. Angie said she wasn't drinking. Jen joked, "What, are you knocked up or something?"

Not a joke.

Lost another set of couple-friends to the dark side.

Maybe having a baby was part of their five-year plan and we didn't know. They seem like planners. But it's possible they looked at us and saw the way their lives would roll out if they decided to not have children and we scared them straight.

Good job.

EIGHT

Fountain Of Youth

"AFTER FORTY, a woman has to choose between losing her figure or her face. My advice is to keep your face and stay sitting down."

- Barbara Cartland

"IF FREE I TAKE! If free I take! Aiiiieeeee!"

Fletch heard the screaming long before I reached his office. When I arrived, he leveled his gaze at me over his dual monitors. "I see you've finally completed your descent into insanity."

"No! I'm getting a new face!" I sang, while dancing all around the room.

When he frowned at me, deep furrows formed on his forehead. "Do you need a new face?"

"Um, *duh.*"

I explained how my nurse esthetician Maureen had just

117

called because her plastic surgery office/med spa was having an open house. She sought a demonstration model and I'd previously volunteered. The deal was, I could have any injection I wanted, as much as I needed, all of it free of charge, and the only stipulation was that people attending the open house could watch. I asked her if I could leave my pants on, to which she replied, "Why would you take them off?"

I was so freaking *in*.

"Kid in a candy store!" I squealed. "I'm going to have everything I ever wanted, all at once! Completely on the house!"

"You don't accept free stuff," he replied, which was true. In the ten years of receiving propositions due to my social media platform, I'd almost never taken anything gratis, less because I had so much integrity, and more because no one ever offered me anything I wanted.

"No, I always said if I was going to be beholden, it'd be for Botox or British cars, not some stupid t-shirt or a discount vacuum cleaner. Now, half of my dreams are coming true! If free, I take! Woo!"

Dryly, he replied, "You're happy about this."

"Yes, because... she's doing you, too!"

Fletch's initial shock and dismay registered all over his face, *exactly* why he needed injections, too. While he was not thrilled to have been drafted, I knew he was bothered by the bags under his eyes. I prepared to give him the hard sell. As it turns out, I didn't have to persuade him that much. I mean, who wouldn't dip their foot [read: face] in the fountain of youth, given the chance?

If free, we take.

_____

A FEW WEEKS LATER, Fletch and I were watching television and he ran across a listing that sparked a memory.

"Did I ever tell you about our exchange student?" I asked.

"Yeah, four thousand times," he replied, eyes not leaving the guide. "He's where you got your mantra '*If free, I take.*'"

After being with the same person for more than two decades, we've developed a conversational shorthand. We can communicate entire ideas/reference adventures with but a single word or phrase. That means Fletch was already well-versed in our former exchange student's philosophy of gladly accepting anything offered–from cubes of cheese in the grocery store to brochures passed out on the street–provided it was at no cost.

The upside to our instant understanding is that we dominate every team in Catch Phrase. The downside is that it's rare for either of us to share a new story. In that respect, I don't dread the onset of senility or dementia because we'll feel like newlyweds!

I said, "He's been on my mind because of the *if free* business, and I just had an epiphany when I saw *Sixteen Candles* come up on the guide."

Fletch held up a hand. "We are *not* watching *Sixteen Candles* again. Talk about your four thousand times."

"That's okay." Although I'd have gladly accepted the opportunity to sigh over Jake Ryan for the four thousand and first time, I wasn't suggesting it. This is a subtle [*but crucial*] difference that every woman of a certain age will understand.

I continued, "I realized yet another reason why *Sixteen Candles* is still one of my favorites. The exchange student in it, Long Duk Dong? That grandma and grandpa 'make-a work-a washing machine?' You know that totally happened at my house? My dad used to go on and on about how the lawn never looked better than when we had our exchange student. I suspect my parents took advantage of the free labor."

Fletch made a noise somewhere between a snort and a laugh. A *snortle*, perhaps? "You're just *now* figuring that out?"

"I mean, he didn't have to do more than my brother and I did, but he was definitely put to work," I replied.

"How long was he with you guys? A semester?"

"No, three years."

"*Three years?*"

I shrugged. "He was really good at cutting the lawn. He made it look plaid the way he crosshatched. That's not the funny part, though."

"Don't sell yourself short, it's plenty funny," Fletch replied. He patted my knee for emphasis.

"No, the funny part is when his parents came from Japan for his high school graduation. They spoke almost no English, but they were cute as could be. Occasionally, his mom would come up with a word and she'd get all excited. I remember we were driving somewhere and she saw an RV. She poked me and yelped, 'Camping car!'"

"Cool story, bro." He began to tab through the channels again. Some nights, we'll lose an entire half hour to the cable guide. Him trying to settle on a show is like me with soda at the gas station. When faced with too many choices, a decision is impossible.

"My point was, we had a houseful for three days as my Noni and Grampa were there, too. I'm talking seventy-two hours of no English from his parents, save for 'camping car.' Our poor exchange student and his brother had to spend the whole time interpreting."

The few moments the guys weren't in the room, we did a lot of smiling, nodding, and pointing, which was less awkward than it sounds. Really, the family was darling.

I continued, "We're trying to get ready to go to the ceremony and the scene is like something out of a John Hughes film. The dad literally has three cameras around his neck and he's making us pose all over the front yard. If I tried to write this up as fiction now, people would come after me with pitchforks for perpetrating unkind stereotypes, but it happened. Anyway, I'm wearing spiked heels for the first time and I keep shrieking because I'm sinking in the lawn and getting stuck. I thought I was going to strike oil or something."

Fletch nodded. He was listening but his eyes were glued to the screen. The great irony is that whenever he can't pick something, he ends up watching *Super Troopers*.

Every. Damn. Time. That movie is his crack.

"When we're finally done, we're already late for the ceremony because no one expected Asian Ansel Adams to have to frame the perfect shot first and we're all trying to pack into one Volkswagen like a bunch of circus clowns. Then we scramble out, falling over each other because there's a bee trapped in there. The whole scene is chaos. Neighbors are watching. And in the middle of it, my Noni turns to the Japanese mom and goes, '*Hello, dear, are you from around here?*' like the three days of non-English-speaking togetherness didn't register. No one thinks this is odd except for me. I keep saying, '*Something isn't right with Noni,*' and no one believes me. At the time, they thought I was being bratty, like I was a troublemaker."

"This was the grandmother who had Alzheimer's?"

"Yes."

He frowned at me. "You say that's the *funny* part?"

"In retrospect, not so much. Really, it's more of an example of how no one ever listened to me."

"I'll stop the presses."

Fletch kept tabbing through the listings while I reminisced about our exchange student. He flipped past a bathroom renovation show and that brought forth another memory. "We used to hear weird noise coming from his room."

"Weird, how? Like unholy?"

"Like, crazy-loud bangs and kapows and crashes."

Fletch glanced over at me. "Was he fighting the Joker on the Adam West version of *Batman*? Were the floors suddenly tilted at a forty-five-degree angle?"

I replied, "Construction noises. We had no idea what was going on, but it sounded like he was building something in there. Turns out, he'd been sawing a hole in the closet wall between his room and the bathtub. Then he poked out all the grout between the tile so he could spy."

"A *Porky's* scenario?"

[For those too young, too old, or too discerning to have seen Porky's, the male students in this film drilled through the wall of the women's locker room to watch the ladies shower.]

"Exactly. I didn't piece together what he'd done until years and years later, but once I did, I felt kind of violated, you know? That's why I rarely *like* his Facebook posts."

"Social media purgatory, the ultimate punishment."

"I'm not mad. He was just a kid, too. I'm sure he's mortified now. Still, it's disconcerting."

Fletch shrugged. "Somewhat, but I'll give him a A-plus for ingenuity. Kids today don't appreciate how easy it is to see anyone naked now. This is our generation's version of walking five miles uphill in snow to get to school. They're just a search term away from every perversion you ever hoped to imagine. Porn took *effort* back in our day, and if you did see boobs, damn it, you *appreciated* them."

"That wasn't the takeaway I expected you to have," I said. "Anyway, you'll love this bit. My mother fixed the grout with toothpaste."

Fletch made a pained face at this. I loved that it was the shoddy craftsmanship portion of the story that caused the grimace and not the peeping.

I continued. "That means I never told you her response, either. She goes, *'Please, Jennifer, he wasn't looking at* you. *I'm sure he did it so he could watch* me.'"

He *snortled* again. "No."

"Oh, yes. What teen *wouldn't* prefer stretch marks and a hysterectomy scar over hot jailbait? This is back before gravity was a factor, by the way. Samantha Baker had nothing on me; I *embodied* perky."

He ran his hand over his beard, as he always does when trying to wrap his mind around something. "Holy shit."

"Right?"

Fletch was quiet for a long time, before finally saying, "'The upside here is that's a completely new story."

He returned his focus to the television and continued to read every single listing for all nine million channels... at least until he figured out which network was running *Super Troopers*.

As he endlessly tabbed, I thought about that era. Back then, I was subject to unrelenting pressure about my appearance, particularly from my hyper-competitive mother, although my father would occasionally chime in, too. *"My God, Jennifer, you're getting fat,"* was his go-to phrase, even though I was five foot seven and approximately one hundred and twenty pounds, about the same dimensions as your typical Miss America contestant. My being imperfect was the one topic on which they could agree.

Nothing fucked up there.

My hair, my face, my figure, all were ripe topics for conversation and prime sources of criticism. There were so many expectations on how I should look, on standards of beauty by which I should abide, yet I wasn't supported with any resources. No one *helped* me find ways to look my best. Instead, they took pride in me when I pulled it all together and punished me when I didn't. Case in point, the summer after my freshman year of college where I was forced to lose two pounds a week or be grounded.

Grounded.

In college.

For having gained the Freshmen Ten.

My errors were gleefully cataloged when I went awry. *"That does* nothing *for you,"* was one of my mother's go-to phrases whenever I made what she considered a poor choice.

Until I worked with a therapist, I assumed other families operated the same way as mine, that every parent was obsessed with their kid's appearance. That they all demanded credit for their children's successes, regardless of how hands-off they might have been in the events leading up to it. I figured everyone's folks left their offspring to fend for themselves, disciplining them when they got it wrong. And when that inevitably would happen, the norm was to bring up the incident again and again, never allowing those children to forget their mistakes because, "That's what builds character."

I couldn't even fathom the notion of "helicopter parenting," as I had no clue people could be so unconditionally invested in their children. My God, my father wouldn't even have a conversation with me, unless we were talking about himself. That's why I'm so obsessed when I see moms and dads really being there for their kids; I never realized that was an option.

That's why my goal growing up was to figure out how to be "the good one," how to be as faultless as I could, as thin and pretty and meticulous as possible, a rule follower and a hard worker with the kind of grades that would keep me under everyone's radar so I wouldn't be the butt of family jokes, so that I could avoid being bullied by those whose only obligation was to love me without condition.

I guess it's no wonder that I finally declared my liberation by getting fat.

———

WHEN I DID FINALLY START SHAKING off the extra pounds, I did it for me. In all the years I've been with Fletch, he's never once commented about my weight. He wouldn't even reply to questions on whether certain pants made my ass look big.

[Because he is smart.]

With the help of my emotional eating counselor, I developed a healthy relationship with food, and, subsequently, my weight. But I guess some of what was drilled into me as a kid hasn't been as easy to shed as the weight. While I'm a lot better with my body, I have become fixated on my face, specifically with holding back the ravages of time.

What I've learned is that fat is the fountain of youth. Cheeseburgers are better than botulism when it comes to plumping fine lines. And while losing weight is the best thing I could do for my health, it blows goats when it comes to appearing younger.

My skin looked amazing after the first thirty pounds. My turkey-wattle disappeared and I was starting to see a tiny bit of definition on my jawline. My head was demonstrably less potato-shaped, but none of the little lines had made an appearance yet.

I looked *fresh*.

To say I was satisfied with myself and my progress at that time would be an understatement. When raised in a house with those who are impossible to please, with those who continue to move the goal line, you develop coping methods if you want to stay sane.

You must become your own cheerleader.

You figure out how to self-soothe with positive affirmations. If you don't, food can be a dangerous but attractive alternative. A donut can give you the kind of hug from inside that celery just can't muster.

Cake loves you unconditionally.

For a long time, I used a layer of fat to buffer myself from the rest of the world. Once I let go of what had been keeping me down, the weight came off and a more genuine type of confidence returned.

Around this time of perfect anti-aging stasis, Fletch and I were visiting the poppy installation at the Tower of London. Artists had crafted 888,246 ceramic flowers, meant to commemorate each British life lost during World War I. The exhibit, called *Blood Swept Lands and Seas of Red*, filled the moat around the Tower with what resembled a river of blood. I was incredibly moved by the gravity of the scene, and the extent to which the Brits honored their heroes. However, there was a tiny, vain part of me delighting in realizing that my bold lipstick choice–a color I was too timid to wear when I was heavier–matched the poppies perfectly.

[*I know, I know.*]

Fletch captured this moment on film. In the shot, I'm grinning like a goddamned lunatic and there's an elderly British woman to my right, casting an almost unfathomable amount of side-eye in my direction. The worst part is, while I totally deserved her scorn, I still love the photo.

After we returned home, and as I continued to work on my health and fitness, my face began to deflate. The loss of that collagen was horribly aging. While I felt terrific, I looked haunted and hollow and gaunt.

The paradox here is I'm fine with my age and happy to tell people how old I am. I have one friend who has lied for so long that she's not even sure exactly how old she is. She literally must look on her driver's license. Although, I've had to do that, too. I'm always whatever age I've turned for the first three months after my birthday and beyond that, I round up. I forgot that I wasn't *already* forty-eight and I was thrilled to receive a bonus year of life on my last birthday.

The wrinkles, though? Not a fan. I wanted my outsides to match the way I felt inside.

And that was finally about to happen, because if free, I sure as hell was going to take.

———

I'VE DONE light maintenance by way of injectable and filler over the past few years, never to the extent of a Real Housewife, though. That's not because I think those ladies look plastic; rather, it's that Maureen refuses to over-fill, no matter how much I beg. Honestly, I wouldn't mind if I trended a bit blow-up doll.

When I went in for an appointment after the first fifty pounds, Maureen explained all the different, non-surgical ways we could fix the damage. As budget's always a factor and if I wanted to stay married, I couldn't fork over an amount equivalent to college tuition.

For a minute, I considered what would happened if I *didn't* want to stay married, imagining a world in which all my old stories were new again. Then I'd probably have to set up an online dating profile and I literally cannot memorize one more single password, I am at capacity. Plus, I hated the idea of losing at Catch Phrase, so the thought was fleeting.

Instead of replacing the flat tire that was my face, I'd simply retread it with Botox and some filler around my eyes. While an improvement, I didn't look as fresh as medical science would allow and folks had stopped carding me at the grocery store. That was kind of a bummer. The sign says they ask for ID if they think the customer is less than forty, so I felt sad when buying my High Life with over-forty abandon.

Fletch and I had to consult with Maureen before the event so she could make sure she had the right products on hand. Knowing that the cosmeceutical companies were supplying the syringes and that we'd be doing the practice a favor by being thorough, I went in with a laundry list.

We'd start by eradicating the lines on my forehead. When not immobilized and I'm able to make expressions, such as surprise, I feel that this area resembles a package of hot dogs, each furrow in a tidy stack on top of another, a veritable tower o' wieners. Clearly, it needed work.

Next up, crows' feet. I am anti-any portion of my body resembling an animal part. [See also: Bulldog Jowls, Cat Bunghole Lips.] We'd then travel slightly south and plump up my cheekbones with mid-face filler. The benefit here is: (A) new cheekbones where I never had them before, and, (B) Juvederm Voluma acts as a winch, hoisting up everything below. Goodbye, flabby chin skin, hello, getting carded at the grocery store again!

Every time you see a celebrity and think, "They've had work done. Bad work," it's because they filled up lost volume in the apples of their cheek, instead of over their orbital bone. Rookie mistake. Always fill the sides, not the front.

Next up, we'd replenish the deep wells in my tear trough, which is the under-eye area. While I didn't love the idea of anyone wielding a needle so close to what I use to see, I must reiterate, if free, I take.

We'd move on to re-inflate my cupid's bow, not to the extent of giving me Duck Bill/Trout Pout, but so that my lipstick wouldn't bleed. We'd finish up by injecting the marionette lines, which is where the face loses volume on either side of the chin below the bottom lip.

Oh, and if Maureen could come up with anything else I could do, that would be fine, too.

When Maureen sat Fletch down, she asked, "What are you thinking?"

He peered at himself in the small mirror she'd handed him. "I don't like how I seem kind of tired under my eyes. Like I need a nap, even when I'm well-rested. If we could work on that, I'd be good to go."

"That's it?" she confirmed.

"Yeah, I'm okay with that," he replied.

"No," I interjected. "He needs *everything*." I began to rattle off all the parts of his face that could be improved.

"Thanks a lot," he said, regarding himself in the mirror, a hand gingerly touching all the newfound trouble spots. "I didn't realize I was so hideous."

"Listen, this isn't for you, it's for me. I've gotta see your face every day over the breakfast table. You can't be all droopy when I'm fabulous. If I'm going to look younger, damn it, so are you."

———

I HAD NEVER BEEN MORE excited for an event in my life, not on my graduation after *eleven years* of college, definitely not when I was married. The time had come for the Plastic Surgery and Med Spa Open House!

The sane, therapy-graduating portion of my brain kept telling me to slow my roll, that there wasn't anything wrong with my face at present, that I was under no obligation to meet the impossible expectations of being the prettiest and the thinnest and the best. I told myself that I'd earned every spot and wrinkle through all the experiences in my life. Really, I should be regarding those imperfections as badges of honor. Yet those thoughts were quickly drowned out by the rest of my brain which was screeching, *"Imma get my free, young face on!"*

When we arrived at the doctors' offices, every room was mobbed with Lisa Rinna doppelgängers, from the reception area to the surgical suite, each double-fisting glasses of white wine and inspecting one another for visible hairline stitches.

Fletch whispered to me, "Why are they all wearing hairy vests and spangled bell-bottoms?"

I glanced down at my nautical striped top and red Dankso sneakers. If their sartorial choices were what's hot, then I was very cold. Frankly, I'd been stuck buying clothes in the plus department for so long that I had no clue what might be in vogue. While I'd finally been able to start shopping in regular stores, I found I still bought the same preppy things, just in smaller sizes. LL Bean sold my favorite navy and white French sailor's shirts from XS to 3X. Whatever size I ended up, they had me covered.

We worked our way through the crowd and found the room where Maureen would do her demonstration. She sat me down, covering my face with numbing cream, which would take full effect in twenty minutes. As clientele would trickle in, she'd explain what was about to happen. My Before shots played on a loop on the large flat-screen to my side. In my head, I kept saying, "*See you in hell, Oldie Hawn.*"

Once numb, she began the injections, which feel like small pinpricks. They don't hurt, per se, but the sound of the needle puncturing my skin causes a noise that normally makes me flinch. However, because I had an audience, I kept on my game face, smiling the entire time. I was a pro. I'd be the best model they'd ever had.

A woman of indeterminate age came in to observe. Her skin was like someone had covered it tightly with Saran Wrap. While she didn't have a single line or pore, all her features were about an inch higher than where they'd originally started. I couldn't see her ears under her curtain of blonde extensions. If I had to guess, I'd say they were located somewhere on the back of her head. Still, if this makes her happy, then I had no room to judge.

Until the bitch began to judge *me*.

"Oh, my Gawd," she gasped, as Maureen touched my forehead with the tiny syringe, the needle's tip about the same width as an eyelash. The woman couldn't move her mouth when she spoke, so it was almost like she was her own personal ventriloquism dummy. She clutched her glass of pinot grigio as though it were a life preserver, pressing a hand to her cat-fur vest. "I would *never* do an injection. Needles? No thank you, ma'am! Anytime I start to see wear and tear on the old kisser, I tell the doc to put me under and lift it all! Needles full of poison are just crazy! You're crazy!"

After she sashayed off and the room cleared, I said, "Wait, so she'll risk going under anesthesia, spending twenty grand on a facelift, losing all that recovery time, instead of dropping a couple of hundred bucks on Botox a few times a year? And *I'm* the crazy one?"

"You understand she was bragging, right?" Fletch replied.

Huh. I did not.

Maureen waited to do the Juvederm Voluma in my cheekbones until the room filled up again, because the Befores and Afters are the most instantaneous and dramatic. While the Botox would take a couple of weeks to fully set, the fillers would change the shape of my face immediately.

With an expert hand, Maureen inserted the filler on the left side of my face and then had everyone move in to look at me. Ten sets of eyes peered down at me and I got a contact buzz from the wine fumes. Everyone was impressed at how much one syringe could do.

"Here," Maureen said, handing me a mirror. "Look at how different the right side is now." My jowls were gone on the left, as were the deep, asymmetrical trenches on the side of my lip. *[I have the bad habit of speaking out of one side of my mouth only, as though I'm a gangster in a '30s film.]*

"That's amazing!" I replied. "Fletch, Fletch, lean in and see! This is what I'll look like after I have a stroke!"

At one point during the night, Maureen said that because of my Mediterranean skin, I've aged better than those with thinner skin. That's when I mentioned how old I was and the entire audience gasped.

They weren't shocked because I did or did not look my age, but because I dared mention *the number.* They all recoiled as if I'd screamed *"Voldemort!"* in the banquet hall at Hogwarts.

When Maureen was finishing up my lips, a leathery woman shuffled in and asked about cost. She wanted to know how she could erase the years. Maureen gave her a rundown of options and then handed her a price list. The woman immediately began to complain in her deep smoker's voice. Were my eyes closed, I'd have sworn she was one of Marge Simpson's sisters.

"That's all too much," she barked. "I can't afford any of this."

I totally understood. Nothing we were doing was cheap. I was there only because I'd exchanged my dignity for a couple of syringes.

[Suddenly I understood how people could ruin their lives for one more hit of heroin.]

"We do run specials," Maureen offered. "Next month, for example, we're offering twenty percent off all fillers."

"That's still too much. What else you got?"

Maureen tapped the sheet. "We have so many other options. You might consider a few rounds with the laser, as that will eradicate the brown spots and bring up the clear, younger skin underneath them."

To me, that sounded like a reasonable alternative. I always associate liver spots with old age.

She looked at her sheet. "Pfft. Still too expensive."

"Perhaps if this is something you want, you could set aside a portion of the cost each month and save up."

"Nope, that doesn't sound like me."

"Girl... me either," I thought.

"Then perhaps you'd want to invest in some our skin-care products, like moisturizers and sunscreen."

Seriously, it's always possible to slow down the aging process, no matter how old you are. While the price of some beauty treatments can be exorbitant, there's always lower-cost alternatives. For example, I swear by Oil of Olay Regenerist. South Korean snail mucous only runs about twelve bucks on Amazon, and it's a lifesaver once you get past the idea of it. *[It feels like egg yolk and there's no odor. It's seriously fine, don't be a big baby about it.]* The drugstore's full of low-cost options, too, like Vitamin E oil. And anyone can shave off years without spending a dime through adequate hydration and enough sleep.

"Couldn't you just give me some free injections now? I'll do whatever you're giving her." She gestured towards me and moved as though to stand in line behind my chair.

Maureen replied, "I'm sorry, I already have all my models for tonight."

"Then when are you doing this again? I want to get it done and I don't want to pay for it."

I appreciated how Maureen could stay focused and patient while she shaped my lips, as I'd stopped feeling empathy. In fact, it was all I could do to not kick the lady in the gooch with one of my red sneakers.

Maureen sighed. "Why don't you give them your name at the desk and I'll see what I can do?"

The woman nodded and left without another word, not even a "thanks."

"This is why you're a professional," I said. "I'd have been all, '*Take your forty bucks and buy yourself another carton of cigarettes. Really, go the other way and* exacerbate *the aging process. Just smoke more.*'"

Maureen said, "I didn't know what to say to her. She's not a client and I've never seen her here. I asked you to model because I've known you for five years. This is a thank you for being a loyal customer."

"I really appreciate it!" I replied. "This is a vain girl's dream come true."

I would have smiled, but I had a needle in my lip.

When I was done, I traded places with Fletch. He handled everything like a champ, like he was meant to get injections, like he was born to be a lady who lunched. I wondered if the spangled bell-bottoms were growing on him.

As we offered our thanks and said our good byes, Maureen cautioned us that we might bruise or experience some swelling over the next few days, which is typical. Again, not my first rodeo.

I saw Fletch's face before I saw my own when we woke up the next morning. He appeared to have traveled back in time fifteen years during the night. I half-expected to turn on the radio and hear Destiny's Child or Matchbox Twenty.

Fletch looked like he'd been on a relaxing tropical vacation, only to return home to find he'd won the lottery, whereas I looked like a victim of domestic violence.

My tear troughs had swollen up to the size of deviled

eggs and I was bruised all about my mouth and chin. Every place the needle touched had doubled or tripled in size. I knew this was possible, especially in having so many procedures at once, so I'd planned to stay in the house for the next few days. The bruising was entirely my fault, though. I'd forgotten to stop taking aspirin a week before the procedures.

Fletch had to go to a meeting unexpectedly, where everyone praised him for, "A fresh haircut? New shirt? A different workout regime? Whatever you're doing, keep it up!" His coworkers didn't know what happened, only that it had agreed with him.

Meanwhile, I had to take my cat to the vet, where everyone at the front desk assumed I'd been mouthy. The more I tried to explain that I wasn't punched, the less likely it sounded, particularly since our previous two visits had been when Libby and Hambone had gotten into it. Nothing says "classy" like a pit bull fight.

While Fletch basked in the glow of his fantastic new visage and youthful good looks, I spent the next week pressing bags of frozen peas to my face, ignoring the fact that I (temporarily) looked worse than before I started.

Eventually, the swelling went down and the bruising disappeared, making way for my younger face. But that's not the best part, nor is it that everything was entirely, blessedly free. Or that when I see myself in the mirror, I still look like me, only a slightly better version of it and now my outside absolutely lines up with how I feel on the inside.

The best part is, Fletch and I finally have a new story to tell, a new conversational shortcut we can take, and a guaranteed laugh whenever the other person says, "Just smoke more," or references cat-fur vests and spangled bell-bottoms.

Wait, no; that's a lie.

The best part is being carded at the grocery store again.

––––––

FLETCH'S LAST WORD:

I am never going to understand cat-fur vests or spangled bell-bottoms.

NINE

Little Pink Houses

"PRIVACY-LIKE EATING and breathing–is one of life's basic requirements."

- Katherine Neville

"LOVE IS AN ACTION VERB."

"Kiss each other every day."

"Never stop dating your spouse."

"Yeah, okay," I say to myself, reading the *Huffington Post's* words of wisdom from married people to newly-weds, *"but that's not everything."* While all this advice is important, they forgot the most important component to long-lasting happiness:

Never share a sink with your spouse.

I'm not saying you can't double up on a toilet or tub; that's doable. Not ideal, but doable.

But God have mercy on those who share a sink.

The sink is a trouble zone, far more than the commode

or shower. Sink habits vary greatly from person to person. It's rare that two people have all the same proclivities. For example, I have a friend who's the greatest girl in the world. She could not be more kind, more giving, more present in conversation. Yet what she does to bathroom surfaces is unthinkable; it's like she paints the walls with Sensodyne.

Add a partner who shaves into the mix and that's a fight waiting to happen. Every damn day, cocked and ready to blow. No matter how tidy Fletch is in all other aspects of life, something happens when he picks up a razor.

Something *untoward*.

I suspect he shakes his head all wet-Golden-Retriever-after-a-swim-style once he cleans up his neck beard. That's the only logical explanation for the tiny hairs strewn from one side of the counter to the other. Even on the days he doesn't shave, stubble leeches from the walls, like crystalline efflorescence migrating from masonry.

It's maddening.

So many things can go awry with a shared sink area. From improperly squeezed tubes of Crest to lids left askew to leaving the bar of Irish Spring wet in the soap dish to not quiiiiiiite turning off the tap, the sink is the Fallujah of household.

The sink can and will break a relationship.

This is why I pray for those couples who decide to move into a "tiny house," especially when the kitchen sink is the only one in the whole dwelling.

I was not initially opposed to the "tiny house" phenomenon. When images started popping up in my Facebook feed a couple of years ago, I'd click over to inspect the blueprints, marveling at how the designers managed to wedge so many amenities into two hundred square feet. I loved the clever details, such as stacked shelves doubling as staircases and all-in-one washer/dryers. Plus, a lot of the tiny houses had wheels, meaning someone could take their place with them should they need to relocate. How cool is that?

Tiny houses, which range from one hundred and fifty to four hundred square feet, are basically mobile homes with better PR. I've always had a soft spot for trailer living. My father's parents (Nanny and Gaga) bought a massive mobile home in New Hampshire after they retired. Their place was a triple-wide model, located on an acre of rolling green lawn. The spacious kitchen accommodated a table for eight. Nanny had plenty of room to prepare her signature roast beef, seasoned to perfection. The large living area held two huge divans, where three generations could gather to watch *Donny & Marie*. They had a couple of bedrooms that could house one king bed, or in my grandparents' case, two twins, separated by a nightstand. The trailer was bordered by wide expanse of metal awning that created a shaded patio, perfect for listening to my Gaga spin his crazy yarns about *[what I thought was the fictional land of]* Nova Scotia.

From end to end, Nanny and Gaga's manufactured home was far longer than our house in New Jersey and it boasted better amenities, such as a full pantry, a dedicated laundry room, and walk-in closets. Everything was pristine and sparkling, but built on a 7/8ths scale. I loved it.

I always preferred to stay with the New Hampshire grandparents, as my maternal grandparents' house was... vaguely terrifying. My Noni and Grampa grew up in abject poverty after having immigrated from Italy, so Noni was loathe to dispose of anything for fear she may need it later. Nothing that came into her home was ever permitted to exit, so even though their place was sizable–two stories with a full basement and a vast attic–every room was packed full.

For example, Noni had three refrigerators in her kitchen, yet a pair of them were non-functional for the entirety of my childhood. These dead behemoths served no purpose, save for squatting on valuable kitchen real estate.

The one working fridge was easily fifty years old, short and wide, wedged into the back of a narrow pantry, its shelves groaning under the weight of pots full of mystery meat sauce.

[Squirrel? Possum? Raccoon? No one knew for sure.]

The appliance had an external motor that would grind away, reeking of petroleum and old cheese. Because said engine produced a hum like that of a Panther Airboat, my extended family would compensate for the noise by yelling over their ravioli and Sunday gravy.

Noni's fridge was manufactured before freezers were included/invented, yet she patently believed any frozen item placed inside would stay in that state through her sheer force of will. She was perpetually pissed off when this didn't happen. The upside is that when the pints of stored ice cream would inevitably melt, brother and I could pour the contents on cereal during our visits.

Ironically, last summer when Fletch didn't properly close our fridge door, the motor burned out. We called an authorized Sub-Zero repair service and found out that the repair would cost three thousand dollars.

Not kidding again.

Three thousand dollars.

In addition, we couldn't replace the broken fridge with

anything more affordable as no one makes them that specific size anymore. [*This model is twenty-eight years old.*] We'd have to tear out all the cabinetry around it and either rebuild or live with a fridge that didn't match the separate freezer and had big gaps all around it. Every solution we researched was more expensive than the one before it. Fletch thought maybe he could fix it himself, but parts weren't available.

So, I moved everything to the cheap beer refrigerator in the laundry room and found myself using the empty Sub-Zero to hold stuff, resigned that a kitchen full of dead appliances was not only my fate but also my cultural heritage. We lived this way for three months until it occurred to me to call an *unauthorized* repair service.

I've never been so happy to write a check without a comma in it.

Anyway, after my Nanny and Gaga passed away, my mother, brother, and I spent the summer on their property, as it was only minutes from the beach. We'd splash around in the ocean all day, often returning with Samantha, our dog, in the evenings. Sam loved to dive into the warm tidal pools formed in the wake of submerged boulders. My dad would come up for weekends and vacations and he'd buy me a new book of paper dolls every visit.

Given a bit of distance, my parents found time to miss each other, and I can't recall any fights that summer. This was the happiest time in my family's life. That's why I always associated mobile homes with paradise. Trailers were clean and nice and new, so orderly, a calming medley of old gold and avocado green, where grandmothers used salt and cooked meat she didn't trap herself.

That's why I was absolutely Team Tiny House.

Until I watched the show *Tiny House Hunters.*

I wasn't a viewer initially. In fact, HGTV was three seasons-deep before noticed that Facebook had reached critical mass regarding despising everyone/everything about the phenomenon.

I enjoy nothing more than being righteously indignant over that which is trivial, so I set my DVR. I wasn't even annoyed at first, didn't understand the fuss. My inaugural viewing involved a funky, older Canadian woman looking to simplify her life. She was tired of being shackled to a mortgage and yearned for the freedom and mobility a tiny house might offer. *[I bet she'd never be expected to fork over three stacks to fix a fridge in a tiny house.]* As she inspected various tiny houses on wheels, each as neatly appointed as a small yacht, I understood the appeal.

Despite my claustrophobia, the idea of being in such a compressed space didn't bother me. Each of the tiny houses she saw smacked of coziness, like living in the ultimate reading nook. Human beings are a lot like goldfish, able to adapt to any size tank. Ultimately, they'll be fine in any place that gives them a sense of peace.

While waiting for the next installment of *Tiny House Hunters* to record, I stumbled across a different tiny house show. In this one, the hosts give the buyers a couple of big paper grocery sacks and tell them they can only bring what fits into the bags.

I almost had a panic attack.

Personally, I could adjust to living in fewer square feet, but winnowing down ninety-five percent of my stuff? No way. The prospect is too daunting; I'm exhausted just imagining it. I never want to have to make that many assessments.

Because I overthink everything, I stress out when faced with multiple choices, even when they're all fine options, with low stakes. I literally feel my heart pounding when looking at the beverage choices in a 7/11. Am I more in the mood for a hot drink or a cold one? Do I want a cappuccino from the machine or would I prefer a hazelnut coffee? Would I be better off with water, and if so, do I want the kind with or without electrolytes? Do I get a regular Slurpee or one of the lower sugar options? And if I decide on a carbonated beverage, do I want it from the fountain or in a bottle or can?

If I feel this way deciding on a soda, I can't imagine weighing the merits of every possession. I like *things*. Perhaps this is a character flaw, but I'm willing to live with it. Of course, Fletch never has this problem. He'll opt for Diet Coke every time, unless he's thirsty and then he chooses water.

Soon after, the DVR picked up a second episode. In this one, an artsy woman relocated to Asheville, North Carolina, and was hunting for a small space of her own while she figured out her second act in life. She viewed a few darling options and chose the cute little home that felt like an enchanted treehouse.

Why was this show making everyone in my timeline so insane? I didn't *despise* the ladies I'd seen; I wanted to read contemporary women's fiction about their lives! I'm not looking to live tiny, but I understand the overarching desire to abridge, to streamline. Sometimes it feels like all Fletch and I do is address things around the house, whether it's repairing, refurbishing, cleaning, or beautifying, and, Christ, I'm tired. I love our home, but occasionally I wish we could spend more time *living* in it and less time *tending* to it.

I roped Fletch into viewing the show after our weekly take-out run. I'd told him our friends had been hate-watching and maybe we could enjoy deriding it together. During the *Chicago Fire* season, our tradition is to spend our Tuesday nights eating cheeseburgers and pointing out plot holes or clumsy dialogue.

Tuesdays are the best.

Now, a caveat about hate-watching. This term is a misnomer. Having affection for the show you hate-watch is key. I don't want to spend time consuming anything I don't like because life's too short. Fletch and I never critique *Chicago Fire* because it's bad; parts are exceptional. Instead, we're more like Statler and Waldorf on the balcony at the *Muppet Show*, shouting constructive criticism where the program *should* be better, i.e. the episode where Severide blithely rifled through a suspected drug house without ever acknowledging his was an illegal search. We'd both turned into *Arrested Development's* Lucille Bluth that night, shouting, *"Get a warrant!"* between bites of fried pickles.

We'd missed having something to mock, so we hoped *Tiny House Hunters* might take *Chicago Fire's* place during hiatus. Luckily, the two episodes I'd already seen were an anomaly, as everything that came after was prime material.

I suddenly understood Facebook's collective scorn when we saw the episode where two assholes decided to abandon their sprawling suburban property for a tiny home on a secluded mountain range… with their pack of huge mutts.

"They're basically buying a dog house," Fletch said, gesturing towards the screen with a French fry. "If we turn sixty and decide, *"Hey, let's live in a dog house!"* Then we've made a lifetime of bad decisions."

"At least they didn't pawn off their pets at a shelter," I

replied. While I reviled the tiny home buyers, their pups did seem to be delighted with the new digs. "I feel like the dogs are happy living so close with their pack."

He said, "These morons have a dorm fridge and a single pantry shelf! You know much food they can store? Two days' worth. The first blizzard is gonna hit and they'll be stranded up there and their precious dogs are going to eat the owners' faces. Mark my words."

He was probably not wrong.

I fully embraced the hate after an episode where two smug hipsters blathered on about how wasteful living in anything but a tiny house is.

"They are *the worst*," I said.

"America's still the Land of the Free, which means if I want to heat and cool a superfluous guest room, that is *my* business," Fletch said.

That set of hipsters was not actually the worst. Instead, we passed the crown to the two who decided to live in a camper. Not a tiny, mobile house, but an actual old-school, toilet-in-the-shower, see-you-on-the-open-road, hundred-and-forty-square-foot camper.

"Do you get the feeling that the girlfriend in this scenario isn't going to stick around for long? The guy seemed way more into everything than she did," Fletch said.

"She kept gritting her teeth. She's going to meet an investment banker with a Manhattan townhouse *and* a summer house in the Hamptons and she'll leave his sorry ass so fast," I replied once I swallowed the Kalamata olive from my Greek salad. "How do the toilet/shower combos work in those little campers, exactly? The 'wet baths?' Wouldn't the seat always be damp? How do you keep the toilet paper dry when the whole room's a shower?"

Fletch bit into his Vinnie Burgerino [*double beef, mozzarella, and* giardiniera, *delish!]* and shrugged.

I added, "At least they have an actual toilet. Remember the people last week with the dry-flushing? Ugh."

The dry-flush model is even more disturbing than the wet bath or the composting toilet, another popular choice in tiny homes. Composting systems entail eliminating in a hole and then covering the contents with wood chips, which aids in the process of biodegrading. With dry flushing, there's not even any wood buffer between you and your business. Instead, waste is encapsulated in a plastic bag and then it just sits there in the cartridge, mere inches below the seat, each deposit steadfastly awaiting your return—much like a faithful hunting dog—before you finally dig in and collect everything, reunited once more before bidding the whole lot a proper goodbye.

As for me, once I'm done *going...* well, I want it gone, not someday, but right this damn minute. I'm talking Viking funeral here, one flush and it's off to Valhalla. I don't want my own personal refuse hanging around like some regrettable Spring Break hook-up who can't take a hint.

And there I was, thinking *sharing a sink* was bad.

With each progressive episode, we marveled over the potential buyers' expectations. We contemplated creating a drinking game for every time someone complained about the lack of closet space, but quickly realized our livers couldn't process that much alcohol. *"The whole thing is a closet!"* we'd holler. We loved all the ridiculous objections, too, such as, "Where shall I keep my antique samovar collection?" *"Bitch, please,"* we'd say. *"You have room for two juice glasses and a spork."*

One night while Fletch was out of town, I discovered a

cache of episodes on Netflix from a previous season. I grabbed a bowl of popcorn and settled in. I planned on watching each chronologically, until I stumbled across this gem of an episode description:

Family of Six Goes Tiny

"*This is going to be good,*" I thought. I considered waiting for Fletch to come home so we could watch together, but the potential siren song of stupid was too great.

The family decided they needed to abandon their comfortable, gracious twenty-five-hundred-square-foot home in lieu of a tiny house. They were aiming for one hundred square feet of space per person. The family hoped to grow closer in the experience and wanted to decrease their footprint.

I abhorred them with both passion and immediacy.

Here's the thing; I care about the melting ice caps. I do. I want to protect the environment as much as the next person. It's my moral imperative as a human being to monitor my own consumption, to conserve, to be mindful. The thing is? By opting to be childfree, I'm responsible for *zero population growth*. My biological line ends *here*.

I'm *it*.

I'm the only branch on a tree that dies with me.

Yes, while I do have a superfluous guest room, I've never bought a disposable diaper. I don't load up landfills with broken plastic toys and abandoned athletic gear after my fickle progeny decided lacrosse is for losers. Pre-packaged Lunchables, bottle liners, Gogurts? Never put any of those in my shopping cart. I'm not spending all day, every day for an entire decade in a giant SUV, as I ferry little people to soccer practice or ballet recitals or math tutors. There are many days where I don't even use the car, and when I do, it's just to zip the three miles to the gym or grocery store. I can go six weeks without refilling my gas tank. Also, my house stays parked in the same place so I'll never burn precious fossil fuel to move it when I feel wanderlust. In actual numbers, my not having a child saves more than nine thousand metric tons of carbon. That's why I'm very unhappy when people like the smug bastards in this episode feel compelled to lecture *me* about *my* ecological obligations.

Motherfuckers have four kids.

While enthusiastic procreation is absolutely their right, if each of them has four kids, and then they have four kids, and so on and so on like that campy old shampoo commercial, the family tree expands out to infinity, which will result in a metric shit-ton of beings eventually consuming resources like so many locusts. So kindly get off my jock if I don't choose to share a sink with my spouse.

As I watched, I noticed that the four children were profoundly less enthusiastic than their folks about the prospect of living in a tiny house. They each wore the same shell-shocked expression that I'd donned when the certified Sub-Zero repairman handed me his estimate.

Those poor things.

I got the feeling that it's them who are obligated to be the grown-ups in their family. Even the Realtor in the episode was, like, "You're not seriously doing this, right?"

The parents toured a handful of properties, each worse than the one before, not just in terms of size, but also regarding condition. One of them didn't even have a bath-room, only an outhouse.

Which means no sink what-so-goddamned-ever.

In two out of the three homes, the four children would have to share a bedroom with their parents.

Share a bedroom with their parents.

I'm sorry, did we lose a war or something?

On the bright side, whatever money they'd save on mortgage payments could go directly to the therapists tasked with fixing the kids after hearing their folks celebrate their love on the futon across from them.

Listen, lots of kids grow up angry or resentful with their family for something. It's my opinion that while this is inevitable, it's the parents' job not to throw gas on the fire. And making your offspring share a bedroom with you is a spark and a puddle of Kerosene.

At least each of the houses under consideration were terrestrial-based, and not on wheels, which meant they'd have their own yard. That was something, at least.

While I still quietly appreciate a home with mobility, inevitably the other Tiny House buyers end up parking on a family member's lawn. Across the country, thousands of unwitting brothers and sisters are sipping their gins-and-tonic through clenched teeth at their tennis clubs, wondering if they're ever, *ever* going to get their idiot siblings off their grass.

My guess is no.

The fourteen-year-old seemed to be taking the downsizing the hardest. I hope that when she pleads her case to become an emancipated minor, she'll use the footage from this episode.

[I kid you not, my mind is still reeling at the idea of six people and one sink. I swear to you, I'd rather be two girls and one cup than six people and one sink.]

Each show ends with a jump forward in time so we can see the family adjusting to life in their tiny house. Author

Chuck Wendig predicts that every tiny house purchase conducted by couples will eventually end in murder-suicide, but our outlook is slightly less grim. Fletch and I envision more of a divorce scenario or the purchase of a second tiny house, which will live next to the original on some long-suffering sister's lanai.

For the family of six, they all came across as happy in the last scene of the episode and the parents did a fine job of maximizing every inch of space.

Truth? I was impressed.

This family was able to eke three bedrooms from a house that had only one, without adding any square footage. I'm sure plenty of folks in big cities live in more confined quarters, without benefit of backyard. While this isn't my choice, I can see how it works for them.

Of course, the cynic in me wonders if the kids are truly content, or if they're just resigned. I'm curious if the oldest girl keeps a calendar in her corner of the bedroom that she shares with her sister, up there under the eaves where standing is an impossibility, if she quietly marks off each square until freedom, waiting for the day that she won't have to wait in a line six-deep to wash her paws.

To her, I say that when she grows up, she's allowed to inhabit the world in any manner she'd like, spread out as much as she wants. I hope she has *fifty* sinks to herself, if that's her jam. If she'd rather live like free-range cattle, as opposed to a veal calf, it's all up to her. In fact, she can have as many superfluous guest rooms as she might fancy. When this girl yearns for a big swimming pool and a rolling green lawn, then go for it, with budget and imagination as her only limitations. The one piece of advice I'd offer is that she locks the fence that goes around her yard.

Because I guarantee *someone* in that family will try to park a tiny house out there.

When Fletch texted to say that he'd landed and would Uber home from the airport, I placed an order from Seamless. Then I tidied up because nothing says "Welcome Home!" like a hot meal and clean house.

I didn't touch his bathroom, though.

Because his sink was *his* problem.

——

FLETCH'S LAST WORD:

Two things:

1) I only skimmed through this, but the point is people need space. Notice most people moving into tiny houses are either single, newly paired with their significant others, or hermits.

2) My father joined the Army Air Corps in 1944 after working as a coal miner. He flew over thirty missions in a B-17 over Nazi-occupied Europe, and lost two crew members on their last run. Then he came home and went back to work in the coal mine, and lived in a house with no indoor plumbing when he married my mother who gave birth to my eldest sister. He did not do that so idiots could live in a closet and shit in a bag.

TEN

The Champagne Of Sports

"I HAVE TAKEN MORE out of alcohol than alcohol has taken out of me."

- Winston Churchill

I'M a Miller High Life kind of gal.

I love fruity tropical drinks while on vacation. However, when I'm home, there's nothing better on a hot summer day than to float around the pool with my Kindle in its protective plastic coating, slowly sipping a red Solo cup full of the Champagne of Beer.

Because I'm a philistine, I'm not above adding ice, either.

High Life's the official beverage of Poolyball, a game that Fletch and I created. This sport's the bastard lovechild of volleyball and water polo, but there's so much more to it.

To backtrack, a couple of years ago, I sent Fletch to

Target to buy Fourth of July supplies. We weren't having our usual party because our dogs had fallen out and we weren't yet sure how to manage them around company. Because I knew we'd be alone, I'd asked Fletch to buy something "fun." I figured he'd pick up a big float or a couple of squirt guns.

When he returned home, I was outside watering flowers. He announced, "I bought something fun!" and before I could turn around, he pelted me in the kidney with a freaking *cannonball*. Said cannonball then bounced into my prize Peace Rose bush and bent a cane.

"*What* the *hell* was *that?*" I shouted.

"I bought you a dodge ball!" he replied. "You wanted something fun, I bought something fun."

"A ruptured spleen is not fun. A dodge ball is *especially* not fun," I groused, trying to mend the crooked stalk.

Fletch just stood there, grinning like a loon, bouncing his stupid rubber instrument of torture.

"P.S.?" I added. "I still have nightmares about junior high dodge ball." Dodge ball was the third amigo in the unholy trinity of what was wrong with seventh grade, which also included getting my period while wearing white pants and being hassled by the mean ninth grade girls who threw tampons at me, after having had my period in white pants.

[Did I make the situation better for myself by retorting to said ninth graders that they lacked creativity, as this exact thing had happened to Carrie in Stephen King's novel of the same name? Did I improve the situation when I then feigned surprise at their ability to read at all?]

[Oh, I think you can do the math, gentle reader, perhaps ascertaining that I wasn't always a "victim" so much as

someone who "didn't know when to shut the fuck up" and, on occasion, in fact "asked for it."]

Still, dodge ball took the whole shame crown and scepter back in 1979, as it was multifaceted in all the ways in which it mortified. First, there was the humiliation of getting picked last for a team. Every. Damn. Time. Then, there was the degradation of being hit square in the tinted glasses, especially painful when the blows came from one's own team. (There was nothing friendly about that fire.) The topping on the whole shit sandwich was having to get bare-ass naked in an open shower bay with twelve out of twenty-four girls who openly loathed me for making my team lose. Let me just say this; Heidi Klum, who I imagine looks fantastic in her birthday suit, might have left that locker room in tears, too.

Good times.

Fletch promised, "You'll see, this is gonna be great."

I said, "I doubt that," and returned to my roses.

By mid-afternoon on a quiet Fourth, Fletch was restless. He wasn't satisfied at the prospect of floating and reading and sipping. He grabbed the dodge ball and began tossing it into the air.

"You wanna play?" he asked.

"Play what?" I replied. "I can't throw or catch and I can only kick with one leg." I was still in physical therapy for my Achilles at the time. "What does that leave us?"

"Maybe you can kind of swat at the ball in the pool?"

"I guess?"

"Lemme crank the tunes and we can figure out something."

He'd recently seen an episode of *Mockpocalypse* about '70s Yacht Rock, so he put together a playlist heavy on Boz

Scaggs, Steely Dan, Pablo Cruise, the Eagles, and all things Michael McDonald.

Turns out, music is key for Poolyball.

We've since determined that you *must* listen to Yacht Rock for Poolyball. Yacht Rock is a big, fat audible Quaalude, washed down with a glass of sangria, laced with trace amounts of cocaine. Yacht Rock is a summer breeze blowing through your mustache and up your bell-bottoms. Yacht Rock smells like Coppertone and piña coladas and Sex Panther.

Yacht Rock is the boss.

SiriusXM agrees; they even have their own channel from Memorial Day to Labor Day now. And don't get all bullshitty, trying to substitute Ski Lodge Rock, because half the fun of Poolyball is the Yacht Rock discussion, marveling over exactly how many songs included pan flute solos back then.

Fletch and I began to toss the ball back and forth and I was shocked to realize that I could not only kind of catch, but also sort of throw. My time in the gym had afforded me enough body awareness so that I was no longer completely uncoordinated. I was a partial Poindexter at best. Had someone been picking teams for gym class, I'd have been selected in the bottom third. Yassss!

The beauty of Poolyball is you don't have to throw or catch. Instead, you can bat, you can bear-paw, you can stick your foot out of the water and kick, you can head-butt all Mel Gibson-style in *Lethal Weapon*. Whichever way you choose to propel the ball from one end of the court to the other is A-okay.

I positioned myself in the deep end on a fun noodle (AKA "horse") while Fletch stayed in the shallow end. My position took more exercise, which was fine with both of us. You don't even need a pool. Any body of water will do. The only constants are a ball (whatever kind floats) and some Yacht Rock.

As the game progressed, we made up increasingly elaborate rules regarding score. We determined that's where the real fun comes in; this is less a game about athletic prowess and more about who can bullshit quicker and with more authority. For example, on one of my serves, I knocked over Fletch's High Life, so I awarded myself one hundred points. However, Fletch allowed that to happen only once, so now beverage spilling is verboten and an automatic penalty. Plus, the tosser loses an additional hundred points if the drinker first quotes the *Big Lebowski*, saying, "Hey, careful, man, there's a beverage here."

After one serve, I got nailed in the face. Fletch said I had my hands in place and they were positioned to catch. However, in sensing the ball's imminent approach, my mitts were suddenly afraid and fled the scene. While you'd think being tagged in the face would be automatic points for me, Fletch awarded himself a bonus for my hands being cowards.

While I was trying to determine if my nose was broken (it wasn't) the most significant thing of all happened; *The Wreck of the Edmund Fitzgerald* began to play. We ceased the game immediately to hoist our drinks and pay homage to those twenty-nine lost lives. This song has since become Poolyball's official anthem, played at the kickoff and during the seventh inning stretch, with mandatory toasts to the early gales of November, to Wisconsin, to Cleveland, to the rooms of Gitche Gumee's ice water mansion, to the old chef, and to the wives and the sons and the daughters.

We came up with all kinds of rituals that afternoon,

like going boneless to Christopher Cross tunes. We didn't mean to halt play, but his music does temporarily turn one into Jell-O. There's a mandatory sing-along for Rupert Homes' *Escape* and if *Tequila Sunrise* is in the rotation, everyone must consume something tequila-based. (The one time this happened, I had a margarita. Fletch mixed Cuervo with Gatorade, which I dubbed a Tequila Sad-rise.)

Point?

On that fateful Fourth of July, history was made.

The nice thing about Poolyball is that it's so athletic, I don't get liquored up at all. I'm at the age where I opt to stop drinking after I feel buzzed. I don't like to be super-impaired and the last thing I want is a hangover. What's fun and adorable at twenty and easily cured by a McDonald's fountain Coke, is un-freaking-bearable in my late forties.

Fletch and I played Poolyball all summer. We kept asking ourselves, "Should it *be* this fun? Would normal people like this? If we have friends over, are they going to laugh at us behind our backs? *[More so than usual?]* Is this stupid game as awesome as we think?"

The big test was a weekend where we finally invited a crowd, believing the dogs to be ready. (They were. Yay!)

That week, I worked out at the gym at the same time as Ryne Sandberg and Brian Urlacher. I was so excited, not because they were celebrities, but because they were potential recruits for my side. I envisioned bringing them in as ringers. I kept mentally plotting, all, *"Let's see... Fletch, you can have our old friend, the patent attorney, and... I'll take my new buddies, the Hall of Fame Second Baseman and the ex-Bear."* Then I realized I'd be better off with the quick-quitted lawyer who could come up with point-grabs on the fly. Also, that way I wouldn't be banned from my gym for bothering the famous dudes.

That Saturday marked the first official Poolyball game. Many of us playing were the same ones who'd been picked last in seventh grade gym class. Our techniques were sloppy and balls flew everywhere. No one cared. We went boneless during *Sailing* and we sang along about getting caught in the rain after using classified ads to cheat on our long-time lovers. We inadvertently knocked over each other's High Lifes, demanding points and issuing penalties with abandon. While we splashed and shouted, Bertie Higgins reminded us about that time that we had it all down in Key Largo.

Fletch and I looked at each other from our opposing sides of the pool and we nodded. Yeah. The stupid game was as awesome as we thought. So Poolyball and High Life have gone together exactly as well as peanut butter and chocolate.

And then I go and almost blow it all up.

I'VE JUST RETURNED home from the trip of a lifetime to Turks and Caicos. Six months earlier, a travel agency had asked if I'd be willing to travel on their dime to the luxury, all-inclusive Beaches resort they were trying to promote. My only obligations would be to post on social media beforehand and hit a couple of group dinners once everyone arrived at the resort.

[Yeah, I could probably pencil that in.]

The whole trip was better than I could have imagined, like a five-day-long bachelorette party, minus the strippers and pornographic drinking straws. We spent each minute as a group, as we quickly discovered we shared the same dark sense of humor. The women who came may have started as fans, but left as friends, complete with memories to last a lifetime and our own inside jokes.

[Game changer!]

Prior to departure, the travel agents sent us checklists of what to pack. One of their tips was to bring a thermal cup to keep frozen drinks cold. "Please," I'd scoffed to Fletch. "I don't need a special cup to keep my drink cold. That's what my mouth is for."

Luckily, Alyson brought Joanna and me darling floral print thermal cups as a surprise. Turns out, the travel agents were right, because they are *travel agents* and this is what they do all day, every day. They are *agents* who understand every aspect of *travel*, including what you need to do about the whole resort drink sitch. The tumblers were so important because they were three times bigger than the glasses Beaches served. One day I forgot to bring mine down from my room and I felt like I was trekking back and forth to the bar every twenty minutes.

My intention on the trip was to load up everyone's tumblers and then teach them to play poolyball as we had our choice of pools and ocean. However, there was no way for us to commandeer the resort's sound system, so no Yacht Rock. Plus, no one wanted to relax so actively. The whole vibe of the trip was way too laid-back, even though some of us worked out on our own in the mornings. If I'd been all, "No, no, we must play, regardless!" that would have gone against the group's energy.

Poolyball could wait until our next trip.

The very best day was when a group of us were lazing around in the azure water, as warm as if we'd drawn a bath, about twenty feet away from the pristine white sand beach. There's such a high salt content that floating was effortless. The six of us bobbed and sipped our mojitos.

[I'd been drinking dirty bananas for the past few days, but switched after watching how they were made. Each regular-sized drink contained a whole banana, so when I used the tumbler, I'd have three bananas. Over the course of two days, I calculated I'd consumed at least twenty-five bananas, which seemed... excessive.]

As we floated, our group would laugh at all the wind-surfers and paddle-boarders who kept falling. We'd narrate what we thought they were saying whenever they'd biff, all *Mystery Science Theater 3000*-style.

We observed that each time a water sportsman would venture too far from the coastline, lifeguards would hop in a motorized raft and tow him or her back to shore. We could tell the guards weren't pleased about this by their body language, which made it even more amusing to watch.

Our group made up *a lot* of dialogue each time that happened.

One woman—who was fine, let me state that up front—had paddled well beyond everyone. Each time the guards went to rescue someone, they bypassed her, even though she seemed to be in the direst of straits. With each mission, the wake from the boat would knock her off course/off her paddle. In saving everyone else, the guards practically drowned this woman.

In retrospect, this sounds like a terrible story, except this woman's friends were floating in the water right by us, laughing the whole time, holding onto their own giant thermal cups. We learned her name was Emily and they weren't at all concerned for her safety. In fact, they mocked her mercilessly while she struggled. We stopped making fun and allowed her friends to do this by proxy; they were so much better at it.

We learned that an hour earlier, Emily had lectured the rest of her party on the dangers of day-drinking. *"While you slothful people suck down your adult beverages, I'm going to exercise! Do you even know how many calories are in those things?"*

This speech had not gone over well with the rest of her group.

Now, watching her struggle in the deep water had become a bit of a spectator sport with her crowd.

"Hey, Emily, how's that paddle-boarding working out for ya?" "What's your target heart rate?" "You feeling the burn yet?" her friends would shout, tumblers waving, even though she couldn't see or hear them, as she was but a speck on the horizon.

Emily was humbled when she finally did drag her exhausted self onto shore, collapsing onto the sand. Her friends gave each other knowing side-eye before bringing her a bottled water. Grudgingly, they forgave her and accepted her back into the fold. I think she even took a sip of someone's cocktail.

At no point did the guards ever glance in Emily's direction; I got the feeling she's pulled this kind of shit before.

[The lesson here is if you go on a group vacay, don't be an Emily. Nobody likes to travel with someone who's a pill. Be the person everyone tells stories with *afterward, not* about.*]*

That day was my favorite, but every day was magical, filled with heartbreakingly beautiful sunsets, pastry shops where you could have as many tarts as you could carry (if free, I take,) and a breeze that perpetually smelled of coconuts.

Once I'm home, I still have a taste for the islands. I long

for heartbreaking sunsets and the scent of coconut in the air. But it's so cold here that the pool isn't even open yet.

When Fletch pulls out the dodge ball the first official summer weekend, I eschew my usual Miller High Life. I decide I'll recreate a little slice of Turks and Caicos here in my backyard. I pull out my pretty tumbler, clip some mint from my garden, and make myself a frozen mojito, following a recipe I find online.

"Hey, this is good, even better than at Beaches," I say, offering him my glass. "Have some."

He takes a sip and pulls a face. "Taste like gum. No, thanks."

"Seriously? I think it's delicious."

The mojitos at the resort were tasty, too, but the flavor was different than this. They reminded more of, say, a spearmint Slushie. I suspect they used more ice and a lighter pour. What's funny is we had our tumblers with us all day, every day and at no point did I ever feel tipsy. I wonder if that's because the bananas sucked up so much of the alcohol?

We commence play and I take a drink now and then. This mojito is going down fast and smooth and my breath feels extra-fresh. Twenty minutes into the game, I knock my serve out of the pool. When this happens, whoever says, "Fuck outta here," first is exempt from having to retrieve the ball.

"Fuck outta here," I say.

[This is an esoteric expression I picked up from Ed Lover when he had Fuck Outta Here Fridays on his Backspin show. Like I said, some of the rules are beyond obscure, but that's why it's fun.]

Fletch climbs out to grab the ball. Usually it's him who knocks it out, as he's always trying new serves. I like to volley, seeing how many times we can send the ball back and forth, because then it feels like a real sport.

We begin to discuss our friend Tracey's suggestion that we add *Wildfire* to the playlist. Fletch is vehemently opposed. "Absolutely not," he says. "It's about a ghost horse. From Nebraska. Who dies during a blizzard? That is some bullshit. You can't have a Nebraska ghost horse on your Yacht list. There's zero Yacht about it. Does not work."

I smack the ball out of the pool again. "Fuck outta here!" I say, watching the dodge ball bounce across the yard into a bush. I swim over to the side and suck up some more minty, minty deliciousness.

Fletch sighs and hops out of the pool. He tosses me the ball and then jumps back in. "She also suggested *Horse with No Name*. I'm considering it, but leaning towards *no*. He's been through the desert and all, but then it turns to water. At first glance, that's hard to argue. He talks about the ocean being a desert with its life underground, but I can make a case that-"

"Fuck outta here!" I can't stop giggling as he hauls himself out yet again.

"In the beginning, that was funny. Now it's getting on my nerves," Fletch grumbles. He rounds up every spare dodge ball he can find in the yard so he doesn't have to climb in and out quite so often.

I help myself to my mo' mojito in the interim. Mmm, island-y. I can almost taste the sunset.

"I'm starting to have thoughts on bands named after places," he says. "I heard Kansas on my way down to the barber shop. I hated *Carry On, Wayward Son* growing up, but, my God, in the moment, it was perfect. But if I let Kansas onto the list, then what? Do I open the door to

Chicago? What about Boston? Will that lead to anarchy? We're going to need to look at this from every angle."

I've been saying his list is too restrictive, so I'm delighted that he's opening his mind a bit, loosening his standards. I indicate my agreement by raising my tumbler and cheering, "Mojito!"

We have a decent volley until Benny Mardones's *Into the Night* begins to play and I must stop for another drinking break. I say, "They don't make enough songs about statutory rape, in my opinion. Seriously, what A and R guy was all, *'Wait, this is about an adult male who can't seem to leave his sixteen-year-old girlfriend alone? Why, that's not crime, that's* romance, *baby!'* What's next, songs about stalking?"

"You mean like *Every Breath You Take*?" Fletch replies.

Okay, Sting. You're on the list now, too.

I say, "You know who I blame? Those fucking *Love Is...* kids. They are playing soccer in cleats but no shorts or shin guards, riding around on mopeds, wearing helmets but no goddamned leathers. They're protecting all the wrong bits! Do you know what kind of road rash they're gonna get if they skid? Fuck outta here, the both of 'em."

We play some more and I continue to work on my cocktail, which has melted surprisingly quickly. Maybe my cup isn't so thermal anymore?

Eventually, I adjust my serves and whip up a second batch of mojitos, which is even better than the first.

Dave Mason's *We Just Disagree* comes on and I change the lyrics as I sing along to make it more mojito-centric. *"There ain't no mo-ji-tos/There ain't no mo-ji-tos/There's only mo-ji-to and we just mo-ji-to-o-o."*

"You know, I recall this game having been more fun last summer," Fletch says. He paddles over to the side where his towel is and wipes off his sunglasses again. I've long since stopped lobbing serves out of the pool and now they've been landing like the perfect curve ball, breaking and dropping right as they get to him. Each time I send the ball his way, he's being sprayed with great plumes of backsplash.

"I'm going to need you to stop that, please."

"Mojito?" I reply.

"Is that a question?"

"Mojito!"

A few minutes ago, I stopped using every word in my vocabulary, save for "mojito."

"I'm going to need you to stop that, too," he adds, his own words coming out more clipped.

"Mojito?"

"Not kidding."

I take a big sip of my drink and nod. "Mojito."

"Maybe you should slow down," he suggests.

Well, now I'm offended.

"Schlow down?" Okay, the slurring? Not making my case for me.

I try again. I say, "This is only my second drink! I had, like nine of these on Emily Day and then we went kayaking. P.S. Joanna made us tip over. She's not allowed to be captain again. I had to tow the damn boat back to shore myself and the whole time Joanna was holding up her glass all, 'I saved my drink!' Yes, she knocked us over, but she rescued her drink. But she's no Emily. She's the anti-Emily. Don't be an Emily. I should have a shirt made with that on it."

He points to my floral cup. "How strong is that thing, exactly?"

I shrug. "I followed the reppice."

"The *reppice*?"

I take a drink. Minty! "Yassss. Two cups ice. One handful mint. Two cups rum-"

"Jesus Christ. Two cups of rum? You've slugged down *four cups of rum* in less than two hours? It's like you got broadsided by the Bacardi truck."

I take a slurp, draining my tumbler. "And now it is gone! I have made it disappear-ed! I am the David Copperfield of rum drinks! I shall have another! You there–make me a mojito!" I shout, twirling around the deep end on my fun noodle. "Two cups ice! One handful mint! Two cups rum! One cup simple syrup!"

"You're all hopped up on sugar, too? You're cut off."

"You can't cut me off. You're not the mojito police! No mojito polito." I grab a dodge ball and throw it at him. "Make me a mojito!"

"No."

I throw another ball. Perfect splash! "Two cups ice! One handful mint! Two cups rum! One cup simple syrup! Make me a mojito!"

"Never going to happen.

"*Love Is...* two naked kids who make me a mojito! One handful mint! Two cups rum! One cup simple syrup! Make me a mojito!"

"Stop."

"Mojitos are Yacht! Make me a mojito! One handful mint! Two cups rum! One cup simple syrup! Make me a mojito!"

Apparently, I go on like this for a while. I don't remember while it's happening, as I've yet to feel the full impact of being run over by the rum truck. Fletch is kind enough to film it for me, just in case.

It's bad.

At some point, he hustles me into the shower to sober me up, to no avail. At least he doesn't tape that.

Now, I wish fewer of my stories ended with, "And then I woke up *sans* pants on the bathroom floor," yet here we are. I do not throw up, but if I had, I imagine the effect would have been like vomiting mouthwash, again and again. Emily was right. Day-drinking is bad.

Make Me a Mojito Day ruins rum for me and I can't imagine I'll ever drink it/them again. In fact, I almost hurl just looking at the sauce served with my poppadum when I order Indian food.

I can't even chew Doublemint gum.

Once something's made me ill, I can rarely return to the scene of the crime. In fact, chocolate covered cherries used to be my favorite food until I had the stomach flu right after eating a few at Christmas in 1979. I've never touched them since.

[Can't be said enough, seventh grade was a bitch.]

I'm seriously worried that I won't be able to play Poolyball again, or listen to Yacht Rock, that I'll forever associate the game with nausea and dehydration and the feeling of ten thousand anvils being dropped on my head at the same time.

When I finally do ease myself back into the water after an overcast week, an iced Solo cup of High Life at my side, some *Deacon Blue* coming through the speakers, I discover that we're cool again, no worries. The beer is as smooth as Donald Fagen's vocals.

Summer is saved.

Miller High Life, I shall never forsake you again.

———

FLETCH'S LAST WORD:

Songs People Think are Yacht, But Are Not

Horse with No Name: *America:* Riding through a desert on a horse is the opposite of Yacht, especially when the horse is a metaphor for heroin. And abandoning a horse after six days in the desert has to be felony animal cruelty.

Wildfire: *Michael Martin Murphey:* What the fuck is with people thinking songs about horses are Yacht? You can't have a horse on a boat. The song about a ghost horse that died in a blizzard, and maybe its ghost rider that possibly perished while looking for it, has zero Yacht. In fact, it has negative 36 Yacht. Yacht Rock is either fun and tropical like a mai tai, or smooth and smoky like a fine scotch. This song is… sucks.

Come Sail Away: *Styx:* "But, Fletch! It has 'sail' right in the title!" Cool story, bro, but the sailing vessel turns out to be a starship full of extraterrestrials. And you know they have anal probes. The chorus should be:

They said come get abducted, come get abducted

Come get abducted with me

Come get abducted, come get abducted

Come get abducted with me

Afternoon Delight: *Starland Vocal Band:* We all know what they're talking about, and that's not the problem. This song is not Yacht because of its blatant country influences and '70s variety show production style. Yes, Donny and Marie did perform it on their show. Now I need a shower.

Anything by Jimmy Buffett

ELEVEN

Crazy Cat Lady

"FIVE CATS AND A WOMAN. That is all I need in life."

- Alejandro Jodorowsky

"HEY, I GOT YOU A LATTE."

I'm home from running errands and I have a coffee for Fletch. Unless I'm just going to the gym, I try to never come back empty-handed, whether it's lunch or an éclair or a hot beverage. I'm all about small gestures because we're not huge gift givers. In fact, he's forbidden to acknowledge my birthday. No card, no cake, no tidings whatsoever.

This came about because I spent my whole life trying to figure out how to be in England on November 5th, which is Guy Fawkes Day. *[That's the date Fawkes was caught before he could burn down Parliament.]* Growing up, I was so psyched to share a birthday with what sounded like such a cool holiday.

Every Guy Fawkes Day that passed built my anticipation for when I could finally be there to celebrate along with the rest of the country. After forty-some years waiting to be in England on that day, I started envisioning Brits carrying me around Cleopatra-style through the streets of London. Children would throw candy at me. Bands would play. People would cheer and try to kiss me in pubs.

While this expectation had no rational basis, there we were.

The closest parallel I can draw would be like if a Brit, let's call him Nigel for the sake of this example, came to the US and expected Americans to be all fired up because Nigel and George Washington share a birthday. No one would be shooting off liberty cannons when Nigel got here, or releasing flocks of bald eagles carrying flags in their beaks. At best, Americans would be all, "Huh. Interesting coincidence. There might be a mattress sale you could check out."

For Nigel to expect anything else would be odd, an irrational leap. Yet there I was, in London, profoundly and deeply disappointed to discover that *no one* was trying to carry me around or kiss me in pubs.

After London, I realized that I was ready to let go of my birthday, too. Didn't need it. Now, as far as Fletch is concerned, the day should be SERVPRO®: *Like it never even happened.* I don't miss it.

Actually, I've never been big on gift-grab holidays because I think they create too much pressure as an adult. For example, we stopped exchanging anything on Christmas, save for stockings, a few years ago. Now we spend the season doing fun things like decorating and baking and entertaining, instead of making ourselves nuts about who has more of what under the tree.

[Let me be clear, if you have children and you unilaterally adopt this policy, I cannot be held responsible for your kids' actions.]

Because we don't go crazy on the major stuff, I make sure there's a never-ending stream of small treats all year. For example, I know Fletch's energy flags in the afternoon, so I figured he could use some caffeine.

"Hey, where are you? I have coffee!"

Nothing. No answer. For all his admirable qualities, he has the uncanny ability to vanish the second I arrive home with heavy bags to unload from the car, yet magically reappears the moment the items are all put away. The second the last can of refried beans goes into the cabinet, poof! He's like Lance Burton, materializing out of thin air. I'm not surprised, as I'm just back from the grocery store and Target with a trunk full of soup cans and cat litter.

Really, it's like he has a second sense.

I begin hauling out items myself. Of course I bought two hundred and fifty pounds of driveway salt today. *Of course* I did. I dump the sacks in the corner of the garage by his car so I can get to the rest of the purchases.

I finish unloading all the bags while Hambone supervises, trotting along behind me. She's a small ball of muscle and sinew, compact and powerful, her eyes, nose and face the same shade of burnt umber, the only contrast provided by the kind of sharp, white teeth that belong on a dog three times her size.

I love her so much, but good Lord, this creature looks possessed, especially when she's excited and her eyes glow red. One is tempted to reach for holy water, maybe summon a priest.

I toss her a cookie for her efforts, but she just looks at it. She's what I call "Hamorexic," sometimes eating only every two or three days. She's not food-motivated, which I simply cannot fathom. Like those old commercials that used to ask what I might do for a Klondike bar?

Untoward things, I suspect.

As I unpack and stow, Hammie does The Lean, where she presses her whole midsection up against my calves. There is no higher compliment one can receive from this dog, no greater sign of trust and affection. I stoop to pet her and she wiggles with glee, flopping over to show me her taut, clammy, hairless belly.

You'd never know that this sweet little thing suffers from terrible anxiety. At first, we thought she'd become aggressive when she started to fight with Libby three years ago. Turns out, she's an enormous coward and the whole world scares her. After we started keeping them apart, *Frozen*-style, we also discovered the full extent of her separation anxiety.

[If you need to know how to replace a chewed-up door jamb or clawed-through sheet of drywall, lemme know, we're experts.]

Between exercise, training, and medication, we've made enormous strides in increasing her confidence. She has a happy life because we will not give up on a pet. She's worth the effort.

However, we've not done as much work as we'd like in bringing Libby and Hammie back together recently for two reasons; first, Loki has taken additional care lately. He has trouble getting around because of hip dysplasia and he's experiencing increasing symptoms of canine senility. He's been a very good boy for a very long time, so we both cater to his comfort.

More pressing is that our blind-in-one-eye cat Odin *[of Clan Thundercat]* has required a lot of extra help lately. He recently lost a leg through a series of unfortunate events, all of which are his own fault. Fletch summed it up as, "Play stupid games, win stupid prizes." However, I feel it's more of an object lesson on *Why You Don't Date Rape Your Brothers*. While I chose to have his damaged leg amputated, the vets at the specialty clinic could have saved it for ten thousand dollars.

Ten thousand dollars.

Not a typo.

That's how much my Achilles rupture surgery cost, and that price included all the physical therapy.

While I fully admit to being a crazy cat lady, I am not a *crazy* cat lady so I didn't automatically agree, all, "Yes, yes, whatever it takes! I shall sell my hair and my antique pocket watch to make it happen!" I wanted to explore all the options, so a team–a team!–of orthopedic surgeons came into the treatment room to explain why I should save the leg through surgical intervention.

"Will he be able to function on three legs?" I asked.

"Yes," the first orthopedic surgeon admitted.

"Will he miss it if you take it?" I pressed.

"No, they do pretty well, especially since it's a back leg," said the second orthopedic surgeon.

"What's the difference in the recovery time?" I asked.

"Amputation's a couple of weeks and the surgery's about two months of confinement," said number one. "Of course, he might need additional surgeries after that, if the hip should have to be replaced."

I could literally hear a cash register chiming as they spoke. When they told me how much less expensive it was to amputate, and really, how much easier it would be on the ol' pervert, amputation was the logical choice. A part of me felt sad about his delicate little striped grey leg being tossed in a garbage can, all alone and forlorn, but not *ten thousand dollars*-bad.

"Listen, if he breaks his other back leg, then there's nothing we can do," said the second doctor, miffed that I opted to discard a perfectly good limb in lieu of buying, say, a used Honda.

"If he breaks another leg because he can't stop molesting his brothers, then he's on his own," I replied.

Odin has recovered brilliantly and at no point has he noticed that anything's different. His fur's growing in over his scar and he likes that he can snuggle even closer to me now when we're watching TV together. He's even back to trying to mount his brothers, Chuck Norris and Gus. Sweet recidivism!

Odin looks up at me with his one good eye, stretching and yawning as he repositions himself in the basket I keep for him at the end of the wide-plank farm table in the kitchen. A while ago, we gave up trying to chase the cats off said table. We figured, they're going to sit here anyway, we may as well make a place for them so they stop trying to cram into the fruit bowl. I set down the Starbucks cup and knead the soft fur around his neck. His purr reverberates through his whole body.

I wonder where Fletch is?

He should be popping out of the woodwork by now. His latte's going to get cold. I kiss Odin and grab the cup to go look for Fletch. He's not in the great room off the kitchen, so I run upstairs to his office. His dual computer monitors are off and he's not in the media room, either.

Where is he?

I open the door to the guest room where Patsy, our cranky old-lady cat, lives. Ham's been on my heels the whole time. While I greet Patsy, Hambone hops up on her special chair, which is covered in a fuzzy pink blanket.

[Ham and Patsy are BFF and spend lots of time together, so Ham has her own bed in here.]

Patsy has lived by herself ever since we lost Edina, her sister, to kidney failure. I didn't realize exactly how much the sisters despised each other until Eddy was gone. While this sounds sad, Patsy's never been happier. She's like Highlander; there can only be one.

I serve Patsy some Bonito flakes, which are wafer-thin bits of dried, smoked fish that taste like lox. She's the only cat who gets this treat. I go to the Japanese market to buy them especially for her. I guess this is her reward for being a sociopath who refuses to be near other cats.

Patsy woofs down her flakes and then we hang out for a few minutes. I let her bite me, as this is the only way she knows how to show affection. Her breath smells like brunch and her teeth are tiny white needles.

[Fletch says it feels like we're running a VA hospital for pets, between the amputees, the elderly, and the PTSD patients.]

Ham decides to hang with Patsy–she's excellent with other species–so I leave her in here while I resume my search.

I close the door and head back down the stairs.

"Fletch, where are you? Got you a coffee." I enter the weird sitting room off the master, which is accessed through a Jack-and-Jill bathroom. The layout of our house is flat-out bizarre. While we have the kind of spaces we want, none of them are in logical spots.

Libby and Loki are chillin' in here. Loki's pleased to see me, greeting me with an "aww-ooo-ooo" howl. We had a DNA test done on him once and it came back "Labradoodle," which was absolutely a mistake and incredibly funny. Google "black wolf" and there he is, his fur, his shape, his howl, his temperament, everything. If there was any poodle in his sample, it's because his ancestors ate them.

In his prime, he was truly magnificent. Now the poor old guy can't even climb onto his favorite couch anymore. I bought him a fantastic orthopedic bed, washable and breathable, super-soft and specially made of memory foam for arthritic senior dogs. He enjoys sleeping next to it. The old man's still got a sense of humor, I'll give him that.

Libby's arranged on top of a pile of pillows on top of the couch. She lazily thumps her tail. One is reminded of Jabba the Hutt. (Fatty does not share her nemesis Hambone's commitment to physical fitness.) They both get a treat. Libby chokes hers down without even chewing, sort of like a duck. Loki eats his with a smile on his grayed face; this pleases me. There are only a few grains of sand left in his hourglass, but it delights me to see him relish experiences during the time he has left.

I turn the corner into the master, assuming he's in the bathroom.

"Jesus, Fletch, I've been looking all over. I have coffee for you. You'll probably have to nuke it by now."

I expect to hear the exhaust fan whirring away as I approach.

Nope. Where the *hell* is he?

I come back into the sitting room and Loki greets me with an "aww-ooo-ooo." He either completely forgot he saw me thirty seconds ago or he's messing with me. Either is possible. This earns him another cookie, which delights him again. His reaction tells me he's messing with me. I kiss him on the top of his head, which is warm and threaded with bits of white fur. Fletch and I always say his head heats up when he's thinking hard.

You do you, you sweet, old gentleman. You do you.

I exit through the bathroom and Libby joins me as I check out the basement. This is the only logical place he could be. Fletch doesn't usually noodle around down here during business hours, but maybe he's trying to fix a router or something.

We search every corner as we have *[meaning I have]* a bit of a hoard accumulated and I want to make sure he's not trapped under anything heavy.

Nope.

Where is he?

I'm not worried, per se. I'm just confused. This is so out of the ordinary. He wouldn't have gone anywhere without his car as we're not in a walkable neighborhood. Well, we're walkable for *me [humblebrag]* as I'll often run the dogs to their vet appointments a mile away so they're calm upon arrival.

In theory, he'd walk Hambone or Libby to the vet if I asked, except he doesn't possess that kind of time management. He'd make a mental note and plan for the walk all day. Then he'd take one more call or attempt to finish one more Visio diagram and then he'd look at the clock and realize the appointment started five minutes ago. Then he, and whichever dog was due for shots, would hop in the car, he'd drive it like they stole it, and they'd arrive at the vet in a state that's the antonym of calm. Also, I've already seen all the pets and no one has an appointment today.

Maybe Peter, his boss, picked him up for a late lunch or something? Peter lives only a few miles away. That would explain why Fletch's car is here and he's not. I'll just confirm by looking in the drawer in the kitchen where he keeps his wallet and keys. They'd be gone if he were out.

Hmm, they're here. His phone's plugged into the dock, too. Double hmm.

I wonder if he's in the yard? This winter has been almost entirely without snow and strangely warm, so it's possible he's working on something outside, but wouldn't I have seen him? He's been eyeing that dead fir tree in the corner of the driveway for a while. I keep telling him, "It's WAY too big for you to cut down yourself," but he's all, "No, all I need is a winch, and I'd save five hundred bucks!" but then he'd cost us *five thousand bucks* when the damn thing took out the roof of the garage after it came crashing down because it's way too big for him to cut down by himself.

We have this conversation *a lot.*

I look out the kitchen window and don't see him by the dead fir. Then I put on my coat and Libby and I traverse the entire backyard. He's nowhere. I call and call and hear nothing back in response. It's too bad there's no snow out here because then maybe I could see footprints and track him down.

Okay, this is kind of weird.

Obviously, no one's kidnapped him. If someone did, I imagine the minute Fletch starts going into granular detail about what data lives on the cloud, and the best way to back up files, and blah-di-blah, or he does that God-awful *horking* thing, or he hears the water heater clicking and he tells them he can fix it and the next thing the kidnappers know, they're taking pirate baths in a bucket for three days instead of showering proper, then we'd have ourselves a *Ransom of Red Chief* situation on our hands right quick.

What would be another logical explanation?

Rapture, of course.

I swear, that's *always* where my mind goes when someone's completely missing from where they're supposed to be.

There's no cashier behind the counter at the bakery?

Rapture.

No one's answering the phone at the hairdresser?

Rapture.

My package didn't arrive from UPS when it was supposed to?

Rapture.

Okay, I need to admit something you may have already suspected. There's a small glitch in my Matrix sometimes. While I pride myself on embracing reason, on making rational judgments, this is not my default mode.

My default mode trends towards paranoid delusion, with a side of religion-based bugfuckery. I have to work really hard to override some of my original programming so I don't automatically leap to batshit, monkey-dick, banana-sandwich insane conclusions every moment of my life.

The problem, from what I've come to understand, is all about neural pathways. These neural pathways are how the nerve impulses travel. Basically they're what connects the whole brain together, kind of like an interstate system. When we're young, these neural pathways are still forming. The paths get deeper and more defined the more the information travels down them, like a knee-jerk reaction. And mine was forming during a particularly stupid era of in my life, namely Sundays during seventh grade.

I can thank the fundamentalist Baptist church I was forced to attend for the default-to-assuming-everyone's-being-Raptured-without-me neural pathway business.

They ingrained the Rapture in me, but good. I'm talking All Rapture, All the Time.

[It's germane to note that my Sunday school classroom was located at the top of a rickety, narrow wooden staircase in a room that always smelled of methane gas. With its singular door and complete lack of windows, to me, holding classes in this death trap was truly an act of faith.]

Every week, I'd hear about the inevitable Rapture. My teacher explained the Lord was going to come for the true believers, and they'd be spirited away to His home in the sky, leaving nothing behind but their shoes. The chosen would float up into the Heavens while all the sinners were left on earth to perish in a lake of fire.

I had a lot of questions about this, especially at first, having come from an unremarkable Methodist church in New Jersey.

First, why just leave the shoes? That part bothered me. Also, what if really good people didn't accept Jesus Christ as their personal Lord and Savior, say, they were a different religion, or they lived in Africa and were unfamiliar with JC's playlist full o' miracles? But what if they were still nice to kids and dogs and other grown-ups, and did a lot of awesome things for the world? Why couldn't they be Raptured, too? The Methodists taught me that Jesus wasn't the type to exclude others from the party based on a technicality; he'd bring enough cupcakes for the whole class. In my opinion, he seemed like a cool dude, like he'd "get it." Why did the Rapture have to be the last chopper out of Saigon?

My teacher would answer each question the same way, saying, *"Because that's how the Rapture works."*

Honestly, I suspected said teacher was full of shit, but I didn't want to *not* believe, lest I be left on earth with all the rest of the suckers still walking around in their sinful shoes.

It was a dilemma.

When my class wasn't actively discussing the specifics of the Rapture, we'd scour our scripture for clues that might give us the exact date for the Rapture so it wouldn't catch us when we were in the shower. That would be embarrassing.

Once after a Bible-based, Rapture Easter egg hunt, my Sunday school teacher held up his brick-sized Texas Instruments calculator, explaining how the devil was most likely going to come to us through it.

[Holy shit, is this why I'm afraid of math?]

He punched out 6-6-6 on the digital display, the Mark of the Beast. The squared-off numerals had an evil red glow about them. Then my teacher nodded knowingly.

I clamped shut my smart lips, not daring ask if "Shell Oil" and "Boob" were also the Devil's handiwork, as they could be spelled on the calculator, too.

Occasionally, my teacher would suggest we burn all the rock records that had backward masking on them, but these plans were nebulous at best. We never did have that big, Satanic bonfire. I guess if you're going to be brainwashed by a zealot, it's better if he has a bit of a lazy streak.

Before I was finally able to talk my way out of having to attend Sunday school, I learned we're all eventually, "Going to have microchips implanted under our skin so we can be controlled by the Trilateral Commission. Mind you, they're orchestrated by the Masons."

Our teacher pulled out a dollar bill so he could show us the Mason's symbol on one, you know, as proof. He explained how all these men of power met under this gigantic mountain in Colorado. I recall being bothered, less because this happened, and more because my teacher insisted there were no women of power.

Looking back, I suspect the church's gas leak was more problematic than any of us realized.

[I should also mention that in addition to teaching Sunday school, this guy taught at my middle school. I was exposed to his philosophy six days a week. While sometimes I exaggerate for comedic effect, unfortunately, this isn't one of those times.]

What's even more messed up is that I sometimes attended services with my Pentecostal friend, where everyone spoke in tongues, literally convulsing when filled by the Holy Spirit. Worshippers weren't allowed to trim their hair, wear pants, or watch television, either. By comparison? My Baptists seemed as insipid and vanilla as the Methodists we'd left behind in New Jersey, like so many pair of abandoned shoes

The point is that my head was filled with some bizarre shit during formative times, so some of my neural pathways shortcut to dead ends. Occasionally, these misfires cause me to take an illogical leap.

[Put a pin in this; it's about to become important.]

Anyway, I doubt Fletch has been Raptured. There's no way *he's* getting Raptured before *me*. I'm the better person. I'm the bringer of coffee, the maker of treats. The rescuer of pets. If karma were a game, I'd have the higher cumulative score. Regardless, something has clearly happened to him and I must figure it out. Whatever it is, I'll just roll with it.

That's when I spot him through the kitchen window, out there sniffing around the fir tree.

Okay, this is not what I expected, *not at all*, but I knew something odd was afoot. I knew it! He circles the tree, eyeing it up and down, tiptoeing around it on little cat feet, probably because he doesn't want to alert the city he's going to whack down a tree without the proper permit. Scofflaw! I can tell by the tilt of his head he's doing geometry right now, just trying to figure out a way to fell this thing.

Again, he's not in a state I *ever* expected to find him, but at this point, it's as good an explanation as any. Plus, Hamlet didn't say, *"There are more things in Heaven and earth, Horatio, than are dreamt of in your philosophy,"* just 'cause it made him sound deep. He meant sometimes phenomena occur that can't be explained by what's taught in books. Stuff can happen outside of the norm. Weird stuff. Inexplicable stuff. *Stranger Things* stuff.

I leave Libby indoors, grabbing the Starbucks cup, the contents long since gone tepid. I head out the sliding glass door, passing through the fence and into the driveway. I walk to the end where the tree looms, casting a spindly shadow, its few remaining needles brown and dry.

He watches me as I approach.

"I have no idea how this happened to you, but we're just going to accept it," I say. Frankly, I think it's awfully cool on my part.

Christian, even.

He looks at me dead-on, but says nothing. I catch him glance at the tree out of the corner of his eye.

"All this and you *still* can't stop thinking about cutting this thing down yourself? Yes, you're good at home improvement stuff, and, sure, you did an outstanding job replacing the water heater, even though it took longer than expected. I lived without hot water while you figured it out, I lived with the pirate baths. Did I complain? No. But this is different. And you can't say it's not, literally."

His gaze is intense, his left eye ever so slightly more squinty than the right. This is the look he always gives me when he's thinking.

Am I getting through to him?

I press on. "Number one, holding onto a winch supporting a downed tree is like carrying a million grocery bags at the same time. Number two, considering how much trouble I have getting you to bring in one grocery bag, I can't imagine you with one million of them concurrently. Number three, you can't do a goddamned thing without thumbs. So, please, just come inside."

I start walking towards the house but all his feet stay planted.

"Really? You're just gonna stand here? And, what? Let the coyotes get you?"

Okay, I am not playing his cat and mouse games.

"Let's go."

Nope. He doesn't say it aloud; his look conveys this for him.

"Then guess what, you're coming in, like it or not," I say, bending down to scoop him up.

Behind me, I hear Fletch say, "Do not bring another animal into this house, we are full-up. No room at the inn."

I drop the black cat I've just grabbed. He scuttles up the fir tree. I'm completely flummoxed. "Wait, what? Where did you *come* from?" I ask.

He holds up a machete. "I was cutting brush in the woods out front. So, hey... why are you standing here arguing with a cat?"

"Because I thought he was you!" I shout. "I thought you'd somehow been, I don't know, turned into a cat."

He mulls this over for a moment, studying my expression to see if I'm joking. I'm not. "Why would I have been turned into a cat?"

"Because that's how the Rapture works!"

He nods and holds the machete closer. In a mild tone, he says, "Sure, yeah, in no way does that sound crazy."

I try to explain, "You were missing. I was starting to panic because it was so weird to not have you here and I looked everywhere."

"You didn't look in the front yard."

I exhale hard and my breath comes out in a white plume. "Fine, I looked everywhere but the woods in the front yard, where you've never been once, never, ever. Then I saw the cat out the kitchen window. I noticed that he has your posture, he did that squinty left eye like you do and he was glowering the fir tree you hate. I figured something super-fucky and *Stranger Things* and post-apocalyptically inexplicable had happened and that you had turned into a cat. Then I thought, *'I should get my husband inside before a coyote eats him.'* I was trying to be considerate."

"The fact that you weren't trying to pet-hoard actually disturbs me more."

I cross my arms over my chest, still holding the cup, saying nothing in response.

He continues. "You honestly thought I turned into a cat. You couldn't find me and your first thought was that I turned into a cat." Then he full-out starts laughing at me, I'm talking big guffaws, with fat, wet tears rolling down his face.

"The more you laugh, the more insulted I am. It made sense in my head. I should have just left you, but, no. I'm considerate. I do nice things for you all the time, including saving you from coyotes."

"Saving me because I was a cat. Because it's the only logical explanation." He blots at his damp cheeks with his sleeve. That's when he notices the Starbucks cup in my hand. "Hey, is that coffee for me?"

I glance down, tightening my grip.

"No."

———

FLETCH'S LAST WORD:

No one ever died from two days of taking sponge baths.
    Net savings on DIY water heater = $1,200.
    I'm not gonna justify the rest of this nonsense.

TWELVE

No Cause For Alarm

INSANITY IS DOING the same thing over and over again and expecting different results."

- Albert Einstein

"I'M *OFFICIALLY* GOING to kick a lung out of someone. I don't know who, and I don't know when. But it's going to happen."

Fresh from another scale-based failure, I am pissed. Trainer Brett pales a bit, takes a step back from me, slightly nervous. I don't blame him. I'd be afraid of me now, too. "Should we work on throwing things?"

"That might be for the best," I tell him. He hands me a fifteen-pound neoprene bag filled with sand and I start with slams. The sound of the sack hitting the floor reverberates throughout the whole gym. Thwack! Thwack! Thwack!

That does feel a bit better.

I've been gaining weight, ever so slowly, yet ever so steadily. Not huge amounts, just a pound here, then a pound there. This is not like previous times in my life when I've been all, "I'm beefing up and I have no idea why!" when I knew goddamned well it was because I was eating my feelings.

Also, pie.

Then I'd run to a place like Jenny Craig, take no ownership whatsoever, and be disappointed when I didn't have a magical transformation after complying for a day or two.

I first assume I'm seeing a difference in the scale because of muscle, but muscle isn't squishy. Muscle doesn't dimple. Muscle doesn't collect in the no-man's land between the bra straps and the arm crease. *[Back fat is the WORST.]* Muscle doesn't make buttoning my skinniest shorts an exercise in futility.

That's some bullshit right there, because I'm at the gym all the time. I recognize everyone who comes anytime between nine and noon on the weekday. I even know the jerk who talked about how fat people should put tape over their mouths during my first run at Lose to Win two years ago. This past year? In January, when the people who'd made resolutions were hogging up all the good machines for the first two weeks of 2017? He and I exchanged a glance and we rolled our eyes together, like, *"Can you believe this shit?"*

[Hey, look at that! I finally got picked first in gym class and now I'm co-captain... of Team Asshole.]

So, putting on so much as a pound without having changed any of my habits for the worse? No. *Hell*, no.

Fortunately, I am the data queen. After the first few pounds creep on, I commence logging into MyFitnessPal. Instead of rounding down, like the calories don't count if I don't commit them to spreadsheet, I round up, overestimating them. I pay attention to my macros. I balance my carbs and proteins and fats. I tweak my percentages. I exclude my caloric burn from my daily counts, too, to see if that makes a difference. I buy a food scale and measure everything.

[I previously learned my eyeballs are notorious liars. They'd be, like, "Nah, bro, that brick sized slab o' Manchego is an ounce, max!"]

After years of bad habits, I've messed up my metabolism, so I lose super-slowly. I accept this. When I participated in Lose to Win in 2016, one year post-Achilles, I worked out twenty-plus hours a week and limited my calories to sixteen hundred per day. I felt like all I did for six weeks was wash gym clothes and complain about sore glutes.

[I kept asking Fletch to walk on my butt, dig in with his feet. He would not. I'm still salty about it.]

My total loss was somewhere around twelve pounds. Sure, I'd have liked to have lost more, but I gave it my very best effort.

Those twelve pounds have since returned.

Fuckers.

When Trainer Brett goes on vacation, I work with Trainer Aaron, a perfect human physical specimen. He body-builds on the side, but not in the veiny/gross/mutant weight class, just the super-buff one. He's someone you'd look at and say, "I bet he could carry a safe up nine flights of stairs!" and not "Can't guess how many steroids are coursing through his bloodstream right now, so Imma back away slowly."

During our session, Aaron asks me about my diet. I tell him what I eat in a typical day. He says he'd like to see me rely more on real food, and less on Quest bars. Instead of grabbing a protein bar for breakfast, he suggests I try egg white omelets, packed full of vegetables. I do it his way.

When I still don't see the scale heading in the right direction, I buy a heart rate monitor. No, not a Fitbit, either. Fitbits are bullshit. Fitbits exist for the sole purpose of selling Fitbits. Fitbits are the participation prizes of health monitoring. I've had a Fitbit, as well as a Jawbone. I'm pretty sure they both counted my M & M hand-to-mouth action as steps. *"You got in ten thousand steps today!"* my devices would cry in congratulations. Sure did! Ten thousand *delicious* steps. My new monitor is the no-nonsense kind that straps around the chest and measures actual heart performance; it's supposed to be the most accurate.

I find the harder I try, and the more data I record, the fewer results I have. Fasting? Nothing. Cutting calories? Nada. More weights? More pain. Also, more gain.

I'm mad at myself for being mad at myself for getting heavier, even though it's not that much. While I absolutely believe you/I/we are worthy at any size, I'm happier being healthier. I full-on cabbage-patched that day in my doctor's office when he said I was through with high blood pressure pills. Because *I* did that. Myself. Through discipline and effort. Then I may or may not have pulled off my shirt, flexed, and told him to, "Check out the gun show."

[He can't tell you, either. Hippocratic oath and all.]

I'm bugged because higher numbers on the scale equate to less healthy, at least in my head. Plus, I like all the fringe benefits that come with getting smaller. I like wearing sleeveless shirts for the first time since 1994. I like not having to pack a seatbelt extender when I fly. I like not telling a tremendous lie on my driver's license. I like buying workout tanks with pithy sayings on them, such as *'Oh, my quad, Becky, look at her squat.'*

I like how I feel, inside and outside.

Please note I'm making it sound like post-Achilles, I had this huge and wondrous transformation regarding exercise, but that's not true. I had to trick myself there for a long while. All I wanted to do for the two and a half months I was on the knee scooter was use the exercise machines, like the elliptical. Then once I finally hopped on them, I thought, "Hmm, I don't care for these as much as I thought and I am ready to quit."

So, I'd save my best/worst shows to watch during my cardio sessions, like *UnReal*, and *Housewives*, and *The Bachelor*. They would be my reward. I made the most lit playlists in the universe and I could only listen to good songs if I was moving. I forced myself to have a habit until it became a habit and now on the days I don't sweat, I feel weird and off, like I've forgotten to brush my teeth. The positive feedback loop is real. The more you do, the more you want to do.

Through embracing healthy living and fitness, I've discovered something about myself that I never realized... I am a hyper-competitive douchebag, not only just in life *[sort of had an inkling about that]* but also in the gym.

One life-changing day, I discovered that if I amped up the torque enough in spin class, I could top the leader board because while I'm not thin, I have a shit-ton of ballast. Oh, my God. Every time I take a class, it's all I can do to not send my consistent number one rankings to my seventh-grade gym teacher.

[Who deserves a C- now, Mrs. Baker, huh?]

As I've always had poor coordination, I was unaware

that I had the makings of an athlete inside me. I didn't know how much weight I could press, how many watts I could generate on the bike, how far I could row on the ergometer, how long I could keep my heart rate in the orange zone, how I could beat far more fit people in classes where metrics are measured.

Frankly, now that I'm aware, I'm a complete dick about it.

One could argue that embracing fitness has made me a *worse* person; one would not be wrong.

That's why I'm furious that something's off and that I can't figure out what. Is it too much cardio? Not enough calories?

[Have I been invaded by an alien life form, because I never dreamed these could be questions I'd ask myself.]

[Also, lest this sound too braggy-braggy, yay-me, I've yet to see one-derland. This is all relative, your mileage may vary, etc.]

I'm flummoxed.

––––––

MY PRIMARY CARE physician sends me to an endocrinologist, because he's flummoxed, too. He was there when my weight was a perfect bowling score. He knows how far I've come, he's aware this isn't denial, or me trying to blame-throw.

As I want answers now, now, now, rather than wait until March (March, March) when his referred doc has openings, I make an appointment with another guy.

I arrive with a big stack of paperwork. I've printed all my food logs and two months' worth of workout data from my heart rate monitor. Let's do this. The endo introduces himself and takes a seat next to me. I notice his South African accent immediately.

Uh-oh.

This is going to be a distraction. Anyone who came of age in the late '80s saw the movie *Lethal Weapon II*. Fact. Mind you, I didn't much care for Mel Gibson back when it was a law to fangirl Mel Gibson. *[Although, why am I suddenly obsessed with mentioning Mel Gibson in this book?]* I was dragged to the theater with a bunch of sorority sisters. I'm so glad they coerced me to see it, as this is one of the most iconic movies of that time. I'm talking an actual generation-definer. There are two unforgettable lines that people still quote today. The first is when Joe Pesci cries about how, "They fuck you in the drive-thru."

The second line pertains to the villain. He's an evil old white government dude from South Africa at the height of Apartheid. He and his henchmen are wreaking havoc in LA and they keep getting away with it; cops can't touch them. This is really working (Gibson) Riggs's nerves. At key moments throughout the film, the bad guy says, "Diplomatic immunity," in his thick accent, real slow and evil, as way of justification.

[Spoiler alert: eventually it all works out, in the film and in real life.]

As this doctor speaks, all I can do is imagine him saying, "Diplomatic immunity," for the first fifteen minutes of our appointment. I must bite my tongue to keep from asking him to please say this for me.

What the hell is wrong with me?

[I feel like Gibson may bring out the worst in people ever since The Unpleasantness.]

I spend an hour talking to the endo (and listening for forty-five) explaining everything I've done. Because he's part of the medical group I've been seeing since moving to Chicago, he's able to pull up my blood test results all the way back to 2003 when they went online. In comparison, there's no comparison. He tells me I've earned my healthy living bragging rights.

Cool story, bro, but *why are my pants tight?*

I pepper him with questions.

"Am I eating too much? Am I eating too little? Am I eating all the wrong things for my metabolism? Am I going into starvation mode because I'm doing too much cardio?" I demand. "Do we test my daily burn rate? Or bone density? Is it possible for my bones to be getting fatter, is that a thing? How about we try an elimination diet and we'd see if I'm reacting badly to certain food groups?"

Do you know what he says?

"You're going to drive yourself crazy. At some point, you need to accept that getting bigger is a simple fact of aging because your body slows down. Plus, now your body's used to you being healthy and it's adjusted accordingly. You can't fight this."

Then he says the thing that almost makes me go all *Lethal Weapon.*

"Have you considered signing up for Jenny Craig?"

———

I LEAVE the endocrinologist with a prescription for Metformin, a drug with particularly unpleasant side effects, meant for those who are diabetic even though I am not diabetic, nor I am pre-diabetic. He'd said he had some patients with symptoms like mine who used it successfully to get past a plateau.

Okay, but I don't want to go the Big Pharma route yet.

I haven't exercised every other alternative first and Metformin seems like going nuclear. I'm not yet ready to walk away from the bargaining table, you know? *[He also wanted to put me on an experimental bladder control drug that has been linked to weight loss. How about... no.]*

When I tell my primary care physician about this, he refers me again to the original endo who couldn't see me until March, March, March, and not now, now. He's kind enough not to say, "Told you so."

My friend Gina suggests my plateau / gains stem from chronic inflammation due to reactive foods. I kind of don't know what this means, so I consult Dr. Google. Basically, while I'm not flat-out allergic, there may be food my body says "do not want" after I eat. Which might explain why I gain four pounds every time I have one slice of pizza. One slice!

I decide to start the Whole30 plan on January 1st. Whole30 takes alcohol, dairy, grains, legumes, soy, and sugar (real, artificial, all forms) off the table for a month. While my diet has been (mostly) nutritionally balanced for the past two years, I eat at least four of the above five triggers daily. I'm not sure if I'll be pissed or relieved if I discover that low fat Greek yogurt and oatmeal have been the cause of my plateau.

To prepare, I do a big Whole Foods grocery run on New Year's Eve. I want to make sure I am loaded for bear here. I stock up on new, preservative-free condiments and salad dressings, reading every ingredient before I decide to buy it. While shopping generally takes me half an hour, this time, it's more like an hour and a half. There's nothing in my cart that isn't grass-fed, free-range, or organic, nary a pesticide nor chemical nor artificial color to be seen. And sugar? Please. Not a grain, not a gram. Nary a drop of honey. I'll make my own sweetness *from within*.

I am one smug earth mother as I push my trolley full o' goodness around the store.

When I fork over what is essentially a mortgage payment, I am considerably less smug.

New Year's Eve night–my last hurrah–is a Christmas cookie, cheese, and bread-filled orgy, supplemented with champagne. When I wake up, I am seven pounds heavier than when I went to sleep.

I know I did not eat *seven actual pounds* of cookies. Not that I couldn't; my arm would have just gotten too tired bringing it all to my mouth.

["Congratulations! You got in ten thousand steps and *ten thousand calories!"]*

I fix a black coffee, unsweetened, and sip it while I make eggs. I serve them with pan-wilted spinach sautéed with garlic, a side of sliced avocados, a few blueberries, and a piece of prosciutto. I mention this because: (A) everything is amazing and absolutely on plan, and, (B) a prominent editor told me that she was sick of reading what white ladies ate for breakfast. Sorry, but it's relevant here.

Over the course of the day, I have a nice arugula salad with steak strips and Tessamae dressing, handfuls of almonds, and chicken with pan roasted vegetables for dinner. Everything tastes great and I'm not at all hungry.

The only down side is that I don't love black, unsweetened coffee.

But I can live with that temporarily if this helps me get some answers.

DAY THREE: I like everything I've eaten and I'm not fixated on food. No headaches, no cravings. I did not tackle Fletch and steal his wine on Sunday, nor did I slap the Bissinger Peanut Butter Maple Oat Chocolate bar out of his hands last night. And I can live with drinking black coffee; my breakfast beverage doesn't have to taste like mocha ice cream to start my day.

It *should*, but doesn't *have* do.

Melissa Hartwig, the diet's author, is a fan of saying that kicking a drug habit is hard, drinking coffee black is not.

Because my sugar intake's so much lower and I'm not having insulin spikes, my hunger level is nil. My energy level is off the charts. My joints feel better, my fingers seem less sausage-like, and my perpetual stuffy nose is clear without spray or decongestant.

The plan says not to count calories or weigh myself, but then there are no metrics, and I love me some data points. If I can't measure it, I can't manage it. If I can't manage it, I can't fix it. Naturally, I'm tracking calories. I've taken in the same amount I've been consuming for the past six months. Bottom line, I feel good.

By the way? I'm down six pounds.

Six pounds since Sunday.

I'd settle for five if I could have a splash of cream and a packet of Splenda in my coffee, though...

DAY FOUR: Thus far, no problems with the plan itself. I attribute this to having been so ready to try, eager to discover if food-based inflammation caused my plateau. Also, I have nothing going on this month. I have no parties, no travel, no day job, no picky kids to feed, so I have fewer barriers to entry. (If you're doing the program despite these hurdles, you are a damn hero.) While I can't imagine living so restricted forever, if in the next twenty-six days I learn that oatmeal is my own personal Satan, then I can plan accordingly.

THE GOOD: I'm reexamining my habits. For example, I'm in the throes of finishing a project. Last night around 5:45, I realized I'd given no thought to dinner. Often when I'm busy, I opt for delivery or takeout.

However, I don't know how to find what I'm supposed to have outside of my own kitchen. (I haven't read that far in the book.) I needed to cook.

From start to finish, assembling chicken thighs and vegetables on a sheet pan took ten minutes, less time than I'd need to leave the house and return with dinner. While the organic chicken is pricier than what I usually buy at Costco, home cooking is far less expensive than my usual alternative. Plus, I wrote while dinner was in the oven and the chicken was excellent. I never bought chicken with the skin on because I thought it was supposed to be horrible for you; actually, the numbers aren't so bad. And chicken skin is an edible jacket made from flavor.

THE LESS GOOD: Fletch keeps telling people, "We're doing Total30." Number one, no. Number two, I'm sorry, WE? After *we* had our healthy Whole30 dinner, *he* ate a piece of cake the size of an anvil. That's fine. I just want to clarify that he's not "doing Whole30" so much as he is consuming the breakfasts and lunches I've started making for him, in addition to our usual dinner. Again, happy to do nice things for him, but credit where due, please.

THE SUMMARY: Again, all is well. If I fall into a vat of chardonnay between now and next time, I shall make note.

DAY SEVEN: Today is Incident Day. First, we almost have An Incident with the string cheese when I'm trying to give Loki his pills. There's cheese stuck on my fingers and I go to lick it off and I get the cheese to my mouth and it's there, just waiting to be swallowed and I panic. I end up spitting it out on the floor.

Why does this stuff always happen right as Fletch walks into the room?

He's like, "Please don't spit on the kitchen floor."

I don't even try to explain.

Then I head to the grocery store. I go there every goddamned day now for something. Glad I'm not busy with a day job. The sample lady is not only giving out bites of my favorite cheese—Belle Etoile triple crème brie—but pairing it with a generous Dixie cup of champagne. I stand there so long, watching other shoppers quaff their champs and eat their cheese, that it gets creepy. Now I'm obligated to hit a different store tomorrow, as employees already suspect I'm casing the joint, because who legit goes to the supermarket every day?

In other news, I buy cashews in bulk and divvy them up into single-serve snack bags. Then I spend ten minutes giggling about "my nut sacks" because I am twelve.

Finally, we install a new alarm system. Our old system did not have a dummy panic code setting, but the new one does. Apparently this one is a few fat-fingered digits away from our nightly-setting code.

FYI, the Lake Forest PD has quite the response time and they are not impressed by braless women in flannel pajamas. I feel like we could have avoided this, had cheese been an option.

At least I have found NutPods, an almond-based creamer that foams beautifully in a cappuccino. At least there's that.

DAY NINE: Would I like to bite into a wedge of Port Salut cheese like an apple? Yes.

Have I bitten into a wedge of Port Salut cheese like an apple whenever I grab some to give the old fella his pills?

No.

What I'm finding is that this plan is all I talk about; this is my singular focus. Suddenly I'm sorry for mocking every vegan and gluten-free person I've ever met.

So, when I assault strangers who have not asked with information they do not seek, I tell them I'm not following the plan for weight loss, per se. Instead, I explain I'm trying to determine if food sensitivity is the reason for my plateau. I'm not restricting so much as establishing a baseline. If I lose weight on X calories/day without grain, sugar, dairy, alcohol, or legumes, and I gain again on X/day with these foods re-introduced, I'll know problem is what I eat, not how much, and I can adjust accordingly. I haven't had problems with my caloric baseline because I'm not terribly hungry outside of meal time. When I do get hungry, it's more like a "I'm a bit peckish" feeling and less a *"I will kill you and everyone you ever loved for a Twix bar"* thing. A bonus, yes?

I've been sharing this journey *[minus ten points to me for using this word, especially in a non-ironic sense]* on social media in real time and I'm getting some push-back. Again, perhaps it's because no one is asking. Some commenters question why I can't simply accept the fact that I may be at my "set" point right now, being content with the results I've had so far. That's a legitimate concern, especially as I'm a huge proponent of loving yourself at any size.

The short answer is vanity, which is also why I highlight my hair, do Botox, and never leave the house without coloring in my eyebrows and lips. I don't take these actions because I'm unhappy; rather, I like myself so much that I want nice things for me.

The longer answer is that I'm stubborn. I've never worked harder than I have in the past two years, yet I've stopped seeing tangible results from these efforts and *that is unacceptable*. Not because I have a ridiculously high and incredibly narrow definition of the standards of beauty, but because I refuse to let an arbitrary or outside force define my limits.

I will always fight my way around an obstacle.

[Um, hello, decision to publish my own memoir.]

From a systemic standpoint, my health continues to improve, but I want to SEE it. Pictures or it didn't happen. Again, it's not because I don't like me or feel like I'm not worthy regardless of size or age or ability to create a smoky eye.

My analogy is that if I had a job where I crushed goals and smashed expectations, eventually, I'd hope for recognition. Maybe a raise, a promotion, a bigger office. Something. While we feel innate satisfaction for a job well done, ultimately we work so we can live our lives indoors. What would make me want to quit that position is if the company said, "Now that we see your extraordinary capabilities, perform at no less than this level all the time or else you're fired."

In the above case, it would be hard to not turn in my notice. Yet since the "job" is maintaining healthy habits, quitting's a terrible option.

To finish beating to death the body-as-employer metaphor, I'll say that I don't require the keys to the executive washroom or access to the corporate jet as thanks. But having my photo posted in the break room under the Employee of the Month placard would go a long way towards job satisfaction.

Now, if the plan allowed me to track my weight, I'd tell

you that I'm down ten pounds in nine days... not that you asked.

I still miss cheese. Just not as much as I did.

DAY FOURTEEN: We're doing a home renovation project this weekend.

Looks like I picked the wrong month to give up drinking.

DAY SEVENTEEN: I screw up the alarm again, this time on my way out the door to go to the grocery store after I finish at the gym. I'm still pulling out of my driveway when the police arrive. We're going to get a bill for this soon, aren't we? The officer who reports looks like a young Tom Cruise. He's very nice and doesn't call me an idiot. Out loud.

DAY TWENTY-TWO: Have been cleaning out the pantry while on Whole30, so every day the squirrels get something new. Thus far, their favorite item is stale ice cream cones. There's nothing cuter than stepping outside and hearing a dozen squirrels chomping on their cones up in the trees. P.S. They hate All Bran cereal.

[Crows go crazy for saltines. Nothing else. Just saltines. I never see them around the yard, but if I toss out a few, it never fails that within minutes, we'll have a murder. Of crows. In case that wasn't clear.]

I feel like I should have more to complain about, or maybe exclaim about, but this plan is ideal for anyone who's ever been an emotional eater. Food truly has become fuel and what I eat, I enjoy, tasting everything that's fresh and good about the pure, whole ingredients. Every bit of pressure has been removed from the equation, every bit of guilt.

Instead, the *feeeeelings* have been replaced instead with stacks and stacks of dirty dishes from all the cooking.

Not a terrible tradeoff.

DAY TWENTY-NINE: I bought two kinds of kale at the grocery store yesterday; I didn't even know there WERE at least two kinds of kale prior to Whole30.

Every week I've completed a Sunday Run Day 5K on my treadmill. Today I shaved three minutes off my time since last week! Now my speed is only pathetic and not tragic. Progress! Also, I didn't know I had IT bands prior to this, but I do. Apparently, they hurt like a bitch when you run with a bad gait. Today's progress comes from having fixed my gait, as well as saying to myself, "What if I just ran instead of stopping to walk?"

Next Sunday, I have my eye on you.

Finally, even though I'm a day away, I can't take it anymore. I put half a Splenda in my NutPod cappuccino today. Tastes like chemicals and not sweet, sweet cream. I do not see that coming.

DAY THIRTY: My Whole30 experience is over. I made it, save for the half Splenda, and I can't be mad at me for that.

I got in the habit of having a stocked kitchen and cooking every meal. Everything I made tasted good, not a dog in the bunch. Or maybe hunger is the best sauce, whichever.

Going all organic/grass-fed/pasture-raised was more expensive at the grocery store, but we saved a ton by never having delivery or takeout. We've established better habits, which will be key moving forward. I'm talking *breakfast salads*; never thought I'd live to see that day.

Even though it's against the spirit of the plan, I consistently weighed and measured myself throughout because I wanted to compare the data from last January when I was doing the Lose to Win program. I worked so much harder and ate so much less a year ago, yet I lost more weight this time with far less exercise and more food. I'm down... twenty pounds!

THE GOOD: I made positive strides towards my health without going nuclear. It truly does all start with food. I enjoyed feeling like a part of the Whole30 community, from reading message boards to sharing recipes to interacting on social media. I liked being part of a team.

With an emphasis on animal fats, this is not meant to be a lifelong diet, per se. Instead, it's a hard reset for the body and in that respect, it worked well. Now it's up to me to figure out what does and doesn't work as I add in foods.

THE BAD: I've never washed so many damn dishes in my life. Thankfully I discovered parchment paper before I ruined too many baking sheets.

[Yes, this implies some were ruined.]

To celebrate the end of what proves to be both a challenging and invigorating month, Fletch and I head down to the city to meet up with Gina, Tracey, and Lee for a nice Italian dinner on Saturday. I skip my usual wine, opting for Tito's martinis. As I'm now a paragon of clean living, I'm only going to contaminate myself with the *pure* liquor.

After three drinks, I learn that my own personal prohibition has turned me into a total lightweight. While Fletch is in the bathroom getting ready for bed, I set off the alarm.

Of course I summon the police.

Of course I do.

I step outside to have a conversation with the officers, delighted that this time I look cute from having been out, not all sweaty like when they've caught me post-gym, on the way to the grocery store, or in my pajamas, like the other nights.

[We are so getting a bill.]

I try to explain that this is all a result of my ham-fingers and Whole30 and Tito's vodka. There's some backstory about how squirrels eschew All Bran as well. The officers on the scene are trying not to snicker into their walkies. The lack of inherent danger is clear, at least the danger to anyone but myself, but they don't go rushing away. I'm glad they don't seem resentful at having had to come.

Also, I'm sure we're being invoiced.

"Okay," says Officer Wiseass. He appears to be in charge. "Blink once if you're actually in danger."

I blink. But then I blink again.

"Shit! I need a do-over. Wait, did I tell you about the Tito's?"

THE LESSON: I learned a lot about myself over this month. I learned it's possible to move past a plateau without medical intervention or drastic measures. Don't let someone tell you what's right for you, no matter how many degrees he or she may have. You know your body best. There's no harm in trying a less invasive solution first. And eating the right foods can make all the difference.

The most important take-away is that I learned I'm able to adapt, to change, and to exercise self-control.

Still working on learning the alarm system, though.

THIRTEEN

Moms Gone Mild

"I LIKE THE dreams of the future better than the history of the past."

- Thomas Jefferson

I AM NOT MISSING this weekend.

That's my mantra as I stand here, ticket in hand, waiting to board my flight home from Los Angeles. The airline won't let anyone on the plane until someone gives up a seat because they've oversold the flight. A harried gate attendant makes yet another announcement asking for volunteers.

Right. Like Imma help you out, American?

I have medallion status, yet I'm number *twenty* on the upgrade list, with a fully-checked-in First Class section.

Fat freaking chance.

It's imperative I get home because I have something like twelve hours before I need to be in the car, on my way down to campus. Joanna has been looking forward to this weekend now for thirty-one years, ever since we were freshmen roommates together. Granted, she was sure we'd be visiting *both* our daughters at Purdue for Moms' Weekend. She was half right. Even then, I knew it was only happening for one of us.

Joanna asks for so little. That's why there was no way I was going to bitch about Moms' Weekend not gelling with my business travel schedule. I'd make it work. Unless American bumps me and then we are going to have ourselves An Incident.

Thankfully, the gate attendant suckers someone else into giving up his seat. I love when they say, "Please volunteer or we'll have to volunteer for you." That's not Draconian *at all*.

At least they're better than United, who will *literally* punch you in the face.

I board and make my way to my window seat in the bulkhead, close enough to First Class that everyone up there can be warmed by the burning hot waves of resentment radiating off me. I'm delighted it's a newer plane so at least I have my own personal video monitor, none of this crane-your-neck-to-see-the-one-tiny-hanging-screen-for-six-rows-of-seats business.

I'm less delighted when I discover my monitor is broken. A father and (I'm guessing) ten-year-old daughter follow along right behind me. They have the middle and aisle seats in this row. They brought their own king-sized pillows because I guess they are unaware that pillows exist in Chicago, too.

Immediately the dad shoves said pillows in the overhead compartment, thus filling the entire bin, superthoughtful on a full flight. While he's not particularly tall, he manages to manspread so wide that every single passenger trying to get by must turn sideways and shimmy.

Now I hate him and he should be afforded no additional courtesies ever.

The daughter, clad in a Harry Potter shirt and Harry Potter socks, whips out a bag of Bertie Bott Every Flavour Beans, opens a Harry Potter book, and selects a Harry Potter film on her personal viewing screen.

Her, I like.

The flight attendant finally says something to Johnny Kneecaps because it's taking everyone so long to board around him. What is it about planes that amplifies every single annoying behavior? Other than the fact that you're trapped and you can't just leave and the off-chance you might accidentally die due to the earth's gravitational pull and I think I just answered my own question.

We take off on time and without additional incident. Once we're in the air, I log onto the Wi-Fi, which doesn't work. Of course it doesn't, why would it? You know, I'd probably be distracted from my worries about corkscrewing into the ground from thirty-five-thousand feet, were I able to check Doug the Pug's Instagram feed. I bet he's saying something pithy about pizza right now and I'm missing it. Ooh, or how about when his owner places her hands in Doug's armpits and makes it look like Doug's dancing with his widdle legs outstretched, and hims neck fat envelopes his whole smooshy face and he seems even more smiley than usual and it's all I can do to not kiss the screen and nom on hims sweet, sweet jelly rolls?

Maybe it's for the best I can't view him right now because, dignity.

I pull up iTunes and none of the downloads I started

completed. *Et tu*, Apple? Do you want me to sit here and read a *magazine* like a *chump*, like it's 1984 and technology doesn't exist? I decide to watch the one thing I've downloaded on Netflix and have not yet seen... *Sausage Party*. If you're unfamiliar, it's Seth Rogan's animated flick about food items in the grocery store having adventures and casual sex.

[I know, I know.]

I'd hoped to view this in the hotel or at home alone, where no one could judge me, but no such luck. I put in my earphones and I start the movie. After a while, I sense a second set of eyes peering over my shoulder. Uh-oh. While animated, the film is not kid-friendly.

At all.

I position myself so the girl next to me can't see. She keeps trying to sneak peeks anyway, which I would totally do, were I ten and saw what looked like a racy cartoon. I turn off the profanity-laden subtitles (I read everything I watch, weird habit) and angle as far away from her as I can. My screen is basically parallel with the plane's window now. She continues to telescope her neck, totally oozing over into my personal space. Her breath smells like marshmallow and watermelon jellybeans.

At this point, I believe I've done my duty. My screen is as sheltered as possible without my actually turning it off. I'm hunched around it like a prisoner protecting his lunch tray from the other hungry felons on Lasagna Day. The dad shoots passive-aggressive looks at me, as though *I'm* the problem here. Why does he feel that his rights in this situation supersede mine? It's not like I'm trying to lure his kid into my panel van with the promise of puppies and Pez.

Here's a thought, Dad; if you don't like the fact that

your kid is crawling into *my* seat to invade *my* privacy and to view inappropriate content on *my* screen, stop her. Distract her. Change seats with her. I'm not the one in charge of safeguarding her.

When I was growing up in the 1970s, every adult could yell at every kid. Totally allowable. That was part of the social contract. I'm not saying it was right, I'm just saying there was a hierarchy. A pecking order, with kids on the bottom. Didn't matter whether these grown-ups were complete strangers; we were obligated to listen. If we were being brats, they could call us on it. I can't imagine turning to this child and saying, "Yo, Hermione, sit your ass down. This movie is not for you." My God, we'd have an emergency landing in Denver and a team of air marshals would cart me off this plane faster than I could say, *"Expelliarmus!"*

Because as a culture we're not doing the whole "it takes a village thing" anymore, it's on you, Pops. Stop airing out your crotch and do your job. Better yet, complain about me to a flight attendant and get me moved to First Class.

That would serve me right.

When the grocery store orgy scene comes on, I close my iPad.

I give up. I'll just read a magazine.

———

I'M HOME LONG ENOUGH to wash some underwear, kiss some dogs and make sure Fletch hasn't gone feral (or vice-versa.) I sleep for a few hours before I head down to pick up Joanna on the way to Purdue.

Even though I have GPS, I've since become a huge fan of Waze because of L.A. traffic and it's the fastest, most effective way to go anywhere. I've preprogrammed everything before I get to Joanna's because I know she's going to want to navigate and that's just not going to happen. In fact, it's why I insisted we take my car.

Joanna still uses Google maps and likes to give directions in retrospect, all, "You should... have exited there!" as we whiz past at seventy-two miles per hour.

As the copilot, she offers instructions by way of mathematical equation, i.e. "We'll want to merge in three times the number of kilometers it took us from the turn off." This is her only fault, the sole flaw in the Hopi blanket that is her life, and it is a charming one, unless you are the driver because then you will want to plow headfirst into a tractor trailer full of steel coils. We've had discussions about how crazy-making this can be, but to no avail. We do not fight ever–too much mutual respect–but if we've squabbled, this is why.

I help her bring her things out to the car and we load them up in back.

"How were your meetings?" she asks, hugging me as she welcomes me inside.

"They went well," I say. Which is true. I have a few projects in play and I was out there talking to producers.

"Everyone was nice?"

I love how Joanna's such a mom, that her greatest concern is for people having been kind to me.

"Everyone's nice out there," I assure her. "I heard nothing but yeses."

I've been doing more business in Los Angeles lately. I find I prefer being there over New York now. If nothing else, an L.A. "yes" is the same thing as a New York "no," but the L.A. yes feels so much nicer.

"Everything will work out for the best!" she tells me.

"You realize the long-shot, million to one, best-case-scenario is a network sale. That means we'd move there."

Joanna looks thoughtful. "Then I hope you crash and burn."

I laugh. "Thought so. Let's load up."

We make multiple trips back and forth to the car. We've both stocked up on festive items for her daughter Anna's sorority's silent auction, as well as snacks for the hotel room. I offer her a fresh, cold bottle of water from the cooler and we jump into the front seats. I'm about to change the satellite radio station from Backspin (classic hip hop) when she starts in about directions.

Call me psychic, because I totes predicted this.

She says, "Okay, I've got Google maps ready. What you're going to want to do is-"

"Don't need it," I say, offering her my widest smile. "I've already programmed Waze. It's a traffic reporting program with directions. They tell you the fastest possible way using satellites. Thousands of users self-report so it's all real-time. There's red light cameras, they tell you about stalled cars, plus it tracks your speed. Really, it's the perfect app."

"Is it going to tell you to take Ogden? Because you're going to want to take Ogden. I don't care what it says, I have to insist you take Ogden."

"Hey, look," I say, pointing at the display, "Ogden."

She argues with me about Waze (ever-so-politely) for the next ten minutes, even though it gets us to expressway more quickly than her route. At this point, I've not changed the radio station.

I know exactly what kind of music Joanna prefers. In fact, I know almost everything she likes, as we share many commonalities. While we're diverse adults, we came together at a point in our lives when we weren't fully formed, so we developed into who were together. At the core, we're much the same. Take our sense of style, for example. Both of us have an undying love for stiff cotton and bold, preppy colors, cut conservatively. A few years ago, she was in New York with me for a press junket. I had to do some media in the Condé Nast building. While dressing, I asked her what she thought of my black loafers and white socks.

"Love," she replied.

She wasn't shining me on, either; she meant it. It wasn't until we were both in the lobby, watching fashion editors swan past in their four inch heels, we realized exactly how in synch and out of touch we were.

"Bodies hauled off after squeezing the trigger, hmm? This is a nice song," Joanna says. I know what she's doing. She wants me to change the station but she's too Lutheran to complain directly. Instead, she'll hint.

Now I must mess with her because of the whole Google maps thing.

That's how people know that I love them, by the way; I bait them.

[If I don't harass you a little, sorry. I guess we're just not that tight.]

"Did you want me to change the channel?" I say. This is officially a power struggle.

"No, it's fine. If *you* like it."

I nod. "I do."

"You relate to it? This music? Does it bring you back to growing up on the mean streets of Indiana? Remind me, did you get your first AK-47 before or after the Miss Huntington pageant?"

"If you *ask* me to change the station, I'll change it."

"I'm fine."

We ride in comfortable silence for a while. I've been watching for a coffee place but haven't seen one. I'm exhausted and could use a boost. Feels like there's nothing but barren cornfields on this stretch of road.

"I am dying for a latte. Are you?" I ask.

"I had coffee at home."

"So did I, but it was two hours ago. Are we going to be near a place to stop soon?"

"Oh, did Waze not tell you where all the Starbucks are?" Joanna asks, her voice the epitome of sweetness and light. She bats her eyes. "Because you should have asked me and Google maps. We could have told you. Sorry, we've passed all of them."

I smile. Looks like someone wants to mess with me, too. We drive on. I turn up the volume. Oh, good. Back-spin threw in a little 2 Live Crew. She'll enjoy this.

"So..." Joanna says, frowning at the speaker. "Talking about 'popping that pussy,' eh? Nice. Very romantic song. Michael and I should have made that our wedding song instead of Frank Sinatra."

I say, "Speaking of? Check this out. I just got another round of edits back on my YA book. You know my character Kent?"

"Sweet, nerdy one?"

"That's him. There's a line where he tells his friend to 'stop being a puss,' when he's freaking out. The copy editor flagged that expression for 'sensitivity,' telling me there's a whole faction who'll go up in arms when referring to female parts when calling someone weak or a coward. Like, I'm not supposed to say that."

Joanna cocks her head. "Has the copy editor met a high school boy? That's how they talk."

"They all know. The editorial team is just trying to protect me from the social justice warriors who are super-easily offended and will come after me, pitchforks waving. But, I caved, I changed it."

"That does not sound like you."

I sigh. "I know. In a lot of ways, I feel like they're not wrong."

Three decades ago, I'd have responded to the email thread with a whole bunch of words I'd never dream of using now. I recall how I was throwing around the *r-word* in my thirties. I even used it in the book *Bitter*. My God, that makes me cringe now.

By any standard, that's inexcusable.

I didn't have friends with differently-abled kids then, I didn't know. I wish I could go back and scrub it from the text, scrub it from existence. I hate how casually accepted the word was at the time, how it was no big deal. Every time I write a check to the Special Olympics, I think, "Not enough." And I'm sorry. I guess if I compensate by over-editing myself in the YA manuscript and if as a society we're hyper-cautious going forward, we'll eventually come to a happy medium in terms of language.

I tell Joanna, "Maybe if I look back in thirty years and *don't* want to punch myself in the face for my expressions? I'll have gotten it right."

———

AFTER THE FESTIVITIES at Anna's sorority house, we're talking to a group of moms and daughters. The whole time we've been here, we've tag-teamed conversations, finishing each other's sentences, recounting shared history and telling tales of all the trips we've taken together.

"This is my mom and this is my Auntie Jen," Anna says, introducing us to another mother and daughter set, right as we're mid-story about our disastrous trip to Italy.

"Nice to meet you both," the mom says, after introducing herself. "How did you two meet?"

"We were roommates freshmen year," Joanna explains.

"Wow! And you've been *together* since then?" she replies.

"Pretty much. We lost touch for a little while. Then we found each other again through Facebook and it was like nothing ever changed, we didn't miss a beat," Joanna explains, squeezing my arm.

The other mom says, "Aw, that's so great."

"It was great," Joanna confirms.

Anna catches on first, laughing. "They're not a couple, they're not my two moms. My mom's married to my dad."

The woman apologizes for her assumption but Joanna and I just look at each other and shrug it off.

"Please," I say. "We could do way worse than each other."

We then head over to Earhart Hall, what we call the scene of the crime, our freshman home. Anna and her roommate live in the exact same spot in this dorm that we did, right next to the resident advisor, across from the bathroom, only three floors up.

While the rest of Purdue has changed so much that I barely recognize it, the dorm is practically frozen in time, our own personal Pompeii. Every single part of it's the same, from the paneling in the lobby to the stained linoleum lining the hallways. It's eerie. What's extra-surreal is that there's this tree outside the window that we must have looked out at a million times thirty years ago and now, it probably appears at the same height here at the seventh floor as it did for us on the forth.

Sunrise, sunset, amirite?

We greet Anna's roommate Nicole, who is still in bed at 2:30 p.m. She's just waking up from a big night. Per Anna, when Nicole finally staggered home, knowing that this was Moms' Weekend and that Anna was trying to keep their room neat, she had the courtesy to vomit in her backpack.

This kid is already my spirit animal.

[I don't think we need a BuzzFeed quiz to determine which roommate is the Jen and which is the Joanna.]

Joanna says we need to get some protein into these girls, so we decide to take them back to our hotel to fill them with cheese and charcuterie and three kinds of crackers. Nicole rolls out of bed in the clothes she went out in and she's ready to go.

Goddamn it, I miss being able to rally like that.

On our way back down to the car, Joanna and I stop outside the elevator to stand by mirror that still hangs there.

"We have to show them what we used to do, Joanna."

"Oh, my God, yes! I almost forgot!"

I tell the girls, "We did this every time before we'd go out on the weekend. Our ritual was that we'd listen to the Talking Head's *Stop Making Sense* album while we got ready. Once we were done, we check ourselves out like this."

Joanna and I stand together in a side-hug in front of the old mirror. We both grin big, cheesy smiles and tilt our heads to the side, as though we're being photographed.

"We might be fifty on the outside, but we're still eighteen on the inside," Joanna says, striking our trademark pose.

"Girl, you let me do something with those grays and I will vanish ten years off you in twenty minutes," I tell her. "We don't even have to go to the salon. Just one box of L'Oréal. Boom. Done."

She shakes her formerly honeyed blonde hair, now shot through with strands of silver. "Nah, I'm happy the way I am."

"Yeah, yeah," I grumble. I'm never going to stop asking her to be my human Barbie head and she's never going to consent. Yin and yang. Our eyes meet and we smile at our reflection.

Anna snorts, "You'd just hug each other in a mirror? Like, that's it? You'd just hug and look? You'd *pretend* to take a selfie?"

"Cool story, bro," Nicole adds.

Are these little assholes mocking us?

"Listen," I hiss, breaking the hug. "We didn't have smartphones back then. We didn't know how to work angles. There was no delete-until-you-get-it-right-gram. Cameras weren't designed to take pictures of yourself backwards, because they had fucking apertures and stuff. They were covered in buttons. They were complicated machines. And, number one, film was, like, a buck a print, and number two, the guy at the Photomat saw every single picture you took. Hell, he made duplicates of the ones he liked! Christ, I *wish* we had cellphones. I would love to see what my ass looked like at eighteen. I wish I'd saved that shit for posterity. You know what happens to your backyard after thirty? Nothing good."

"Mrs. S? Your adult lady friend is making me feel

uncomfortable," Nicole says, again, totally making fun of us.

Oh, I cannot wait for these kids to be on the other side of this conversation in thirty years.

Later, back at the hotel, we realize we don't have a wine key. We send the girls down to the lobby with twenty bucks and the goal to do whatever it takes to find one, but they return empty-handed. They don't even spend my twenty on nonsense. We are sorely disappointed by their lack of industry.

Joanna and I have the last laugh when we manage to open the Chardonnay with nothing but my motorcycle boot and a coat hanger.

Our age has given us the skills these kids won't master for decades.

———

WE EAT dinner with some of Anna's sorority sisters and their moms. One of the ladies owns a second home in a cool resort town out west. She and her daughter have invited Anna and another friend to live there over the summer. Joanna doesn't want her to go, even though everything about the situation is safe and above board.

"Why not?" I ask as we get ready in our hotel room for what Anna calls the "pregame" frat party. We're playing the Talking Heads for old time's sake. "Anything she'd want to *do*, she's had the opportunity already but probably hasn't because she's a good kid who makes smart decisions.

"I know," Joanna admits, pursing her lips.

"You never lived at home during the summer. You always had an internship or something. You turned out great. You know why? Because you were a good kid who made smart decisions, too. Look at me, I was home all the time and I was a freaking disaster."

"I know."

"Honey, you raised a nice girl with strong values. Yeah, she's kind of a smart ass, but that's the best part of her."

Joanna fixes her mascara in the mirror next to me. "I know."

"Then, what? This summer's a great opportunity, and you know how bored she was home over spring break." I meet her gaze in the mirror. "What's stopping you from allowing her to go?"

Joanna's eyes are a little glassy. "I'd just miss her."

I pull her in for one of our side-hugs. It's all I can do.

Never one to dwell on the unpleasant for long, Joanna clears her throat and claps her hands together. "Okay. Are you almost ready?"

I slide on one last coat of lipstick and spray some perfume. "I am."

She says, "Then we are off to the Pike house! Huh. I really never thought I'd say that again."

A couple of the fraternities are hosting Mom parties tonight, which is the cutest thing I've ever heard. I'm oddly excited for this. I say, "I haven't set foot in a frat party since I was legal to go to bars."

Joanna stares at her phone. "Then I just, what, do the Uber?" She downloaded the app for tonight, always having been a taxi cab kind of gal prior to now.

"Yes, and definitely call it 'doing the Uber,'" I suggest.

When our car arrives, even though the driver lives in town and Joanna hasn't been a resident since the first Bush administration, she tells him to ignore the route and directs him via Google maps.

I don't say a damn thing.

We stop to pick up beer because I am not a savage and I can't show up to a party empty-handed. The place doesn't sell High Life, so I opt for a case of Bud instead. I suspect the kids won't mind.

Walking in the door of the Pi Kappa Alpha house gives me a great sense of comfort as my sneakers suction to the hardwood. In a world that can be, at best, confusing, and, at worst, terrifying, it's nice to know that on any given day, the sun will rise, the birds will sing, and the floors of a frat house will be sticky.

When we enter the party proper, I hand the beer to the backwards-ball-cap-boy behind the bar. Judging from his reaction, you'd think I was T.I. rolling up with a wheelbarrow full of Cristal on ice. He takes the red and white case from me with great reverence. His movement is so ginger, so tender, so deliberate, somewhere between handing a newborn and a bundle of dynamite. He stashes his great prize behind the bar.

"Ohmigod, thank you! Wow! Thank you!" he says.

"You're welcome," I reply with a shrug.

"*You* get a clean glass," he says, presenting me a red Solo cup with the kind of flourish reserved for Oprah handing out vehicle keys to deserving audience members.

"It's fine," I say. "I can drink out of a can."

"Whoa."

After the pregame party–which looks exactly like a regular party–the three of us do the Uber [*sorry, Joanna, it's still funny*] up to the more formal fraternity party.

A whole cadre of kids sit at a big table at the door, laptops open in front of them. At first, I think they're studying and this breaks my heart. Then I realize they're running an elaborate system of alcohol control and management, coordinating security and paring up guests and sober drivers.

Sometimes I wonder how any of us made it out of Purdue alive back in the dark ages, especially me.

We head down to the party in the basement where the DJ spins nothing but '80s and '90s tunes. With each song by Guns N' Roses or Bon Jovi, the moms in the group shriek and rush the dance floor while their daughters stand to the side, face-palming.

It's so awesome.

Joanna and I are only planning to stay for a drink or two. While Anna seems to be having fun with us now, we don't want to blow up her spot. Also, I'm losing track of who's basic and who's extra and I still can't discern the difference.

A lot of girls here are in rompers, which, why, God, why? While admittedly cute, I have to wonder if the designers got together and asked, *"What's the wearable version of the Rubik's Cube? Really, what would be the hardest item in the world to remove in a public restroom after, say, six Natty Lights? Could we add a feature that makes the wearer perform naked gymnastics while trying to keep said garment off the disgusting floor in the midst of taking said leak?"*

My old neon Forenza sweaters, linebacker shoulder pads, and knickers don't seem quite so stupid now.

[No. They still do.]

Judging from the Pike house and now Delta Upsilon, the party togs du jour for the modern American fraternity boy appear to be a basketball jersey, a khaki short, and a sport coat. While this look is more functional, and somewhat David Letterman in its vibe, I find it equally puzzling. What message does it convey about the wearer?

"I'm up for a game of one on one or *a meeting with the marketing team, your call."*

Despite questionable sartorial choices, these boys are smart. They're all coming up to talk to Joanna and me, knowing this is the way to get to the pretty daughter.

"These guys are all so cute, aren't they?" Joanna says.

"Yes, but they're *babies*," I reply. "Still, just darling. Check out that one in the striped rugby with the dark hair and sunglasses—he looks like someone you would have dated."

"He does, doesn't he? Hey, how about that blonde kid with the *'I have a sailboat'* vibe? I could have seen that for you," she replies. "Totally your type back then. Working that Top Siders and golden leg hair thing."

"Ha! All he's missing are the Madras shorts," I said. "Oh, over there, look at the one giving off all the art school realness. He's legit brooding! He's like, *'I'm intense! I contain multitudes! Look at me but don't look at me!'*"

"Where?"

"By the neon beer sign." I begin to point and then I catch myself. "Aw, shit, Joanna. Do you *hear* us? We just got creepy. Seriously. Do you realize we just turned into Matthew McConaughey in *Dazed and Confused*? *'All right, all right, all right. I get older, the frat boys stay the same age.'*"

Joanna nods. "Ew, yeah, we should go now. I kind of want to wash my hands. Let me hit the ladies room. I'll be back here in a minute and then we're out of there."

As she walks off, a kid in a Lakers jersey and herringbone tweed jacket sidles up to me. "Can I interest you in another Straw-Ber-Ita, m'lady?"

While I occasionally buy Mango-Ritas, they're meant to be consumed on the rocks, by a body of water, not served in a sweaty basement, at room temp, from a can. My Straw-Ber-Ita is vile. I've had more delicious cough syrup.

"I'm good, thanks," I reply.

"Well..." he says, raising an eyebrow. "Do you go to school here?"

I clap a hand over my mouth because this boy is just too precious for words. Every other kid in the place is casting for minnows with breadcrumbs, awkwardly flirting with sorority girls. Here he is, trolling the deep water with the heaviest test line, looking to reel him in a barracuda.

"Oh, honey," I tell him. "You are darling. I mean it. *'Do you go to school here?'* I love that you think that would work. I do. You keep at it, okay? Plug away. Commit to it. No one who isn't an undergrad is going to buy that you think she's an undergrad. But if you're lucky, one of these moms in here, probably someone fresh off an ugly divorce, is gonna want to live out her *Younger* fantasy. And she's going to give you the night of your life."

His smile could light up Detroit. "You really think so?"

The DJ plays that Fountains of Wayne song and the over-forty crowd loses their fucking minds. There's a veritable stampede of higher-waist jeans heading towards the dance floor.

"Trust me, kid. I'm old enough to be your mom."

————

JOANNA and I choke down one beer at our favorite Purdue bar. Neither of us even want that, but when we find our names still carved in the woodwork twenty-five years later, we haven't much choice but to stand there and drink a toast to it.

There's what I think is a hot dog stand next to the bar and I ask for two of their most popular item while Joanna does the Uber. When we get back to the hotel and unwrap them, we discover hot dog buns filled with French fries, mozzarella sticks, a chicken tender, and splashes of ranch and marinara.

I feel like I need Seth Rogan to explain whatever this is to me.

We are ready for bed by midnight.

Party animals.

Thirty years ago, we'd have just been going out at this point.

You know what? I wouldn't go back. I wouldn't trade my life for Anna's. I'd hate to be starting out again. I'm truly happy with where I am. The precipice of fifty looks good, even though I might need reading glasses to help me see it.

Sure, I had fun revisiting my youth this weekend, but there's so much more to me, more to either of us than just old memories. Joanna and I are constantly creating new ones in our lives, together, with our husbands, and even by ourselves. I believe that's the key to staying young.

When we were eighteen, she and I would lay in our respective dorm beds, talking about these elderly aunties that Joanna had. They were best friends, too. Both of their spouses had passed, so these women spent their twilight years traveling the world together, having adventures, coming back with stories to tell. We pledged that someday, we were going to do that kind of thing.

And we have and we are.

How great is that?

WE'RE en route home when I ask Joanna to Google map us a way to get to a Starbucks around Schererville.

Once we have our drinks, we drive in silence for a while, no sound but that of an iPhone playlist I know Joanna likes.

Apropos of nothing she says, "I'm going to do it."

I glance over at her. "Do what?"

"California. I'm letting Anna spend the summer out there."

"Yay!" I cheer. "This will be so fun for her. And we can visit."

She nods and says nothing, looking at the empty fields where stalks of corn will soon flourish. This had to be a hard decision, and the choice she's making is completely selfless. There's no upside for her in letting Anna go, in giving up her peace of mind in always knowing where her daughter is, what she's doing, and who she's with. Joanna was so looking forward to having Anna home this summer. The kid's such a sunny presence, with a wicked sense of humor. She's always willing to help and she's especially sweet and loving with her younger sister.

Joanna and her husband Michael have worked so hard to raise this intelligent, independent young woman, one who'd have the confidence and ability to leave the nest.

And that's exactly what they've gotten.

That realization must be bittersweet.

I tab through my playlist until I find the right song to mark occasion. Fountains of Wayne claim that it's Stacy's mom who's got it going on.

I disagree. In my opinion, it's Anna's.

FOURTEEN

Who's Afraid Of The Dark?

"IF YOU WANT to conquer fear, don't sit home and think about it. Go out and get busy."

- Dale Carnegie

"ARE YOU IN THE HOUSE ALONE?"

I cower here in bed, frozen in panic that my phone will ring and a menacing voice on the other end of the line will ask me the question I've dreaded for most of my life.

"Are you in the house alone?"

Because I am in the house alone. I fear that he knows this.

[Why is it always a he *in my imagination? This is inadvertent gender bias. Not cool. Ladies can be murderers, too. What about Aileen Wuornos? Or Belle Gunness? Or Velma Barfield? They didn't just slaughter* a *person, they slaughtered multiple people. They were legit serial killers!]*

[Wait, why am I so well-versed in female serial killers?]

He has my number. He's biding his time before he calls.

Fletch, my husband, my protector, my own personal Secret Service agent, is across the country on business. There's no one here but me, a lonesome figure huddled in the darkness.

Sure, I have a whole pack of scary dogs who, in theory, could scare off intruders, but they're even bigger babies than me. For crying out loud, Hambone's terrified when I cook meat on the stove. She runs to hide. Yes, she gets a little snarly when she sees the FedEx guy, but if he broke in and fried up some bacon? Forget it. Game over.

Hazy moonlight casts ominous shadows on the long drive leading up to the house. My home is ensconced by trees and bracketed by a nature preserve. The woods are deep around me... providing so damn many places for monsters and aliens to hide.

Thanks for that, *Stranger Things*.

As if I wasn't already neurotic enough.

Our residence is set far back from the main road, shielded from the sight and sound of other homes in the vicinity. These properties are distant oases, their wan pools of light barely breaching the wood line. Whenever Fletch is here, all this privacy is a totally selling point, especially if we were "naked people," which we are not.

[Perhaps you've gathered this already.]

We moved from the city to the suburbs to avoid that which perpetually violated our peace. We were so very *over* Chicago's constant twilight, where the nights never quite darkened, where blackout curtains barely dimmed the bedroom. And do not start me on the noise pollution.

With open windows, we heard every flush of nearby

toilets, the drone of a dozen different televisions, the scrape of steak knife against dinner plate as the feuding couple next door consumed their meals in angry silence in the days before she finally left him, taking the Labradoodle with all his personalized, embroidered sweatshirts.

The last thing we wanted was to see or hear those people.

Okay, that's a lie.

At first, Fletch and I both turned into Gladys Kravitz when they squabbled with each other. "See?" he'd say to me. "I always put the seat back down!" Then I would chime in with, "And I would never leave you less than a whole serving of milk in the carton!" Then we'd congratulate each other for winning at the competitive sport of being the better couple than the people who lived next to us.

As things devolved, we were more and more uncomfortable with our front-row seat at their unraveling marriage. We were an unwilling audience, trapped by proximity. We bought this place to be out of neighbors' earshot.

Yet now I realize we're too far away for anyone to hear me scream.

Motherfucker.

"Are you in the house alone?"

My heart pounds with such force that my pulse throbs in my ears. A steel band of terror constricts my lungs and I can barely catch my breath. The taste of fear is bitter on my tongue. My palms are damp as I wrap the blanket around me. I cling to it, as though the thin cotton could protect me, could keep me safe. I close my eyes, but I know sleep won't come.

I lay here, awake, alert, awash in terror.

And I wait for the phone to ring.

———

FULL DISCLOSURE?

Nothing happens to me while Fletch is away in Boston. Or in Las Vegas. Or Dallas. Or the handful of other places he's traveled in the past few years for business or boys' weekends. I've never had an incident; no terrifying precedent has ever been set.

No one's called to ask me if I'm in the house alone. In fact, on this last trip, the phone doesn't even ring. Of course, that's because the twenty-year IT industry veteran in the house, the guy who's designed millions of dollars' worth of telecom infrastructures for *Fortune 50* organizations, installed a new cable jack in the bedroom a few months ago and now all our calls go straight to voicemail.

Fletch claims that he was working with CAT-5 wire and never touched the basement phone lines, so the malfunction can't be his fault. I claim that when he went downstairs to monkey with the wiring, our landline worked, and, when he came back up, it didn't.

Do the math.

Also, even if the raspy-voiced murderer tries to hit me on my cell phone instead, I won't hear it; I never un-muted my ringer after one too many robo-dialed election calls. Plus, there's almost no scenario that entails me talking on the phone in the first place, particularly to anyone at a number I don't recognize.

Decline. Block. Done.

Still, I'm in full-on, bitch-panic mode about unwanted calls from the second the sun sets whenever he's gone.

Which makes no sense to anyone, especially me.

The irony here is that the dialogue from the *Are You in the House Alone* made-for-TV movie that's scared me since its debut in 1978 *wasn't even about murder*. Instead, the heroine was being secretly harassed by her classmate, a pink-cheeked, teenage Dennis Quaid. And, despite his poly bell-bottoms and propensity for acquaintance rape, Dennis Quaid wasn't spoiling to kill anyone.

The problem is that I've conflated this stupid movie with every other terrifying film I saw/book I read during my formative years. The phrase *"Are you in the house alone?"* has become emblematic shorthand for all the media that scared me growing up. In the late '70s/early '80s, no one made entertainment geared towards middle graders.

Why is that, I wonder?

Were authors too concerned with the Cold War? Did producers assume that twelve-year-olds didn't have discretionary income to spend on movies? Personally, I was babysitting four nights a week back then, so I was makin' it rain, a dollar an hour at a time.

For whatever reason, today's flourishing Young Adult market had yet to exist. Like the rest of my peers, I went straight from *Clifford the Big Red Dog* to *Cujo*. That's like swapping out aspirin for heroin, or going from holding hands to reverse cowgirl.

[I refuse to Google "reverse cowgirl," so I'm not one hundred percent clear on what it means. In my head, it involves spurs and a saddle.]

Generation X 'tweens didn't have *Harry Potter*; we had *Halloween*. We swam out of the kiddie pool and straight into the Marianas Trench. That's why it's not my fault that I'm afraid of the dark.

This is all on you, Jamie Lee Curtis.

Every scary movie was rated-R back then, so I wasn't old enough to see them in the theater. However, my father had the first video disc/VCR set-up in town, *[read: he was the first video pirate]* so we had an extensive horror collection.

Dad duped video discs from Friday night to Monday morning, every single week, building his library. We had *everything*. My folks would never allow me to buy a ticket for something psyche-scarring. But watching slasher flicks in the privacy of our own family room? If free, I take! Such was the impact these films had on me, I spent a good chunk of adolescence assuming that blonde hair + big boobs + shower = inevitable stabbing.

I took *a lot* of baths back then.

No matter how old I am now, I will never not freak out over the "ki ki ki, ha ha ha" score that used to play when *Friday the 13th's* Jason Voorhees would stalk his victims. To this day, I eschew both summer camps and hockey masks. And despite Ms. Curtis not being in this flick, I avoid Activia.

Because I can never be too sure.

Still, I knew the situations in these books and movies were fictional, so why do I let my home-alone fear impact me now? While I'm far from intrepid in the rest of my life, I'm comfortable with plenty of phobias that make others break out into terror-sweat. For example, I've been interviewed on national TV without issue. In fact, I held my own with Charlie Rose who was deeply dismayed to hear that my book *The Best of Enemies* was not about the Nixon-Frost debates, like, *at all*.

I hate being afraid of what might be lurking in the dark outside my front door, which is why I sleep so badly when Fletch travels. I did finally drift off this time, but it took a glass of wine, a Benadryl, then a Xanax, and, eventually, an Ambien.

Fletch says my falling asleep isn't nearly as surprising as my waking up.

I want to learn to deal with this fear.

My only comfort is knowing that a potential murderer's calls will never come from inside the house... because the phone line's still not fixed.

———

"WHY ARE YOU HERE?"

I've been listening to everyone else's answers as we've gone around the room, explaining our rationale for joining Lake Forest's Citizens Police Academy. Fletch has been on me about doing this with him for years and I finally ran out of excuses as to why I couldn't.

He made the point that knowledge is power. He said the more I learn about what I have/don't have to be afraid of when I'm by myself, the better I'll feel. I couldn't argue that logic, so that's why I'm spending the next ten weeks in cop school.

Our class includes twelve other citizens. Their reasons for participation vary. Some are involved in community government and they want to inform themselves about the law enforcement arm. Another woman lives alone and would like to learn to shoot. There's a husband and wife couple who have friends who'd taken the course and heard it was fascinating. One older gentleman has an adult son who had two cars stolen from his driveway here in town. He's interested in what he might do to prevent future crimes.

Officer Instructor [pseudonym] is very kind when he

talks about having been on that case. The son had left both cars unlocked, with the keys in plain sight. The cars–both newer model luxury cars–were stolen, but quickly abandoned when the car thieves found two brand new Mercedes unlocked, with the keys inside, a few blocks away. The sons' vehicles (also Mercedes) were a few years old, and, thus, less desirable.

Apparently, this happens here all the time.

Who *are* these people?

No, not the criminals, I'm talking about the people who go so blithely through life that they're completely oblivious to any bad thing that could ever happen.

I want to be one of them.

Sign me up, please. I'm tired of hiding under the covers when I'm alone at night, terrified of every creak and gust of wind. Their way of life sounds a lot happier.

Officer Instructor smiles at me, waiting for my answer.

I consider making up something that sounds cool, but ultimately, I tell him the truth. I figure he's a cop, he'll know if I'm lying.

I simply shrug and say, "I'm here because I'm nosy."

———

EVERY WEDNESDAY NIGHT AFTER CLASS, I apologize to Fletch, telling him how sorry I am that we didn't do this sooner. Over the thirty-plus hours of coursework, we're learning every aspect of how the local PD operates. Each unit is more interesting than whatever we learned about the previous week, from hiring procedures to evidence gathering to undercover drug investigations.

Fletch is right, the more I know, the more I'm able to relax in my own house. We're doing things right. We're observant. We're careful. We have an alarm and we set it. (So many people fail to take this crucial step, we learn.) We have big, loud dogs, which are the greatest deterrent of all. And if we were to ever happen to be fortunate enough to own two brand new Mercedes, we would definitely not leave them in the driveway with the windows open and the keys inside.

These seem like simple steps, don't they? Like the common sense you'd learn in grade school.

There's one woman in the class who's a pathological hand-raiser. She first came to my attention when she lectured the officers about how it's their duty to tell people to lock their houses, because she does not think these are simple steps or common sense.

This lady's always chiming in on something. Fletch and I had to start sitting in the front row so my inadvertent eye rolls wouldn't be so obvious. At first, she wasn't so bad, but as the weeks have progressed, she's gotten more and more obnoxious. She keeps arguing with the officers about the laws, saying, "No, no, you have it wrong, the law isn't X, it's Y." And then the officers, who are all so polite, will disagree, saying, "No, that's incorrect. In fact, when we were in court last week..." and then they'll go on to explain how the law as they know/have been applying it, secured a conviction.

And *she'll still disagree*.

By the way?

She's not an attorney; she's a Girl Scout leader.

Before the CPA started, I'd suspected that nothing ever happened in Lake Forest. This town was recently recognized as the safest in the state for this exact reason. And that's why my home-alone-in-the-woods fear feels so irrational.

However, while major crimes are infrequent, I've learned they do happen here. The town's bisected by the artery that connects Chicago and Milwaukee, so all the drug traffic going from point A to point B passes by us. There are some deeply gang-infested areas due north, too, so we are less Mayberry than I anticipated. But this isn't a fear that has to keep me up at night.

While Lake Forest did have a homicide seventeen years ago, it was a domestic disturbance. Before that, the last gun discharge happened in 1981. Given the law of averages, I will likely be okay here the six or seven nights a year when Fletch is out of town. So, he was right. Knowledge does make me feel better.

My assessment is that the scariest thing in this town is to be the parent of a teenager. Because I'm writing Young Adult books now, I'm familiar with some of the problems, like rampant opioid abuse. We also have abnormally high instances of teen suicide. My novel *The Gatekeepers* is a fictionalization of a suicide cluster that happened up here in 2012. I wrote this book because I learned that local kids are under so much pressure to perform that they're cracking.

Which puts my scary-noise-in-the-woods fears into perspective.

On top of that, thanks to technology, teens have almost unlimited access to drugs and everything can be consumed in vape form now. Plus, vapes can be made to look like a thumbnail drive; this item could literally sit on a kid's desk and parents would be none the wiser. There's a big trend on YouTube called "ghosting" where teens film themselves consuming illegal substances via vape pen in class. Like, high school class, not college. I can't imagine having balls like that as a high schooler. One day in 1983, I wore a shirt where the sleeves were so capped it almost looked sleeveless. I spent the day on the verge of puking because I thought I was going to get expelled for breaking dress code.

Complicating matters further, teens are becoming accidental pornographers. If your kid participates in sexting, that's considered child pornography under the law. If your daughter sends someone provocative pictures, she's considered a pornographer. If your son forwards them, then he's pornographer. Depending on the circumstances, the judges, the quality of legal defense, etc. these kids could end up on a sex registry database. I'm guessing that would hurt their chances of getting into Cornell.

For one stupid, impulsive decision.

The police tell us that parents think they're on top of this stuff, even the most diligent. Unfortunately, their kids are technologically one step ahead, by doing stuff like hiding the evidence in photo vaults disguised as innocuous apps like calculators.

[The great irony here is, in some small way, my Sunday school teacher might have been on to something.]

This is the kind of stuff that scares me now. I can see how foolish I've been with my indefinable flights of fancy, how much energy I've wasted on nonsense.

The officers say the best thing anyone can do for his or her teen is to buy them a flip phone.

Maybe it's not so bad to be an analog girl in a digital world.

———

FLETCH'S LAST WORD:

It's 2017, a serial killer would never actually place a voice call to a landline to find out if you're home alone. They might text, or just check your social media to see where you checked in, but ain't nobody got time to talk to your about-to-be-hacked-into-tiny-pieces ass on the phone.

FIFTEEN

Ride Along

"*COMMUNICATION IS SO MUCH BETTER when people are vulnerable.*"

- A. J. McLean

"THAT'S WHAT YOU'RE WEARING?"

Glancing down at myself, I reply, "What's wrong with my outfit?"

Fletch cuts me this exact same variety of side-eye every time I eat something off the kitchen floor *[listen, it's called the "five second rule" for a reason]* or whenever I scrape the fender on the side of the garage.

He tells me, "Number one, with your black and white stripes and red sneakers, you look like The Hamburglar, and number two, there's a chicken on your shirt."

"And?"

"*And?*" he says. "There is no *and*. You're about to go on

your first police ride-along in a *chicken shirt*. Don't you think you're getting a little bit *Jen Lancaster Show!* here?"

Fletch says sometimes when I'm in a situation where I feel uncomfortable, I lapse into doing bits, turning on the charm extra-high. I become a caricature of myself. He says this is why I can't see; I'm too busy performing for the optometrist to accurately read the eye chart.

[He may or may not be right, yet I will never admit this.]

I tick my counterpoints off on my fingertips. "Number one, this is my favorite shirt, number two, I'm pretty sure it's a rooster, and number three, how mad will people be when they see me in the front seat? Criminals will be all, *'Got a DUI from Officer Rooster Shirt.'* Boom! Don't drink and drive, son."

He exhales heavily. "I literally cannot argue with that logic."

"Right?"

Besides, my outfit's cute and comfy, which is key if I'm going to be cooped up in a squad car for the next six to eight hours. He's only giving me crap because he's jealous I'm doing my ride-along first. He even offered to switch days with me because I have the opera tomorrow night. He kept saying, "I don't want you to be too tired."

Right.

Like the rest of our Citizens Police Academy group, Fletch needed to check his calendar before selecting a slot, so I grabbed the first open night on the sign-up sheet. My friend took the class last year and her ride-along sounded so fun that I was dying to do mine. She live-tweeted every dispatch call. Her night was filled with teens playing mailbox baseball and drunk college students. Nothing dangerous happened on her shift, so I wasn't at all worried about mine.

Until now.

Last week, Officer Young Tom Cruise [pseudonym, obvi] showed a terrifying YouTube video comprised entirely of dashboard camera footage. I watched in horror as one cop after another was shot or struck during routine traffic stops.

Now, do the officers here handle plenty of calls from homeowners asking them to remove stray waterfowl from their basements? Yes. [Totally true, BTW.] But what Officer Cruise stressed is that his job isn't all life and duck; sometimes it's life and death. Real shit goes down here. Stands to reason real shit could go down while I'm riding along tonight.

That's why I decided to have McDonalds for dinner. I don't want my last meal to be a freaking kale salad.

I want my ride-along officer to be charmed by my wit and good humor (and to doubly ensure my safety) so I stop at Dunkin's to pick up treats before reporting for my shift. FYI, the cool kids on the force don't call them donuts. Instead, they're "power rings."

I'm paired with Officer This Evening's Driver [pseudonym, clearly] and I try not to look surprised that he's so youthful. While I'm generally okay with my own age, I struggle to accept that professional/important/successful people are now noticeably younger than me. A few years ago, during minor surgery, I had to keep my smart mouth shut, lest I inquire if the anesthesiologist's mommy knew she was out by herself. Following the rule of *Never Insult the Person Who Literally Holds Your Stupid Life in His/Her Hands*, I refrain from calling him Officer Baby Face aloud.

Also? He's *thirty*. When did I get so old? I haven't even finished paying off my student loans!

Anyway, Officer Driver gives me a tour of the squad

car, a Ford Explorer. Even though we're mid-shift, he shows me the standard vehicle check everyone does before beginning patrol. He demonstrates the lights and sirens and walks me through the myriad of useful items he keeps in the back of the car, from tourniquets to what's called a "less-lethal" shotgun, as it fires beanbags.

Beanbags!

Frankly, the notion of a beanbag gun is adorable. I envision giant, colorful chairs inflating the moment they leave the barrel, then flying through the ether, knocking their targets down onto a nice, squashy surface.

I… may or may not express this thought out loud.

Officer Driver assures me that being hit with a beanbag round is far less festive than it sounds and I am already concerned he's not charmed by my wit or good humor. *[Is it the rooster shirt?]*

There's a Toughbook attached to the dashboard and that's the car's nerve center. The computer is incredibly sophisticated, linking to every system and database law enforcement could need. For example, if Driver types in a name or birthdate, each incident and attribute associated with that name/date/plate (including physical descriptions, i.e. gang tattoos) populates. So, if he pulls someone over for, say, speeding, he can see if they're a Vice Lord or habitual scofflaw or total first-timer.

The LFPD maintains no "quota," so officers aren't obligated to issue tickets. Most offenses garner a warning instead. Driver tells me the golden rule of traffic stops is that everyone is treated the same and measured by the same standards, period. He's adamant about this and it's a sentiment expressed in class again and again.

Driver explains that the fines are expensive and he doesn't want to burden someone if his or her speed isn't egregious. He says a lot of times, especially at night, people are passing through town quickly to get to their second jobs, or their third, and why make their day more stressful if he doesn't have to?

[I might not be charming him, but, guess what? He's charmed me.]

The system includes a separate chat feature so that everyone on shift can communicate without their conversations being broadcast over the radio. Because anyone with a scanner app could listen in–including criminals–this feature seems not just convenient, but potentially life-saving.

The car is equipped with cameras and microphones to capture everything that goes down during stops or whenever there's a suspect in the vehicle. During the last class, Officer Cruise also showed us a dashboard video of a takedown on US 41. The driver was an escaped felon and his family members had warned area law enforcement that the man was armed, dangerous, and planning to go out shooting. He'd bragged about taking cops down with him.

Yikes.

On the video, we witnessed Cruise yelling to the other officers to cut their sirens before he approaches the vehicle. He explained that he wanted the audio to clearly capture every warning he issued to the escaped felon, who he then apprehended without incident or injury.

"Does all this surveillance bother you?" I ask Driver. "Kind of Big Brother, right?"

He doesn't hesitate to answer. "Absolutely not. The cameras are for our protection; they keep everyone honest."

Huh.

Earlier, I'd joked to Fletch that I'd hoped to be given a

Taser. No dice, but it's for the best as I suspect I'd be all, *"Hey, what does this button do? Zzzt, zzzt, zzzt!"* I don't get a vest that says WRITER on it like Nathan Fillion wears on *Castle*, either. The plus side is that the bulletproof plates would have covered up my rooster.

As I settle into my seat, I realize the bar that's been pressing into my left arm isn't a bar at all. What I'm leaning on is an AR-15 assault rifle. The gun is locked securely in place. I can't decide if this makes me more or less anxious. Then Driver shows me how to use the radio in case something big goes down and he's in a pinch or my life is in danger.

Definitely more anxious, then.

We exit the Public Safety Building parking lot and head over to the northeast corner of the city, which includes the lakefront and the college, but is mainly residential. *[This is the super-fancy part of town, where I do not live.]*

Patrolling this beat is up-close-and-personal real estate porn. I forget that I'm not on a house tour when we pass the majestic 20,000-square foot Schweppe estate and then the Armour mansion *[as in Armour hot dogs, the dogs kids love to bite]*, both practically palaces. We see director John Hughes' former home and Bears quarterback Jay Cutler's place. Lake Forest was founded as a summer residence for Chicago tycoons, once housing business icons like the McCormicks and the Swifts. We cruise by architectural gems designed by Frank Lloyd Wright, Howard Van Doren Shaw, and David Adler. Stunning.

Driver explains that officers in other beats will assist if we require backup, and vice-versa, but this is where we patrol when no one needs us. Outstanding, because there are a few more chateaux I'd like to see on Mayflower Road.

As it's Friday night of Spring Break, the streets are particularly quiet. The parents with school-aged kids are on vacations and the snowbirds have not yet returned to town.

I say, "I was so surprised to hear that there are never more than four patrol cars on the road at any time."

"How many did you think there'd be?"

"I don't know; just... significantly more? Are there ever instances you're all tied up at the same time?"

He tells me, "Once in a great while, if something major happens. Like last week, everyone was directing traffic at the logging truck roll-over on 41."

I ask, "What happens if there's another crime while you're all busy?"

"Well, dispatch prioritizes each call. If needed, we get backup from units in Highland Park or North Chicago or Lake Bluff."

"If I were a criminal, I'd stage a diversion so everyone was occupied and then I'd cruise in and commit my heist or whatever. You know these places have amazing shit inside, like, Picassos and stuff. I'd do it during shift-change, too, when coverage is extra sparse."

Driver gives me Fletch-style side eye. Not charmed. Not digging the *Jen Lancaster Show!*

"I'm not a criminal," I add, trying to win him back. "That's just what I'd do if I were."

We drive around quietly for a while, windows open so we can hear what's happening outside. His eyes are peeled for anything unusual while I gawp at porticos and turrets and gabled roofs, quietly applauding everyone for their outdoor lighting game. The only downside is I'm freezing; I should have opted for a sweater instead.

Circuit complete, we head west, passing the Jewel

grocery store, where an old car idles in a parking space next to the train tracks. Driver mentions this is a trouble zone; they get a lot of calls about shoplifters at the store.

"People swipe roasts and stuff?" I ask. Given the price of beef lately, I can't blame them. With all the grass-fed, pasture-raised, organic meats I've bought for Whole30, my non-existent kids couldn't go to college now if they wanted to.

"No, mostly they take razors, Rogaine, and baby formula."

"Why?"

"They're black market items. Thieves resell them to little bodegas or swap meets for ten cents on the dollar."

Huh.

Before I can comment further, Officer Driver spots a car he recognizes, which belongs to an alleged high school-aged dealer he's been dying to catch with weight on him. I say, "We have TWO Starbucks AND a high school dealer in this sleepy little burg? Why, Lake Forest, you have arrived!"

Why am I making him audience-participate in the *Jen Lancaster Show?* The man gets shot at for a living. No one should be subjected to this, but I can't seem to keep my stupid yap shut. Clearly, I know there are drugs in this town. One of the undercover officers told us that a few concerned parents here have stocked up on Narcan because it stops the effects of an opioid overdose, with the added benefit of keeping This Unpleasantness off the police blotter and out of the news.

I tell myself to dial it back. I don't have to perform, I just need to fucking *be*, okay?

Just *be*.

Driver confirms that I'm buckled up and then we haul

ass to catch up with the dude. We're off and we are going fast. So fast. We're going all-caps, italicized-so-the-slant-makes-it-looks-like-forward-motion *FAST*.

You know, I'm learning a lot about myself in this experience. For example, unlike (Old) Tom Cruise, I can confirm that I do not have the need, the need for speed. In fact, you could even say I'm *afraid* of speed. I look around for something to grip but the only purchase is the rifle, and that seems like yet another faux pas.

My mouth is dry and I'm having trouble drawing breath. I'm no longer chilly, the sweat's pouring off me in rivulets. I surreptitiously pray and stomp on my invisible passenger brake.

My desire to be *liked* supersedes my fear, so I'm just going to pretend to not be having four hundred consecutive heart-attacks right now and I shan't call any additional attention to myself. I feel that shrieking in terror would extinguish what few embers of charm I might still emanate.

Once we catch up to the driver, we slow down and proceed to tail him. We all observe the speed limit. The kid's lights are functional and his plates are current, so we have no reason to pull him over. "Wait, I think the suspect just crossed over the center line," I say, in my most-helpful-Officer-Lancaster voice. "Is that considered probable cause?"

"Technically, yeah, but an attorney would get that stop thrown out in a minute," Driver replies.

We have a whole conversation about "good arrests" versus "bad arrests." In instances like this, the point is less to apprehend ASAP and more to establish a rock-solid case when putting a suspect in custody. Driver wants a bust that sticks; he's not a fan of the kid as he's allegedly selling the hard stuff to his classmates, not just dime bags of weed. In fact, marijuana is so close to becoming legal in this state, possession's a wrist-slap, whereas fentanyl or cocaine is a class-A felony.

I drop a few more points on the ol' charm-ometer when I exclaim, "Blow's in style again? The '80s are back, baby!"

Stuff a sock in it, self. God.

Anyway, if Driver were to make an arrest, the goal isn't to ruin the kid's life. Instead, the hope is to give him a deal so they can go up the chain to figure out suppliers. There's always a bigger fish. Officers are anxious to halt the flow of drugs into our town, as they're ruining the lives of some of our best and brightest.

The State of Illinois has what's called a "Way Out" program for addicts. If you're apprehended and you offer up the drugs before they're found (or if you just come into a police station) and ask for a "way out," you won't face criminal prosecution for possession. Instead, you'll be whisked to the hospital for detox and then into treatment. Even if you can't pay for the rehab, you won't be turned away.

Well done, Illinois. Well done.

The kid heads home so we drive away. I feel like Batman as I glower at his vehicle and whisper to myself, "Soon." We then drive down to check out the park on the lakefront. I point out the cars with steamy windows here and there and I ask if we're going on a raid.

"No," he tells me. "The park's still open until eleven o'clock. They're allowed to be here. Occasionally, we'll check to make sure everyone in the car's consenting, but otherwise, we leave them alone. Again, we're not here to ruin anyone's night."

This is so weird to me. Between the media's narrative

and what I experienced growing up, it's odd to witness the "service" aspect of police work. Even though I never did anything wrong in high school [read: was a total fucking nerd], I was afraid of cops. They perpetually harassed kids when I was growing up in Huntington, *delighting* in ruining people's nights. The police were even worse in West Lafayette during college. They were always arresting students for walking home drunk from the bars. Walking! What were we supposed to do instead?

Teleport?

Drink responsibly?

I was even wary of law enforcement in Chicago. We used to live on a block where the police would never respond to 911 calls, not for acts of prostitution or knife fights or attempted burglaries, even though there would be a dozen officers shopping at the Target a block away all damn day long. After we moved, we'd heard rumors that a crime family controlled our street and that the police were on their payroll, which is why they never came.

I have no idea if this was ever true, but I hope it isn't.

Anyway, in class, we've been discussing how law enforcement has changed. Being a *warrior for* the citizens used to be the trend, but now it's shifted to *guardians of*. The LAPD under Daryl Gates is a good (and by good, I mean *horrible*) example of *warrior for*. The police were paramilitary and they routinely violated civil rights (i.e. stop-and-frisk) in the name of being *warriors for* the community.

I feel like N.W.A. was not wrong, you know?

I have the impression that *warriors for* allows personal prejudices to cloud or influence judgment, which is why we still see terrible injustices and that's a goddamned travesty. There are far too many social media hashtags out there related to questionable moves by the *warriors for*.

The warrior mindset is the antithesis of being a guardian, which is all about establishing cooperation and trust with citizens. Being a warrior means officers look at everyone as a potential enemy combatant when so often, that's not the case. We discussed a quote by Lt. Chad Goeden of the Alaska Training Academy who asked, "If we're 'warriors,' who are we at war with?"

I'm a big fan of the *guardians for* mindset, which is more about protecting and less about dominating. The police force is considered a part of the community; they're not like an adversary or a mean friend, waiting to pounce the moment someone screws up, *ahem*, West Lafayette PD, circa 1991. I see a guardian in action as Officer Driver rolls down his window to talk to a group of kids heading our way. They look to be late teens, having crawled directly out of a Vineyard Vines catalog. Two guys are walking and there's a girl riding one of them piggyback.

Piggyback!

Piggyback is the universal girl-sign for "I just drank five Lime-a-Ritas and I weigh nooooothing!"

[Trust me, I know this.]

I assumed they'd scatter as soon as they saw the car, but instead they approach us. Wait, *what?* They're approaching *us?*

"Hey!" says the one with the *[tipsy?]* girl on his back. "Is Officer Wiseass in there?"

Hold up, these kids know the officers? And they're *excited* to see them? What kind of Bizzaro world is this? How is their first instinct all, "Yay, police!"

Is Eazy-E rolling over in his grave right now?

We chat with them and the kids introduce themselves, each one with a name preppier than the one before, I'm talking the full Lovey and Thurston Howell here. No one shows signs of having been drinking (save for being piggyback, which again, not probable cause) and no one has booze fumes wafting off them. We chat a few minutes more before we part.

I'm struck by the level of respect and professionalism Driver displays with each kid. Of course, the cynical part of me–the portion that knows only the warrior trope–wonders if they'd have been treated differently had their names not all been some variation of Shackleford Hampton, IV.

[This is also a pseudonym, and it's still not as preppy as the kid's real name. What's funny is when I tell this story to my new girlfriends from cop class, they're both like, "Wait, which Shackleford did you meet?" Because Shacklefords exist. I just... wow.]

As we head back up the bluff, Driver points out the big rocks, saying that we have a huge wild mink population at the beach. He knows this because he was bitten trying to move one he thought had died. Surprise! Not dead. While the mink was very much alive when he happened upon it, Animal Control did have to put it down to test for rabies

"Did you get to skin it and keep its pelt?" I ask.

"No."

"They wouldn't let you?"

Side-eye. "I didn't ask. Why would I want a dead mink?"

"Because he bit you! You could make a garment out of it, all, *'Huzzah, I am wearing the hide of my enemy!'*"

Welcome back to the *Jen Lancaster Show!*

He blinks a couple of times and then says, "Yeah, let's head west."

We cruise by Jewel again. The rusty old car is still idling in the parking lot. We thought maybe someone was being picked up at work when we'd previously passed, so we made a mental note and drove on. At this point, the car's been running for at least an hour and the store's closed; the situation is officially suspicious.

We run the plates and get back some questionable information. Latin King tats have been documented in relation to this particular license plate, which gives *me* license to panic. I mean, I have a (half-removed) sorority tattoo which I'd have never gotten if I weren't initiated. A tattoo isn't like just buying a jersey of a team you like; it's a commitment, a pledge of loyalty, a permanent mark of membership.

I wait in the car as Driver exits. He leaves the window down so that I can listen. As he approaches the vehicle, every single damn gunshot video plays again in my head. Is he in danger? Is some shit about to *go down*? Do I need to grab the radio? Adrenaline courses through my veins. Despite being a good five miles from home, I'm sure I could run all the way there. I unbuckle my safety belt in case I've gotta fly.

I watch as he taps on the passenger window with his flashlight and a face appears. In my head, I'm screaming, "Save yourseeeeelllllllllf," as I imagine myself bolting away from the scene. I grasp the door's handle, ready to throw it open at any second and disappear like a vapor trail.

Driver is both alert and nonchalant as he speaks with the Hispanic man inside the vehicle.

What's your 20, officer?! (Also, what does, "What's your 20?" mean?)

The passenger exits the car with something in his hand. *Look out, it's a weapon, we're all gonna dieeeeeee!* No, wait. It's a bottle. The passenger dumps the contents in the bushes and then takes back his driver's license. Then he *shakes hands with Officer Driver* and begins to walk away.

What in the actual fuck?

Upon return, Driver explains that the guy was passed out in the running car, waiting for his friend. The passenger did have an open container of alcohol (which was dumped) and technically, this could be considered drunk driving, although he'd never be convicted. The guy's a caretaker on one of the estates we've seen tonight, so Driver has him walk home, having declined a ride from us.

"The fresh air will wake him up," Driver declares.

Now I feel like a massive jerk for worrying that the non-Shacklefords in town might be treated differently. Certainly, I can't speak for every town and every officer, given the incidents we see reported every day. But right now? There's only one asshole near this car and she's wearing a rooster shirt.

"Were you scared when you approached that guy?" I ask.

"Nope, just business as usual," he says as he documents the incident for his shift report.

"You weren't afraid *at all?*"

I'm glad he wasn't scared because I was frightened enough for the both of us. I have to wonder, though-how did he not quake in his boots, even a little? Has he not seen Officer Cruise's videos?

"I don't have the luxury of being afraid," he replies. "Even if I were, I couldn't show it. I've gotta be confident. There's no other option. The bad guys out there can smell panic on you. You learn pretty fast to get past the fear and do your job or you'll never make it."

"Help me understand," I implore. "*How* do you get past the fear? How is your first response not to run or freeze? Granted, you're more likely to get bitten by a weasel up here than to be shot by one, but still. Where do you find the confidence? Are you born with it?"

He explains, "I'm confident because I'm prepared. Preparation is a conscious, ongoing choice. For example, I've taken classes on how to maneuver vehicles at high speeds and under stress. I work out hard to be in my best shape if a situation turns physical. I study body language so I can anticipate actions and react accordingly. I practice on the range in case I ever need to discharge my weapon. I learn the ins and outs of the law to make sure I'm respecting everyone's rights while building a solid case for arrest. And our commanders are always running us through training drills so that nothing ever catches us off-guard."

"The key is to eliminate any element of surprise?"

"Right, even though it's impossible to envision every scenario. Fear stems from the worrying about the unknown. We do our best to eliminate the unknown."

Makes sense to me, more and more, every day.

Driver's shift is over and he brings me back to the station. I have a couple of minutes before I leave on the midnight shift. As much as I enjoyed being in the car, I know I didn't make a good impression. That bothers me. I wasn't trying to be obnoxious, even though that was the result.

Fletch is right, I can go too *Jen Lancaster Show!* in situations like this. Humor's my side-arm, it's the go-to weapon in my arsenal. If being sarcastic or quick is the only hammer I have, then ostensibly, everything looks like a nail. And, while wit can be effective, it's not everything. I perpetually joke about or mock that which makes me anxious or uncomfortable, which can be off-putting. I often sound glib and insensitive when, really, I'm just trying to desensitize myself.

If I'd just said to Driver, "This experience is scary for me," maybe we'd have gotten off on better footing. I suspect that's why I opted for this ridiculous rooster top tonight; wearing an irreverent shirt is the only modicum of power I felt I'd have in this situation, my only agency over the great and frightening unknown. To extrapolate this point, it's like my sassy mouth is the virtual rooster shirt I wear every day of my whole damn life.

I meet Officer Short Time [pseudonym] for my midnight shift. He has less than a year to go before retirement. I decide to approach our encounter entirely differently.

I'm going to be real, for better or worse, and not try to charm or entertain him. I'm just going to make a genuine connection.

———

I'M BACK in class a week later, having missed a session because of meetings in New York. When Officer Trainer asks me about my ride-along, I offer effusive praise for the experience. I don't mention that I made an ass out of myself with Driver, nor do I explain my plan to dedicate my YA novel to Officer Time. He and I spoke nonstop for hours and over the course of our conversation, I learned how he'd been on the scene for six different train suicides.

I can't even imagine.

I don't know how he got up and did his job the next day, but he did and he has, for almost thirty-five years. In my book [literally,] that merits recognition.

During a break, my classmate Kathy tells me she rode with Officer Driver a couple of days ago. I like Kathy. She comes across as calm and rational and the questions she asks our instructors are always meaningful and thought-provoking.

[The last time I raised my hand, I was curious about where everyone pees and buys coffee on the midnight shift, as the gas stations in town close by 10:00 p.m. After that, I kept quiet.]

Kathy asks me, "Were you nervous when the officer showed you how to unlock the rifle? I was worried about the idea of providing cover, no matter how unlikely the scenario. Then I figured, if he needed me, I'd find a way to be brave."

Fletch spins around in his seat, his gaze flinty, accusatory. "You didn't tell me about the rifle." He thinks I've been holding out on him, keeping the most key detail to myself. He'd waited up for me the night of my ride-along, so excited to hear every detail. He was like my giddy sorority sister, dying to dish about my date with the big man on campus.

"That's because he didn't show me how to unlock it," I say. "Wasn't an option. No gun, no Taser, not even any pepper spray. He said, *'This is how you work the radio if we're in trouble.'* That was it."

"So he was all, *'Here's a whistle. Maybe you could blow on it if a war breaks out,'*" Fletch says, slightly altering a misogynistic line someone once said to Lisa on an old episode of *The Simpsons*.

"Exactly," I reply. "I suspect throwing a box of donuts at him and demanding he find me charming five seconds after meeting him might have tipped him off to my level of competence."

Fletch nods. "I could see how he'd draw that conclusion."

He and Kathy then launch into a conversation about

the pros and cons of the tactical assault rifle while I stew in my seat, finally realizing the extent of the bad impression I surely left.

Stupid fucking rooster shirt.

———

I DO a second ride along with Office Driver, this time with the *Jen Lancaster Show!* on hiatus. I'm not in costume and I don't thrust a box of carbs at him. I'm just me, dialed down and this is key. He seems a lot less guarded around me now because I think my energy before made him nervous. He even shows me how to unlock the rifle.

Progress.

As we patrol, he tells me the very best defense is a nosy neighbor.

[Ha! I knew it!]

Our night is very quiet. Because of this class, I've become a lot less fearful of what's out here in the dark, so much so that I fell asleep before Fletch even called to check in last time he was out of town.

I'm far more familiar with what dangers might lurk in the night. Mostly, it's raccoons, a few foxes, and drunk drivers coming back from the bars in Highland Park. The officers can't do anything about my *Stranger Things*-based concerns, but I'm not nearly as freaked out about random crime anymore.

While it never hurts to be alert, there's such a thing as being paranoid for no good reason. We have other dangers here in Lake Forest, and if I can prevent any of them from harming teens through my YA work, then I feel like I'm doing a good thing.

Driver's shift is almost over. We're about to get gas out

at the Municipal building and he'll take me back to the station for the midnight shift. Then we get a dispatch about two drunk fourteen year females causing a disturbance in a limousine.

Again. Two drunk juveniles. Limousine. Disturbance.

I do not say, "Is it my birthday?" out loud. That does not mean I don't think it.

I am still me, after all.

Driver slides on a pair of protective gloves as he makes his way to the scene. "Drunk juveniles are bad. Drunk juvenile females are the worst."

When we pull up, we see vomit all over the side of the car, having come from the window of the back seat. The chauffeur is outside, pacing, pissed. Driver tells me he'll leave his window open so I can hear what's happening. On the last ride along, I suspect he wouldn't have been so accommodating.

He and another officer assess the scene, talking to the chauffeur and each of the girls. There are two of them. One of them looks scared shitless and the other, I'm assuming she's the ringleader, is standing with her arms crossed, her expression somewhere between defiant and bored.

This kid is fourteen, shithoused, coming home from a party in a limo, getting the business from not one, but two sworn officers of the law, and she's self-possessed enough to be annoyed, all, *"Tick-tock, time is money, can we wrap this up already?"*

I'm guessing if someone doesn't step in, if someone doesn't aggressively parent her, like, yesterday, she's probably going to see some trouble in her life. I'm afraid for her future and for her family, yet at this moment, I think, "I will never in my life be as cool a customer as this girl is right here."

Parents are called and instructed to pick up their wayward offspring at the station, so we take one of the juveniles (not the badass) and the other officer takes the other. Once the kid's all belted in, Driver tells her, "I'm going to drive very slowly and carefully. The station is less than a mile from here. However, if at any point, you don't feel well, tell me to stop immediately and I will."

I want to ask this kid *everything* but I say nothing.

When we're less than thirty feet from the door, the girl begs us to stop. She bolts out and gets sick. We can see that the limo is already parked in front of the station and someone had barfed out of the window on the opposite side, too. Now it occurs to me it wasn't the juveniles having a fit in the limo, it was the guy driving. I can't fault him for being mad. Poor guy did not sign up for this.

The problem is, he doesn't speak their language [metaphorically] so he can't see past the spoiled rich kids trashing his car. I heard one of the moms on speakerphone when the police called her. She was furious, not that her fourteen-year-old-child had been caught drinking, but that she had to drive to the station. She didn't understand why the police couldn't just come to *her.* She was all, "So, I called a limo for nothing?" Maybe the driver doesn't have any experience living in a world like this, where convenience is more important than children.

As for the girls, they have no clue that carting them around could be this guy's second job, or third, and that their shenanigans are costing him a night's wages, that this run could have been the difference between him making rent this month or not.

No one wins in this scenario.

After the girl has finished, Officer Driver asks if she's

going to be okay and her response both warms and breaks my contemptuous black heart.

"I'm not sure officer, this is my first time consuming alcohol."

Because it would be in bad form to hug this young stranger, instead, I fish a still-sealed bottle of water out of my purse and hand it to her. I won't have anything to drink later, but I think she needs it more than I will.

With that, I leave them and go inside to meet my partner for the next shift. One of the guys on midnights is Officer Wiseass, who came to my house post-Whole30. He remembers me. Over the course of this class, I've met *every* cop who's been to my place because of my butterfingers.

At least we've finally changed the code.

———

FLETCH IS WAITING up for me again when I get home. I tell him all about my night, detailing every call. As it's almost 4:00 a.m., I'm about to drop.

"Wait, I almost forgot what I told everyone on the midnight shift," I say. "I walk into the squad room and it's all the youngest people on the force. Every single one of them is adorable. Half my age, and so darling. I told them, *'If the Police Foundation doesn't do a fundraising calendar with you guys, you are leaving money on the table.'*"

Fletch face-palms. "You didn't."

"Of course I did. They work out hard, they eat healthy, they take good care of themselves! Firemen do this kind of thing all the time. The calendar would sell so well."

I say this because I genuinely care about these officers now. The respect they give begets respect. I want the Police

Foundation to raise as much money as possible to keep these brave men and women safe. Personally, I'm going to be on tenterhooks between now and when Officer Short Time gets to retire down to Florida. He has so many plans between fishing and grandkids and learning to salsa dance with his wife! And if calendar sales provide one more bit of gear that will protect not just the officers, but everyone they encounter, then I think it's our obligation to help make this happen.

But I'm exhausted as it's about five hours past my bedtime, so I'm not properly articulating this thought.

I try to clarify. "Not just the men, the female officers, too. They hide their light behind those dowdy uniforms! They want a chance to be pretty, too. Every one of them is attractive. I'd swipe right on any of them. Or left. Which is it?"

"I have no idea."

This is not coming out like I mean.

"Why are you giving me that face?" I ask. "People see these calendars, it might change their minds about law enforcement officers. Most people will never go through a CPA course, they don't know what we know. This was a game-changer for us. But a calendar is visual. Maybe someone who is anti-law enforcement, which may or may not be fair in this day and age, will see this attractive officer posing shirtless with a baby goat on a hay bale. And in their heads, they're suddenly experiencing everything from an entirely new perspective. A calendar would promote understanding! Folks could be like, *'My philosophy has always been, 'Fuck tha Police,' yet I never considered the alternative before. Perhaps I shall reevaluate and I could fuck the police in an-'* Wait, why are you leaving? I wasn't done telling you about the night!"

He shakes his head. "I'm going to bed. You just made it weird."

Yeah.

I do that a lot.

FLETCH'S LAST WORD:

Both officers showed me how to unlock the rifle on my ride along. We even discussed tactics for its employment if a traffic stop went sideways.

"Roll out the passenger side, leave the door open, work your way to the back of the car. Stay low, and provide cover fire if needed." 10-4!

I'm proud of Jen for stepping out of her comfort zone, but I don't have anything to add to this story. However, I do have a story about losing and recovering my latest iPhone.

People who freak out when they lose a phone because their "entire life is on that phone" are doing it wrong. Storing your precious photos, videos, contacts, and credit cards on your phone is a bad idea in the modern era of cloud storage. Keep your shit in the cloud, and your phone becomes an expendable device that can be wiped clean remotely, effectively becoming a paperweight for whoever finds it.

Last week I took the commuter train to our office in downtown Chicago, which is directly across the street from the train station. I crossed the street, rode the elevator up twenty-four floors, sat down at my desk, and realized I didn't have my phone. I immediately checked Find My iPhone, and it was still sitting on the train in the station.

I stood up from my desk, rode the elevator down twenty-four floors, crossed the street, descended into the train station, and began spewing a stream of obscenities that hung thick as the diesel fumes permeating the depot when I saw the train was gone.

I crossed the street, rode the elevator... you know the rest. I went back to Find my iPhone, and watched my phone make the journey to Fox Lake, which is damn near Wisconsin. I don't know if people there would recognize an iPhone, or if they would throw it up to the sky like the Coke bottle in The Gods Must Be Crazy. I remotely switched the phone to Lost Mode, which prevents any attempts to unlock the phone and allows the owner set an "if found please contact owner@email.com" message on the home screen.

I was shocked when I immediately received an email from a Good Samaritan stating, "I found your phone on the train and gave it to a conductor." Hot damn, my faith in humanity is restored! All I have to do is wait for the train to make the round trip from the Land of Packers Fans, Monster Trucks, New Glarus Spotted Cow Farmhouse Ale, and Cheese, meet the train at Union Station when it arrives at 11:23 a.m., find the conductor, and get on with my day.

At 11:15, I stood up from my desk, rode the elevator down twenty-four floors, crossed the street, and descended into the train station again. I found the conductor and, assuming he was expecting me, greeted him with a wave.

"I left my phone on the train this morning, and a passenger gave it to a conductor," I said, thinking, "You know why I'm here, I'll be taking my phone now."

"Nobody turn nothing into me." And the Oscar for best use of double negative goes to... This Guy!

What? That's not possible! You have it, you must have it! Maybe you just forgot.

"Have you checked Lost and Found? It's next to the ticket windows."

Of course I checked Lost and Found! What kind of idiot wouldn't check... oh, actually I hadn't checked Lost and Found. Damn.

The walk from the boarding area to the ticket windows was only two to three miles. Uphill. I finally reached the bank of fifteen windows in about an hour, and two of them were actually open! After standing in line for another hour, I finally stepped up to the window and spoke to a person behind three inches of bomb-proof glass.

The ticket agent's mouth moved, and I could barely hear her voice through the weird intercom speaker thing embedded in the glass.

"May I help you?" She didn't mean it, I could just tell.

"I'm looking for Lost and Found."

The ticket agent may have rolled her eyes, I couldn't be sure through the up-armored window, but I saw her look over the wall towards the closed window to her left, and heard her yell, "Jerry, are you over there?"

I hadn't noticed the gold leaf LOST AND FOUND lettering over the art deco window frame. The window was obscured by mini-blinds that were tightly shut, so I never considered approaching it as an option. But, just like that, the blinds raised about six inches and a face appeared, sideways, peering under the mysterious curtain of bureaucratic solitude.

"Nobody gets in to see the Wizard, not nobody, not no how!"

That's what I heard anyway. Jerry actually asked what I was looking for, and after I gathered my thoughts I told him.

"Nobody turn nothing into me." *And the Oscar for best use of double negative goes to... wait a minute, is Metra Rail fucking with me? Or is this just standard procedure?*

I returned to my office empty-handed. When I checked Find My iPhone again it placed the phone in Elgin, which is damn near Iowa (for all practical purposes), and from here the story *gets complicated and would require a completely separate book to explain.*

Eventually my phone made its way back from The Land of College Wrestling Fans, Monster Trucks, Corn, and Presidential Primary Caucuses, and I finally caught up with it eight hours later and less than two miles from my home. It's like it never really went anywhere.

And that's why you always get insurance on your phone and store your shit in the cloud.

———

WAIT!

Did you think he was going to get the last word? Seriously? Bless your hearts.

The bad news is, the memoir part of the book is over. Fletch and I (and the rest of the gang) must live some more life before we have anything new to document. However, in the next section, there's a whole big chunk of something special I think you're going to dig.

Maybe it's not so much a story I'd *tell* in a bar, but rather, one you'd watch someday. Again, thanks for supporting me in this endeavor. This is the first time in a while that writing a memoir's been fun again. Now, I hope you like this extra-special, special-extra, bonus for sticking around after the credits Ferris Bueller ending!

Bonus

HOUSEMOMS PILOT

Here's a look at the kind of material I've been creating when I haven't been writing books. *Housemoms* is a dramedy pilot. If you're unfamiliar with the term, other dramedy examples include *Desperate Housewives*, *Devious Maids*, *GCB*, *Mistresses*, and *Ugly Betty*.

The background here is that I've been working with a team of agents who pitch my books in the film/TV world. They suggested I also put together an original script to demonstrate I understand the mechanics of writing a television show. That's how *Housemoms* came to be.

While not actively in play now, at least for the fall season, this pilot opened a lot of doors for me in Hollywood, putting me in front of those I never thought I'd meet. *[Trust me, it was badass. Then I went home and had to clean litter boxes, so, as always, perspective.]*

After I reread the script, I realized how much affection I have for these characters, how much more I want to say about their pasts and futures. If you read this and you love them, too, let me know. I'm considering giving these women the narrative arc they deserve in their own novel.

So, now... it's showtime!

TEASER

INT. THE OMEGA LOUNGE BASEMENT - EVENING

We see what looks like a sorority house TV room. An Omega symbol is painted on pastel pink cinderblock walls. A few cardio machines sit to the side. The floor's littered with diet soda cans and hair ties. EIGHT PRETTY COLLEGE-AGE GIRLS, 20's, hang out in baggy sweats and lots of makeup. They text, read celeb magazines, or watch TV.

SOFIA (Off Screen): We take care of the girls.

SOFIA JIMENEZ, 24, enters. She's a petite, serious Latina in a white Omega shirt and simple gold crucifix necklace. Older than her years, she's a classic beauty, even without cosmetics. She walks briskly, holding a clipboard and a giant coffee cup while an anxious TRAINEE tries to keep up.

SOFIA (CONT'D): Omega hired us to maintain order, but our job really is to help. Housemoms are more like therapists or nurses or maids. (laughs) Sometimes? We're even plumbers.

TRAINEE: Do I need to know about pipes?

SOFIA: Nah, plumbing's not a big issue.

CANDY, 21, one of the girls, snorts.

CANDY: Unless it's burrito night, Desiree.

DESIREE, 22, kicks Candy, who flips her off. No one acknowledges their squabble; they're all friends here.

SOFIA: That reminds me, let's talk dinner.

Sofia marches the trainee down the hall into...

INT. THE OMEGA LOUNGE KITCHENETTE - EVENING

Steam trays line the counters. There's a table stacked with dirty plates. Sofia sets down her cup, sweeping everything into a bus tub in one deft motion, then washes her hands.

SOFIA: We serve at 6:00 p.m. sharp. God help you if the food's late.

Sofia gives the trainee a detailed spreadsheet labeled Omega Meal Planning.

SOFIA (CONT'D): Nutritional needs, dietary preferences, allergies. Ariel claims she's gluten-free but those Oreos didn't inhale themselves.

Sofia uses her clipboard to gesture for the trainee to follow. They scurry back down the hall to...

INT. THE OMEGA LOUNGE BASEMENT - EVENING

TRAINEE: Why are you leaving the Omega?

SOFIA: I'm not. Gonna audition for that TV singing show so I'm taking voice lessons a few nights a week. You'll cover those shifts.

CANDY: Girl doesn't need lessons. Her version of *I Will Always Love You?*

Candy points to her fully contoured/highlighted face.

CANDY (CONT'D): Tears. For realsies.

Sofia appears uncomfortable with praise. She touches her crucifix, then glances at her watch.

SOFIA: Ladies? Showtime.

Sofia snaps her fingers. All of the girls except Desiree leap into action, whipping off their comfy attire. They reveal skimpy spangled G-strings and racy push-up bras. They swap their Tom's for platform shoes with clear heels.

We PULL BACK to see a row of lighted make-up tables and a sign that reads The Omega Lounge; Patterson's Premiere Gentlemen's Club.

SOFIA (CONT'D): Main stage in ten. Des, move it, no one's gonna get off stuffing a Jackson into your UGG boots. (considering) At least I hope not.

Desiree's eyes stay fixed on the television. ON THE TV SCREEN, we see a NEWSCASTER showing a photo of CHIP BARCLAY, late 40's, handsome, looks like he lives on a yacht. Chip is with an EFFORTLESSLY BLONDE SOCIETY WIFE, 45.

NEWSCASTER (O.S.): The investigation continues into the disappearance of financier Chip Barclay, who's been accused of --

DESIREE: This dude ripped off his own family and ran away, just like my Uncle Paulie. (a beat) Except he took millions and not my aunt's El Camino.

The trainee sits down to watch. Sofia curtly shakes her head and the trainee jumps back up.

SOFIA: Cool. So, he's bringing his millions here tonight? Then he'll buy enough private dances to cover your son's tuition at that school I told you about?

DESIREE (confused): Well, no, he's missing. Like, maybe even left the country.

Sofia herds Desiree to her dressing table.

SOFIA: Yet Mr. Guzman, your best customer, will be here tonight. He will want to see you sparkle.

Sofia hands Desiree a jar LABELED -- Ultra Gloss Rack Spackle, for the Discerning Dancer.

DESIREE: Guzman sucks. Dude's a drug lord.

Sofia holds up finger in caution.

SOFIA: Alleged drug lord. What's not alleged? Your kid's limitless future if he learns Mandarin.

Desiree rubs glitter cream on her enhanced cleavage.

DESIREE: I dunno, Sofia. That school is --

SOFIA: That school is amazing.

EXT. FANCY IVY-COVERED SCHOOL - DAY

TODDLERS wearing striped rep ties and blue blazers sit on the entry's steps. They READ -- War and Peace.

SOFIA (Voice Over): What I wouldn't give to have gone there.

INT. FANCY SCHOOL/CLASSROOM - DAY

Toddlers stand at whiteboard, solving quadratic equations.

SOFIA (V.O.): With a start like that, maybe I could have finished high school. I'd have other options. I'd be more... cultured.

INT. FANCY SCHOOL/CAFETERIA - DAY

Toddlers eat sushi with chopsticks.

INT. THE OMEGA LOUNGE BASEMENT - EVENING

SOFIA (wistful): I could have gone to college, studied voice. Met a decent guy. Everything would be different.

Sofia sighs and touches her crucifix.

SOFIA (CONT'D): Anyway, heading to my lesson, but I'll see you in a few hours. Ladies, werk.

She dashes down the hall, clipboard still in hand.

EXT. THE OMEGA LOUNGE PARKING LOT - NIGHT

Sofia crosses in front of a Bentley idling by her old beater, held together with duct tape. LUIS GUZMAN AND FRIEND, tough men with scars, hustle into the club. They ignore Sofia.

SOFIA: Hi, Mr. Guzman and friend. (a beat) Bye, Mr. Guzman and friend.

She notices she's still carrying her clipboard. She rolls her eyes and returns to the club.

INT. THE OMEGA LOUNGE MAIN STAGE - NIGHT

Candy twirls on the pole to *Pour Some Sugar on Me*. Sofia steps inside, stopping short when she sees Mr. Guzman and his friend pull AK-47s from their jackets. They spray A BOOTH FULL OF STRIP CLUB GUESTS. We FOCUS ON Sofia's clipboard as it clatters to the ground.

INT. PATTERSON POLICE STATION - DAY

The station is dark and dingy, with case files stacked high on every desk. Sofia clutches her clipboard, shell-shocked, her shirt flecked with blood. She's sitting with a grizzled DETECTIVE, 50's. He looks to have slept in his cheap suit.

DETECTIVE: Thirty people there and nobody saw nothing. Four people gunned down, cold blood, no witnesses. Typical.

FLASHBACK TO:

INT. THE OMEGA LOUNGE MAIN STAGE - NIGHT

GUZMAN (addressing the room): You didn't see nothing.

Sofia and the girls hover by the side of the stage, nodding in mute terror.

END FLASHBACK

INT. PATTERSON POLICE STATION - DAY

The detective makes a note in a thick file labeled Cartagena Cartel. He hands Sofia a business card.

DETECTIVE: Here's my number if you suddenly recall Guzman pullin' a trigger, which I very much doubt. So I guess I'll add this unsolved case to the stack.

He flings his file at the pile, which topples. Exhausted, Sofia cants forward. Her crucifix catches in her clipboard. As she untangles and rises to leave, she pauses.

SOFIA: Theoretically, what if... what if I saw what happened?

DETECTIVE: Theoretically, we'd finally have cause to lock up this dirtbag. Then, theoretically, you'd be placed in witness protection because Guzman's so high profile.

She nods, not sold, but close.

DETECTIVE (CONT'D): Theoretically, your whole life would change. New city, new name, new everything. Witness protection's a fresh start.

Sofia weighs her options. Resolved, she touches her crucifix.

DETECTIVE (CONT'D): You ready to talk?

She sits.

SOFIA: Detective, I'm ready to sing.

END TEASER

———

ACT ONE

EXT. PATIO OF ELI'S HOUSE OF BEANS - DAY
    SUPERIMPOSE -- ONE MONTH LATER
    Sofia sits outside a coffee shop with a giant latte, two battered suitcases to her side. She watches a video on her tablet, idly touching her crucifix. ON HER SCREEN we see --

EXT. GRASSY QUAD AT ELI WHITNEY UNIVERSITY - DAY
    ASHLEY, a perky coed, 22, with long black hair in a high ponytail, cartwheels into the shot. She wears head to toe Eli Whitney University gear.

    ASHLEY: Welcome to Eli Whitney, Central Illinois' premiere public university!! Founded in 1864 --

    Sofia jumps when MARSHALL PAT O'BRIEN, late 40's, taps her on the shoulder. He's a solid type, a man who could kill then cook his own dinner. He sports a neatly trimmed mustache and sense of purpose.

    O'BRIEN: Janelle Smith, I presume?

    SOFIA: No, sorry.

    O'Brien pulls out a chair and sits across from her.

    O'BRIEN: You sure about that, Janelle?

    Sofia, having been given the witness protection name of JANELLE SMITH, buries her face in her hands.

    JANELLE: Oh, no! I keep forgetting my new name. Nice to meet you in person, Marshall O'Brien.

She offers her hand but Marshall O'Brien hugs her, much to her surprise. He doesn't emit a touchy-feely vibe.

O'BRIEN (quietly): Families hug. Don't forget, I'm your Uncle Pat. I'm definitely not the U.S. Marshall assigned to look out for you.

Chastened, Janelle curls into herself, overwhelmed and lost.

JANELLE: Damn it. Will this get easier?

O'BRIEN: Yes, and soon.

She wants to believe him.

O'BRIEN (CONT'D): What will help is your new job. You'll like it.

JANELLE: I'm ready for something different. What's the position?

O'BRIEN: Housemother at Gamma Kappa.

She deflates.

JANELLE: Great. Another strip club.

O'BRIEN: What? No. Gamma's a Greek house, a sorority. The job is sorority housemother.

JANELLE: How does a sorority housemom differ from what I did at the Omega?

O'BRIEN: They're fairly similar. You coordinate meals, you manage the staff. You oversee, keep your girls out of trouble. The difference is, you live there.

JANELLE: That I can do. (a beat) So no one gets naked?

O'BRIEN: Well, this is college.

JANELLE: Will it matter that I never graduated high --

MARSHALL O'BRIEN: You have a bachelor's degree, Janelle Smith.

She straightens in her chair.

JANELLE: I have a bachelor's degree...

MARSHALL O'BRIEN: You feel okay with this placement, like you'll be safe here at Whitney?

JANELLE: Totally. (a beat) No one from my old life would ever look for me at a college.

Hayden, 23, blonde with hipster glasses, approaches. She's an attractive dichotomy, simultaneously fresh-scrubbed and world-weary.

HAYDEN: Something to drink? Coconut milk macchiato? Chai chili latte? Our Earl Gray mistos are legendary.

The Marshall raises an eyebrow.

MARSHALL O'BRIEN: Coffee. Black.

HAYDEN: I'll start a fresh pot.

She exits the patio and enters...

INT. ELI'S HOUSE OF BEANS - DAY

CECE BONDURANT BARCLAY (the effortlessly blonde wife from the newscast) is here. She's regal, elegant, icy as Grace Kelly herself. Perched on a stool in the eclectic coffee bar, she flips channels, landing on the news. ON THE TV SCREEN we see a photo of Luis Guzman --

NEWSCASTER (O.S.): In Patterson, New Jersey, a grand jury has indicted suspected Cartagena Cartel kingpin Luis Guzman --

Hayden starts a fresh pot of coffee, then grabs the remote, flipping to sports.

HAYDEN: TV's supposed to stay on soccer.

CECE: Soccer? So I've raised my daughter to be a communist.

Hayden snorts.

HAYDEN: You've never raised anything but a martini glass.

Cece shrugs. Hayden's palpable resentment is one-sided.

A FRAT BRO in a backwards Whitney U cap saunters up.

FRAT BRO: Hey, you look familiar. You're not Callie, are you?

HAYDEN (curt): No.

Hayden points to her name tag. Dismissed, he leaves, glancing back over his shoulder. A SECOND FRAT BRO eyes Hayden from his table across the room.

HAYDEN (CONT'D): Why are you here?

CECE: There's a law against visiting my kid at college?

HAYDEN: Law? No. Lack of precedent? Yes. Four years of undergrad, one of a master's program, an hour from your Chicago house, yet you've never come. Why now?

FLASHBACK TO:

EXT.   CECE'S   SUBURBAN   CHICAGO MANSION - DAY

Cece is restrained by a MAN IN AN FBI WIND-BREAKER while a TEAM OF AGENTS removes pricey items, including a huge painted portrait of Cece, Chip, and a younger, more bershon Hayden.

INT. BANK LOBBY - DAY

Cece stands in front of A TELLER looking at the BANK MANAGER who vehemently shakes his head. The TELLER puts back the stack of bills and shrugs apologetically.

INT. CONVENIENCE STORE - DAY

CECE grimaces as the STORE CLERK cuts up her credit card and plucks the carton of milk from her hands.

END FLASHBACK

INT. ELI'S HOUSE OF BEANS - DAY

CECE: I'm here because I love you.

A beat.

Both women laugh.

CECE (CONT'D): Fine, I need a loan. The government couldn't seize your assets, so I want you to tap into your trust fund.

Hayden crosses her arms. She's not having this.

HAYDEN: Lemme see, (A) no, and (B) no. I don't touch my trust. Ever.

CECE: Then how do you pay your bills?

Hayden gestures towards her apron. Cece doesn't follow.

HAYDEN: I have a job? I suggest you find one, too, if you want to, you know, live indoors.

The second frat bro approaches Hayden.

SECOND FRAT BRO: You're Callie, the girl from -

HAYDEN: (barks) No.

Sheepish, he slinks away.

HAYDEN (CONT'D): You're here because I'm your last resort.

CECE: I wouldn't say last.

FLASHBACK TO:

EXT. FIRST SUBURBAN CHICAGO MANSION - DAY

A front door slams on Cece.

EXT. SECOND SUBURBAN CHICAGO MANSION - DAY

Another front door slams on Cece.

EXT. THIRD SUBURBAN CHICAGO MANSION - EVENING

A third door slams on Cece.

END FLASHBACK

INT. ELI'S HOUSE OF BEANS - DAY

Hayden spots a small snag in her mother's Chanel suit and her hard expression softens.

HAYDEN: I know dad screwed you over. He screwed everyone. He's a jackass.

CECE: I looked the other way when Chip would lie and cheat. I knew he wasn't perfect. But stealing money from our charity, then completely disappearing? Leaving me with nothing? Not even my dignity? Unacceptable.

Hayden blinks hard, steeling herself against the charming plague that is her mother.

CECE (CONT'D): I'm in a bind until we find Chip or my attorney figures out how to unfreeze my accounts.

HAYDEN: Sell your Mercedes and live on the proceeds until then.

Cece's lip trembles.

CECE: My car is the only piece I have left of my old life.

She gives Hayden wounded-doe eyes. Hayden cracks.

HAYDEN: I guess you could stay with me temporarily.

A slow grin spreads across Cece's face; mission accomplished.

CECE: Outstanding. So, sweetie, where is it that you live?

Hayden grits her teeth.

HAYDEN (mumbling): I instantly regret this decision.

INT. HAYDEN'S APARTMENT - AFTERNOON

With a pained expression, Cece wanders through Hayden's sparse loft. Her tower of Louis Vuitton suitcases sits next to door. Cece gingerly handles knickknacks, checks for dust, frowns at the modern artwork. A desk housing a massive iMac, servers, a camera, and a light bar takes up a whole wall.

Cece fingers the sheets on the platform bed.

CECE: What's the thread count on these? Two?

HAYDEN: That's my bed. You sleep there.

She points at a minimalist futon.

CECE: No guest room with en suite bath?

Cece is pushing Hayden's buttons.

HAYDEN: This is a one room loft.

Cece shudders, but realizes she's out of options.

CECE: Then I guess this will be like camping... only horrible.

HAYDEN (sarcastic): Welcome home, Mummy.

INT. ELI'S HOUSE OF BEANS - DAY

Hayden makes a massive cappuccino for Janelle, who's standing at the counter. Hayden seems stressed. Fresh as can be, Cece sits at the bar.

HAYDEN: Will your attorney have an update soon? It's been a week, a long week.

CECE: She says she has a lead on Chip's whereabouts.

But she's worried that unfreezing my assets could take a while. Told me I should find work for now.

HAYDEN: So, exactly what I suggested last week.

Cece opens a newspaper to the CLASSIFIED SECTION and takes a pen from her purse. She begins to circle ads.

CECE: Sweetie, how many words do I type per minute?

HAYDEN: Zero.

Cece crosses out the listing with a red pen.

CECE: How would you rate my accounting skills?

HAYDEN: Dad stole fifty million dollars from your charitable foundation, so... not great.

Cece crosses out the listing.

CECE: Would I be right for a work-from-home position?

Hayden stiffens.

HAYDEN (snarls): I need you to be in my apartment less often, not more.

Cece shrugs and crosses out the listing.

CECE (reading): Sorority housemother needed ASAP. Manage operations. Oversee staff of cooks, gardeners, and housekeepers. Position includes luxury accommodations. Sounds perfect.

This catches Janelle's attention. She can't help but listen.

HAYDEN: No, not perfect.

CECE: Why?

HAYDEN: Because mom is right in the job description.

CECE: And?

HAYDEN: And you're a terrible mother!

FLASHBACK TO:

EXT. POOL IN BACKYARD OF SUBURBAN CHICAGO MANSION - DAY

YOUNG HAYDEN, 10, flails and chokes in the pool. Is she drowning?

Cece's on the other side of the pool, coaching THE GARDENER as he prunes a bush into the shape of a swan.

CECE: Shh, Hayden, Mummy's talking.

END FLASHBACK

INT. ELI'S HOUSE OF BEANS - DAY

CECE: Yet I'm outstanding at managing a household staff, so you can see my dilemma.

Hayden sets Janelle's coffee on the counter with a bang.

HAYDEN: Jumbo skinny vanilla cap for Janelle.

Janelle doesn't respond.

HAYDEN (CONT'D): Janelle? Skinny cap?

Still nothing. Both Hayden and Cece look at Janelle - she's the only other person at the counter. Janelle smiles before she realizes why they're looking.

JANELLE: Of course that's me. Because I'm Janelle.

She takes her coffee, but lingers by Cece.

JANELLE (CONT'D): I hate to eavesdrop, but I'm a housemom.

CECE: Yeah? Do you like it?

JANELLE: I do. All the other moms are so nice! If you're interested, I'll introduce you to the Dean who oversees the sororities. She's actually here now.

Janelle motions towards DEAN GRACE, 40's, dressed in a bland suit with no-nonsense hair. She's meeting with KAYLEE, her dim assistant, 20's, and a SMALL GROUP OF ACADEMICS IN BOW TIES AND TWEED and an ASIAN MAN.

CECE: I'd love an introduction. (to Hayden) How can you say that other women are the worst?

HAYDEN: No, you say that! You have problems with women, not me!

Janelle and Cece grab a table. Cece smiles as she chats, effusive with charm. Hayden angrily wipes the counter. A MALE GRAD STUDENT approaches.

MALE GRAD STUDENT: Hey, aren't you --

HAYDEN: (snaps, not looking up) No! Okay? No! You don't freaking know me!

GRAD STUDENT: Sorry. Thought you were Hayden from Ed Psych class with Professor Baer.

She's mortified as he spots her name tag. After he leaves, she pulls out her phone and ON THE SCREEN we see -- a pop-up reminder that says pay tuition by Friday or else!!

HAYDEN: Damn it!

We see her tap a few lines. When finished typing, ON THE SCREEN we see -- a very sexy photo of Hayden in booty shorts and a long, red wig. She's biting her finger and eyeing the camera. The caption reads -- Sorry I've been offline. Your camgirl Callie will be back ASAFP!

END ACT ONE

————

ACT TWO

INT. ELI'S HOUSE OF BEANS - DAY

Janelle and Cece chat while waiting for the Dean.

JANELLE: The other housemoms say the key is to

respect the girls, like, really embrace sisterhood. Does that sound like you, Cece?

FLASHBACK TO:
    INT. NEIMAN MARCUS STORE - DAY
    A SHOPPER admires a gorgeous handbag.
    SALESCLERK: That's one of a kind.
    Like a ninja, Cece yanks the bag out of the SHOPPER'S grip while thrusting her credit card at the SALESCLERK. FOCUS ON the name on her card -- Cece Bondurant Barclay.

INT. COUNTRY CLUB DINING ROOM - DAY
    Cece stands by a fishbowl containing names on slips. A group of LADIES WHO LUNCH, all wearing pastel suits and hats, wait in anticipation. Cece draws a name.
    CECE: The winner of the trip to Bali is...
    ON THE PAPER, we see -- Joyce van der Zee
    CECE (O.S.) (CONT'D): Why, it's me, Cece Bondurant Barclay!

INT. BRYN MAWR DORM ROOM - DAY
    COLLEGE CECE, 20, sits on a bed, listening to *Damn, I Wish I Was Your Lover*. There's a poster from the movie *The Bodyguard* on the wall. Her roommate BITSY enters, wearing a Bryn Mawr sweatshirt. ANGLE ON Cece's face -- we only see the madras-clad Chip from behind.
    BITSY: Miss Cece Marie Bondurant, please meet my boyfriend, Chip Barclay.
    END FLASHBACK

INT. ELI'S HOUSE OF BEANS - DAY

Cece sips her coffee.

CECE: Sisterhood is my middle name.

We SHIFT FOCUS TO Dean Grace's table. She sits with Kaylee, the academics, and MR. WU, the Asian man.

ACADEMIC #1: We're recommending the trustees name you Provost next year, Dean Grace.

DEAN GRACE (pouring it on thick): I'm just so honored to be considered for this promotion.

ACADEMIC #2: What would help your case is you finding housing for Mr. Wu's students. His group wants to live together.

ACADEMIC #1: Don't forget, our international tuition prices are three times higher than domestic.

We hear a CHING from Hayden using the cash register. The Dean's smile falters.

DEAN GRACE: Placing all those students in a single location might be a challenge. But we have so many wonderful off-campus apartments that --

MR. WU: One spot. Non-negotiable.

KAYLEE: Wouldn't Greek Row be amaze? International students could have, like, their own neighborhood.

Mr. Wu leans in, very interested.

ACADEMIC #1: The university does own the land up there. Too bad the fraternities have those long-term leases...

Dean Grace's wheels turn. She rubs her hands together in anticipation. The cash register CHINGS in rapid succession.

DEAN GRACE: I'm confident we'll work this out.

ACADEMIC #1: Sounds like a plan, Provost Grace.

Everyone rises and shakes hands. The men depart. Before the two women leave, Janelle approaches with Cece.

JANELLE: Hi, Dean Grace, this is my friend, Cece. Can we have five minutes?

INT. DEAN GRACE'S OFFICE - DAY

The Dean's wood-paneled office is lined with shelves full of leather-bound books. The room smells of academia, mothballs.

Kaylee stands in the doorway.

DEAN GRACE: Yes?

KAYLEE: That lady today - you got her the job at Alpha. No one even checked references because you vouched. Will she be good?

Dean Grace offers a predatory smile.

DEAN GRACE: She'll be a train wreck.

KAYLEE: We want her to be terrible?

DEAN GRACE: That's the plan.

Kaylee scratches her head, bewildered.

DEAN GRACE (CONT'D): What happens when a sorority house is mismanaged, Kaylee? Anarchy happens. You can't manage that many hungry girls without a strong leader, a true adult. So then what happens?

KAYLEE: Um...

DEAN GRACE: Anarchy impacts membership. If the house doesn't recruit enough new girls, they lose their national charter. And when the charter's revoked?

KAYLEE: Um...

The Dean swears it's like pulling teeth with this one.

DEAN GRACE: No charter, no lease. Without leases,

Whitney reclaims the land. (a beat) Which will go to Mr. Wu's group.

The last horse to cross the finish line is... Kaylee!

KAYLEE: But... how do we get rid of all the other housemoms? (whispers) Murder?

The Dean blinks hard. Idiot.

DEAN GRACE: We don't get rid of the moms. What we do is make and enforce new rules. Impossible-to-comply rules.

KAYLEE: Ah, rules. (a beat) That's probably better than murder.

EXT. GREEK ROW/ZETA OMICRON OMEGA FRATER-NITY HOUSE DAY

OVER BLACK

MEAN HELENE (O.S.) (guttural sounds/heavy breathing): Mmmmpppph.

CLOSE ON housemom MEAN HELENE SCHROEDER, 70's. She has the countenance of a grizzled war veteran. Mean Helene lays in the grass of the ZOO fraternity. Clad in a ghillie suit, she uses binoculars to track the academics as they survey the block with Mr. Wu. A ZOO PLEDGE starts towards her, but a ZOO BROTHER yanks him back. The message is clear -- don't provoke Mean Helene.

MEAN HELENE (CONT'D): Mmmmpppph.

Mean Helene makes a note on a small pad. MEAN HELENE'S POV is on the Pi Mu Sigma house, where housemom RAIN LEVINSON (50's) tends her organic garden.

MEAN HELENE (O.S.) (CONT'D): Useless hippie.

MEAN HELENE's POV shifts to a window at Rho

Sigma Tau where MARILEE MITCHELL, mid 30's, stands. She's an African American version of Martha Stewart. Marilee's apartment is a pink and green paean to Lambda Phi Lambda's letters and colors.

We see a framed article on the wall and WE READ the headline -- Lambda Phi Lambda, Whitney's First African American Sorority Moves into Greek Row. The picture beneath shows a younger Marilee in a Lambda sweatshirt holding ceremonial scissors for a ribbon-cutting. WE READ the photo's caption -- Lambda president Marilee Mitchell does the honors. Marilee gazes longingly at the Lambda house next door. She spots Rain outside and waves.

MEAN HELENE (O.S.) (CONT'D): Friendly fire. Hate your troops long enough and they'll turn on ya.

MEAN HELENE'S POV hones in on Janelle waving at Rain while helping Ashley load her car.

MEAN HELENE (O.S.) (CONT'D): Bachelor's degree, my ass.

Finally, MEAN HELENE's POV shifts to the Alpha Zeta Alpha house. Cece has just arrived in a shiny new Mercedes convertible. She doesn't wave back at anyone.

MEAN HELENE (O.S.) (CONT'D): Mmmmppppph. Trouble.

INT. HAYDEN'S APARTMENT - DAY

Dressed in a flimsy teddy and bobbed auburn wig, Hayden sits at her computer. She taps out a few keyboard commands, adjusts the camera, and then...

HAYDEN (into the camera): Hey, y'all... your girl Callie's finally back.

INT. GAMMA HOUSE / ASHLEY'S ROOM - DAY

Ashley wears head to toe Gamma letters. Her curtain of black hair sweeps her elbows. A sign on her door denotes she's the chapter president. Janelle keeps her company as she unpacks.

ASHLEY: I'm loving that we finally have a young housemom! Our last mom was, like, ancient! Couldn't walk up the stairs.

Janelle tries to air out this cramped room. Her progress is slowed by the bright snowboard propped against the bed in the middle of everything.

Ashley unpacks a wall-hanging crucifix.

JANELLE (pleased): You're Catholic, too?

ASHLEY: In theory. My mom made me pack this. She says Jesus's watchful eye will keep me out of trouble. Please. This room is the only place I won't find trouble.

JANELLE: Why's that?

Ashley gives Jane an odd look.

ASHLEY: Because of our national no alcohol or boys upstairs rules? Plus, I'm president so I set the example.

JANELLE: Yeah, right, of course.

ASHLEY: Don't you hate how movies portray sororities?

INT. GENERIC SORORITY HOUSE LIVING ROOM - NIGHT

A pack of HOT DRUNK CHICKS do keg stands while HOT DRUNK CHICK #1 chops up a mountain of cocaine. HOT DRUNK CHICK #2, dances around in a Viking helmet and underpants. HOT DRUNK CHICK#3 leads a live sheep into the party.

INT. GAMMA HOUSE / ASHLEY'S ROOM - DAY

ASHLEY: We'd lose our charter in a hot minute if we behaved like that. I'm, like, have the writers ever even seen a college?

Janelle nods, nervous.

ASHLEY (CONT'D): Anyway, my party days are over. I have a serious boyfriend. He's delish. Goes to law school here.

JANELLE: You're so lucky! I'd love to meet a nice guy. Kind of rare in my life so far.

ASHLEY: You'll meet someone amaze, I just know it.

Janelle beams, because, sisterhood.

EXT. GREEK ROW / ALPHA HOUSE - DAY

Rain approaches Cece in the sorority's portico. Rain's an earth mother, clad in hemp clothes and gardening shoes, proudly displaying her gray roots, as though aging were a badge of honor and not a horrible fucking curse.

RAIN: You must be Cece! I'm Rain Levinson, mom at Pi Mu next door. I'm here to show you around.

Cece coolly regards Rain, underwhelmed by her over-alls and Crocs. Rain offers her hand, but Cece declines as it's caked in soil. Rain laughs, wiping her palms on her pants.

RAIN (CONT'D): Sorry, I've been mulching.

CECE: Don't we have people for that?

RAIN: We do, but I can't help myself around dirt. Former botany professor.

Cece won't even pretend to feign interest.

CECE: Wow, botany. That sounds... stimulating.

INT. ANONYMOUS BASEMENT - DAY

WE HEAR Prince's *Purple Rain*. Under extensive silver ductwork and the glow of grow lights, Rain inspects the flower on a thriving marijuana plant LABELED Purple Rain. PULL BACK to reveal dozens of additional plants.

EXT. GREEK ROW / ALPHA HOUSE - DAY

RAIN: You might be surprised. (a beat) Ready for the tour?

They walk together into...

INT. ALPHA HOUSE / ENTRY HALL - DAY

Rain and Cece enter a legit mansion, with a massive open atrium. A huge floral arrangement, studded with daisies, sits in the center of the foyer. The room's lit by an enormous crystal chandelier. The elegant space is decorated in muted shades of gold and red.

CECE: A catsup and mustard palette? Who's the interior designer? Ronald McDonald? Not lovin' it.

RAIN: The sorority's colors are crimson and maize, so --

CECE: So, I'll change it. I have access to the house checkbook, yes?

Rain's tries to nudge Cece in another direction.

RAIN: Yes, but the sisters move back tomorrow and rush is this weekend. It's better to concentrate on --

CECE: On calling a decorator stat?

Cece shoots a quick text.

CECE (CONT'D): Done.

Cece then sniffs the air.

CECE (CONT'D): What's that God-awful stench?

297

Rain takes a whiff of herself. Not her, not this time.

CECE (CONT'D): It's coming from back there.

They head down the hall to...

INT. ALPHA HOUSE/KITCHEN

LORETTA, 60's, stout with kind eyes. Her apron reads Never Trust a Skinny Chef. She stirs the contents of a large pot. She hums, content.

RAIN: Loretta! Meet Cece, the new mom.

Loretta waves her wooden spoon.

LORETTA: Deee-lighted to meet you!

Cece glowers at the pot like it froze her accounts. She takes a handkerchief from her bag, placing it over her nose.

CECE (muffled): Thanks.

RAIN: That your famous vegan white bean chili?

LORETTA: You know it. Low cal, low fat, low guilt; the perfect lunch.

CECE: (gagging) For livestock?

Loretta's unfazed.

LORETTA: My gals love my chili and it only costs fifty cents a serving.

Cece removes her handkerchief.

CECE: Let me ask you something --

Loretta smiles encouragingly.

CECE (CONT'D): Would it smell better if we were to spend sixty cents?

RAIN: Let's introduce you to the head of housekeeping.

Rain hustles Cece down the hall to...

INT. ALPHA HOUSE/JANITOR'S ROOM - DAY

EDYTA, 40s, brusque but efficient, wears a starched maid's uniform. Her lips are pressed into a thin, white line.

CECE: All I'm saying is that marble floors shine brighter when polished on hands and knees, and not just dry mopped.

EDYTA: Yes, but hand-polishing makes them too slippery.

CECE: That sounds like an excuse.

Edyta clenches her fist.

RAIN: Let's find Bob, the landscaper.

They walk out front to...

EXT. GREEK ROW/ALPHA HOUSE - DAY

BOB, 60's, resembles Santa Claus with his thick white beard. He holds a shovel by the row of daisies that line the drive.

BOB: You want me to take these out and replace them with white tea roses? All of 'em?

CECE: All of them.

BOB: The roses would be mighty pretty, but daisies are Alpha's official flower.

CECE: Who chooses a weed as an official flower? No. Gotta go.

Rain face-palms. Cece is hopeless.

INT. ALPHA HOUSE/ENTRY HALL - DAY

A hub of activity! An INTERIOR DESIGNER shows Cece an array of fabric. A PAINTER stands on a drop cloth on the floor of the entry, changing the wall color. Loretta enters with a snack of shucked oysters on a silver tray.

Edyta is on her knees in the adjoining living area, hand-combing the fringe on the rug. She pauses to wipe her brow. Cece motions for her to continue. Edyta scowls.

Cece spots Bob through the open front door. He's waxing her Mercedes, which is parked next to the new roses. She motions for him to polish harder.

Across the street, Mean Helene watches from her spot beneath the ZOO sign. Her expression is terrifying.

Hayden enters carrying a fern and sees what her mom has wrought. CLOSE ON Hayden wincing.

MATCH CUT TO:

INT. MARILEE'S APARTMENT - DAY

Rain is wincing. PULL BACK to discover she's holding in smoke, a one-hitter in her hand. She exhales a great white plume.

MARILEE: Since when is the new housemom awful? I thought we loved Janelle.

RAIN: We do love Janelle. I'm talking about Alpha's new mom.

MARILEE: Whoa, what happened to Mama Doris?

RAIN: Stroke, three days ago.

MARILEE (to herself): Never the ones you hope.

RAIN: I'm concerned for the Alphas. Yet the universe knows how to right itself.

Rain takes a monster inhale, then offers the pipe to Marilee. She declines.

MARILEE: Going the other way, thanks.

Marilee opens a pill bottle and we FOCUS ON the prescribed name -- Brooke Ames. She swallows the tablet dry.

RAIN: Since when do you take Ritalin, Marilee?

MARILEE: Since Brooke Ames left her script in the bathroom.

RAIN: Hon, you can't do that.

MARILEE: Why not? Tough love. Pay more attention next time, Brookie.

RAIN: Will you ever stop resenting your poor girls for not being Lambdas?

MARILEE: Of course.

Marilee glowers out the window at the Lambda house.

MARILEE (CONT'D): Soon as Mama Shirley dies. Diabetes and high blood pressure, yet still alive and kicking. So unfair.

RAIN: Do you ever wonder if your passion for Lambda is a bit... much?

FLASHBACK TO:

INT. A CHURCH ALTAR - DAY

A wedding gown-clad Marilee shoves her HUSBAND, late 20's, out of the way to pose with HER PINK AND GREEN BRIDESMAIDS.

MARILEE: Everyone say "Lovely Lambdas!"

INT. MARILEE'S FORMER CLOSET - DAY

Marilee shoves all the men's clothing to the side to make way for sorority sweatshirts while her husband watches.

INT. MARILEE'S FORMER LIVING ROOM - DAY

Marilee shoves a Plexiglas box of Air Jordans off a shelf to display her collection of stuffed llamas wearing

Lambda shirts. Her husband grabs the box and walks out the door.

    END FLASHBACK

INT. MARILEE'S APARTMENT - DAY
    MARILEE: No, why?
    RAIN: No reason.

EXT. PATIO OF ELI'S HOUSE OF BEANS - DAY
    Janelle READS a copy of -- *The Dummy's Guide to Sororities*. Oblivious, she's caught the attention of Trevor, mid 20's. Sporty, with freckles and floppy bangs, he looks like he'd help old ladies cross streets. He READS -- *Constitutional Law*.
    TREVOR: Are you going through rush?
    JANELLE: Sorry?
    TREVOR: Do you want to pledge a sorority house?
    JANELLE: Me? No, I, um, already graduated.
    Trevor nods towards her book.
    JANELLE (CONT'D): Oh. This. I'm getting a handle on my new job. Just became housemom at... Kappa Gamma. The Greek stuff is all new to me.
    TREVOR: No frats at your last school?

FLASHBACK TO:
    EXT. NEW JERSEY HIGH SCHOOL - DAY
    CATHOLIC SCHOOL KIDS wearing uniforms mill around the entrance. The sign out front reads St. Sebastian High.

BACK TO:

    EXT. PATIO OF ELI'S HOUSE OF BEANS - DAY

    JANELLE: Not so much.

They return to their books, taking turns stealing glances.

Janelle's phone beeps. ON THE SCREEN we see -- a text from Uncle Pat.

    O'BRIEN (TEXT): Status check?

    JANELLE (TEXT): Everyone's so nice, [heart emoji] it here

Janelle looks around, content.

    JANELLE (CONT'D) (singing to herself) If I should stay, I would only be in your way...

Her voice is soulful and pure.

    TREVOR: Whitney or Dolly?

    JANELLE: Sorry?

    TREVOR: Are you singing the Whitney Houston version or the Dolly Parton version?

    JANELLE: Dolly Parton never sang *I Will Always Love You.*

    TREVOR: Never sang it? She wrote it!

    JANELLE: Impossible. That song was made for Whitney. The legato passages? I die.

    TREVOR: You don't believe me.

    JANELLE: Can't believe you. My girl Whitney owned it.

    TREVOR: Wanna put a friendly wager on it?

    JANELLE: Maybe?

    TREVOR: I'll bet you a --

Janelle's excited to be speaking with a nice guy.

    JANELLE: Coffee?

    TREVOR: Nah, too easy. Dinner? If I'm right, I take you to dinner.

JANELLE: What if you're wrong?

TREVOR: Then dinner's on you.

Trevor pulls out his phone and ON THE SCREEN we see him type -- I Will Always Love You into Google.

TREVOR (CONT'D) (reading): Written and recorded by Dolly Parton in 1973...

Janelle's never been so happy to lose.

INT. ROMANTIC ITALIAN RESTAURANT - NIGHT

Trevor rises from his seat in a busy restaurant, kissing Janelle on the cheek when she arrives. He pulls out her chair. A chianti bottle holding a candle burns on the table.

TREVOR: I wish you'd let me pick you up.

Such manners! He pours her a glass of red wine.

JANELLE: What can I say, I'm cautious. I can't warn my girls about getting into strange men's cars if I do it myself.

Trevor's puzzled.

TREVOR: Do you normally have to speak to them like they children?

JANELLE: Actually, not here. At the old job, yes. We didn't run into many nice guys there.

TREVOR: What'd you do before?

FLASHBACK TO:

INT. THE OMEGA LOUNGE / MAIN STAGE - NIGHT

Candy is bent over and a PERVY MAN tries to swipe his credit card in her butt crack.

END FLASHBACK

INT. ROMANTIC ITALIAN RESTAURANT - NIGHT

JANELLE: Um... troubled youth outreach?

She's flustered, still getting the hang of lying.

TREVOR: Sounds stimulating.

JANELLE: That's a good word for it.

TREVOR: Why'd you quit?

JANELLE: I needed a change of scenery. How about you?

TREVOR: Professional bartender by night, amateur attorney by day. I'm a third year in law school.

JANELLE: Wow! What do you do for fun?

TREVOR: Fantasy football. Snowboard. Stalk Dolly Parton. You?

JANELLE: Don't laugh, but I make lists. I live in mortal fear I'll miss something, so I log everything. Checking off items when I'm finished gives me life.

TREVOR: Ever complete a task, realize it wasn't on the list, and then write it down so you can cross it off?

JANELLE: You just looked right into my soul.

They laugh, clink glasses.

INT. ALPHA HOUSE/ENTRY HALL - NIGHT

NATALIE, 22, a rule-follower, prone to whining, enters the house, suitcase in tow. She stops short, noticing the formal entry has turned into a construction zone. Is this Alpha? She steps out the door to check the address, before re-entering. She pulls out a phone and dials, pissy.

NATALIE: Who approved the renovation? As chapter treasurer, I should have been consulted. We don't have the budget for this.

INT. ROMANTIC ITALIAN RESTAURANT - NIGHT

All the tables are empty, save for Janelle and Trevor's. The candle nub flickers out in a pile of melted wax.

TREVOR: I'm still afraid of rulers. Sister Kathleen was no joke, man. A swing like hers, shoulda played for the Cubbies.

Trevor protectively rubs his knuckles.

JANELLE: For me, it's plaid kilts. My PTSD is triggered whenever I see a plaid kilt.

FLASHBACK TO:

INT. THE OMEGA / MAIN STAGE - NIGHT

Candy dances in a naughty Catholic school girl uniform to Winger's *She's Only Seventeen*.

END FLASHBACK

INT. ROMANTIC ITALIAN RESTAURANT - NIGHT

Janelle shudders inadvertently.

TREVOR: Listen, if we're trying to out-Catholic the other, I'll have you know I played Joseph in the Christmas pageant.

JANELLE: Whoa. Joseph? You win.

TREVOR: I did. Crushed so much sixth grade ass after that.

They laugh. Neither wants the night to end.

JANELLE: Do you remember leaving room for the Holy Ghost at dances?

TREVOR: Yeah, but even the Holy Ghost refused to dance to Nickelback.

An ANNOYED WAITER approaches.

ANNOYED WAITER: Can I get you anything else? Like... a check?

They ignore him, focused only on each other.

TREVOR: Hey, what's on your bucket list? What do you have to do before you die?

JANELLE: Well, I want to sing at Madison Square Garden. Or in front of any audience. Of course, I want to go to col -- (clears throat) Calligraphy classes.

TREVOR: Random, but respectable.

The waiter snatches their water glasses and candle.

ANNOYED WAITER: Really, anything? How about a check?

Janelle and Trevor gaze at each other. He stomps off.

JANELLE: What's on your bucket list?

TREVOR (sly): Right now? Convincing you to come back to my place.

Sparks fly.

JANELLE: Check, please!

INT. ALPHA HOUSE / KITCHEN - NIGHT

Natalie enters in pajamas. She opens the fridge.

NATALIE: Chili time. Time for chili. It's chili o'clock. Where are you, chili?

She looks in plastic containers LABELED -- Cece.

NATALIE (CONT'D): Filets? Caviar? Damn it, Cece!

INT. TREVOR'S APARTMENT / LIVING ROOM - NIGHT

Janelle and Trevor tumble into his front door, kissing passionately over Dolly's version of *I Will Always Love You*.

Trevor unbuttons Janelle's blouse and she yanks off his shirt They pause to admire each other. Then Trevor pulls her to him with such force that he falls backwards onto his couch, taking her down with him. Their lips never part.

We see a skirt and a pair of pants land on the floor. CLOSE IN on the couple's faces; it's go-time.

JANELLE: Hold on, wait.

Trevor stops, alarmed. Did he misread her signals?

JANELLE (CONT'D): Save room for the Holy Ghost.

They laugh and we PAN UP the wall to reveal a crucifix.

INT. ALPHA HOUSE/LIVING ROOM - NIGHT

Another construction zone, with all the furniture gone, save for a couch. Natalie crosses the marble floor in thick socks, carrying books. She slips and falls, disappearing behind the sofa. The books fly everywhere.

NATALIE: Who polished the [bleeped] marble?!

INT. TREVOR'S APARTMENT/BEDROOM - NIGHT

Janelle's wrapped in a sheet on Trevor's bed. Every time she tries to get up, he pulls her down again.

TREVOR: Stay. Please.

JANELLE: Can't. Already called an Uber.

He buries his head in her hair. She slips out of his grip.

TREVOR: I'm not a one-night-stand guy. I don't see you as a one-night-stand girl. That means you have to stay; it's the law.

JANELLE: Most of the girls move in tomorrow. Can't have their first impression of me be the walk of shame.

TREVOR: At least let me drive you home.

Relenting, Janelle grabs her phone.

JANELLE: I cancelled the Uber.

Trevor gets out of bed to look for his clothes.

TREVOR: Hey, where is the Kappa Gamma house, anyway?

JANELLE: I don't know. Why?

TREVOR: Because you live there?

JANELLE: No, I'm housemom at Gamma Kappa.

TREVOR: But you said Kappa Gamma.

JANELLE: I probably did. The letters are tricky, like, it's all Greek to me.

Trevor blanches and crosses the room. FOCUS ON Trevor's desk -- we see a shot of Trevor with his arms around Ashley. His girlfriend. He places the picture face-down.

END ACT TWO

————

ACT THREE

INT. ALPHA HOUSE / ENTRY HALL - DAY

Cece, pacing, speaks on her cell phone as Natalie approaches.

NATALIE: We should discuss your spending.

Cece gives her the one-minute finger.

CECE (mouthing): My attorney.

Natalie doesn't care.

NATALIE: Like, the colors you picked are cool and all, but the cost of --

Cece turns her back, holding a hand over her ear to better hear.

CECE (on phone): That's not how good news and bad news works. (a beat) Then please explain how finding

Chip in a country without an extradition treaty is good news.

Natalie maneuvers around to be in front of Cece.

NATALIE: The cost of the fabric is, like, insane. You do have access to discretionary funds, but you blew through --

CECE (on phone): Where is Madagascar, anyway? (a beat) No, I have not seen the charming film by the same name.

NATALIE: You spent, like, a ton and we don't have the money allotted. P.S. I worked super hard on that budget.

CECE (on phone): No extradition means we can't force Chip back to the US to stand trial. That's why finding him there does not constitute good news.

Natalie taps Cece on the shoulder. Cece shrugs her off.

NATALIE: New member recruitment starts in three days. I don't feel like your renovations will be done in time. Then how will we pay for them?

CECE (on phone): What am I supposed to do?

Natalie chases Cece around the room. She's a small dog yipping for attention.

NATALIE: What are we supposed to do?

CECE (on phone): If he won't return to stand trial, I'm done! My assets will never be unfrozen! I'm screwed.

NATALIE: We can't have rush in a construction zone! Although everyone in hardhats would be kind of adorbs. Still, we're screwed!

CECE (on phone): Make it work? That's your advice? Thirteen hundred dollars an hour to quote Tim freaking Gunn? Argh!

Cece repeatedly stabs the keypad with her finger.

CECE (CONT'D): Hanging up on people was a lot

more satisfying on a landline. Anyway, you were saying something?

A beat.

NATALIE: I'm saying fix this, or we find a new housemom.

For the first time, we see Cece worried.

Outside the window, we see Mean Helene watching Cece with her spyglasses.

INT. DEAN GRACE'S OFFICE - DAY

Dean Grace sits at her desk, phone in hand. SHE DOODLES -- Provost Grace on her blotter. Kaylee enters, handing the Dean a STACK OF MESSAGES THAT CONTAIN WORDS LIKE -- Complaint, Alpha, Terrible, Cece, Help.

The Dean flaps her hands for Kaylee, like she's working a pair of sock puppets, clearly mocking the person on the other end of the line.

DEAN GRACE (on phone): I'm so sorry to hear about the problems you're having, Natalie. (a beat) I agree, it would be awful if Mrs. Barclay's incompetence impacted recruitment. Just awful.

Kaylee and Dean Grace high-five across the desk; the plan's working.

INT. HAYDEN'S APARTMENT - DAY

Hayden's doing a webcast. Her look is Japanese-anime style. She wears a blunt-cut black wig styled into pigtails and a tiny sailor's uniform with thigh-high socks and stilettos. She addresses her webcam.

HAYDEN: What are you looking for your girl Callie to do today?

She reads her viewers' responses on the screen. *[We can't see them.]* *[Could also show screen and have lines blurred because they're pornographic.]*

HAYDEN (CONT'D): Dirty. I can definitely do that.

Someone starts banging at Hayden's door. She ignores the intrusion.

HAYDEN (CONT'D): We'll need to upgrade to a private screen so it's just us. Sound good?

The banging continues. Whoever's here isn't leaving. She reads the screen.

HAYDEN (CONT'D): Um, no, it's fine. I don't have to answer the door.

Bang! Bang, bang! Hayden finds the intrusion difficult to ignore.

HAYDEN (CONT'D) (quietly fuming): Okay, yeah, it's probably my landlord. You're right, I'm sure I will have to convince him to let me pay my rent late.

CECE (O.S.): Hayden! Your mummy is here! Open up!

Hayden rips the computer's power cord out of the wall, ending the broadcast. She stomps over to the door, furious, forgetting to cover her outfit. She opens the door hard.

HAYDEN: What?!

CECE: That's how you greet your mother?

Cece takes in Hayden's outfit. She reaches in her purse for a card, which she hands to Hayden.

HAYDEN: What's this?

CECE: The direct line to my personal stylist at Neiman's. Your taste is a cry for help.

Mortified, Hayden pulls on a robe.

HAYDEN: Do you need something?

CECE: Yes, to move in. The housemom thing is a bust.

HAYDEN: Because you treated the Alpha house like your own private residence?

Cece shrugs, admitting nothing.

HAYDEN (CONT'D): Because you bulldozed the staff, treating them like they worked for you and not with you?

CECE: A lot of things happened, no one can say who's to blame.

Hayden is apoplectic.

HAYDEN: No, it's you! You are to blame.

CECE: That's a gray area.

Hayden tries another tack.

HAYDEN: You know, this is a blessing. This is your chance to finally do something on your own.

CECE: Meaning?

HAYDEN: Meaning you went from your parents' house to your dorm room to your husband's house. You've never been on your own. You don't know how to be an adult. You have no clue what it feels like to earn your own living, to chart your own course. You know, that's why I never took money from you guys.

Cece looks visibly uncomfortable at hearing these truths.

HAYDEN (CONT'D): I'm so afraid of turning into you that I work terrible, degrading jobs --

CECE: You're being dramatic, sweetie. Making coffee's not so bad.

Hayden's white with rage; how clueless is her mom, anyway?

HAYDEN: My point is, I'm proud to support myself. That feels good. I don't owe anyone anything. I rely on me.

Cece's quiet for a beat.

CECE: So I'm not moving in?

HAYDEN: Um, yeah.

Cece's defeated. She struggles for her words.

CECE: Then what am I going to do?

HAYDEN: I suggest you return to Alpha. Get in your car and go back. Right now, they're your only option.

CECE (in a whisper): What if I can't do the job?

HAYDEN: Then talk to the other housemoms. Ask them for help. Make it work.

Before Cece realizes what's happening, Hayden has hustled her out the door.

INT. HALLWAY OF HAYDEN'S APARTMENT - DAY

We hear a deadbolt click behind Cece.

CECE: What is it with everyone quoting Tim Gunn today?

END ACT THREE

———

ACT FOUR

INT. GAMMA HOUSE/ASHLEY'S ROOM - DAY

Janelle knocks on Ashley's open door, carrying folded towels. The room is still in chaos, boxes everywhere. Ashley is at her desk, disassembling her phone.

JANELLE: Clean towel delivery.

Janelle places the towels on Ashley's bed.

ASHLEY: You didn't have to do that, thanks!

JANELLE: I like to help.

Janelle stifles a yawn.

JANELLE (CONT'D): Sorry, need more coffee. Late night.

ASHLEY: Yeah? Anything interesting?

JANELLE (shy): Maybe, we'll see what happens.

Janelle notices the phone parts splayed across the desk.

JANELLE (CONT'D): What's happening here?

ASHLEY: Something's wrong with this thing. My boyfriend said he kept texting me last night, but I never got anything.

JANELLE: Are you seeing your other texts?

ASHLEY: Uh-huh.

JANELLE: Weird.

ASHLEY: Right? You don't think he's lying? Like he's cheating on me?

JANELLE: On you? Impossible. He'd have to be crazy.

Janelle laughs. She has no idea.

ASHLEY: Whew! Don't have to kill him now.

JANELLE: Any woman who'd cheat with someone else's guy is a total skank. You don't violate Girl Code.

ASHLEY: Thanks for that, I was kind of losing it for a second.

JANELLE: No probs. Hey, you want me to recycle these empty boxes for you?

ASHLEY: I'm not done unpacking. But you're the best!

JANELLE: I aim to please.

Janelle's phone beeps. ON THE SCREEN we see -- a text from Trevor.

TREVOR (TEXT)

Can't stop thinking about last night...

Anxious to respond, Janelle exits, phone in hand.

JANELLE: See you later, Ash.

ASHLEY (to herself): Love her!

Ashley opens the box next to her desk. We see that it's full of photos of Trevor.

EXT. GREEK ROW / ALPHA HOUSE - DAY

Cece pulls up, parking her Mercedes out front. She looks at the house long and hard, as though deciding. Resigned, she exits the car, squares her shoulders, and enters the house.

Mean Helene watches through binoculars, intrigued.

INT. ALPHA HOUSE / ENTRY HALL - DAY

The entry hall is a disaster - all the half-done renovation projects have been abandoned. Scaffolding is everywhere. Walls have partial coats of primer, woodwork is stripped, floors are torn up, the furniture is frame-only. Natalie paces, panicked.

NATALIE: They've left! All the workers are gone! What are we going to do?

CECE: Back up, they're gone? Why'd they leave?

NATALIE: I have no idea! All I said was that we didn't have the money to pay them.

CECE: You told everyone that?

NATALIE: I mentioned it to one guy because we were chatting. He was cute. But he had a big mouth and the word spread.

Cece runs her hands through her hair, concerned.

CECE: When does the house need to be ready for rush?

NATALIE: Two days! If we all pitch in, we could maybe finish the painting, but we can't fix the hard stuff! And we have so much recruitment party prep on top of that!

CECE: Can you postpone rush?

NATALIE: No.

CECE: What happens if these recruitment parties go badly?

NATALIE: Then girls won't pick us. We won't meet our quota from national. They'll pull our charter.

Natalie begins to cry. Ugly cry. Baby with a bowlful of spaghetti on his head cry.

Cece attempts to comfort her. Her awkward hug comes across more like a TSA pat-down, but she tries.

NATALIE (CONT'D): Were you ever in a sorority?

CECE: My college didn't have them.

NATALIE: Then you don't get it.

CECE: What's to get? You live together and go to frat parties, right?

NATALIE: No. I mean, yes, but no. We're so much more than that.

CECE: How?

NATALIE: Being in Alpha teaches us how to resolve conflict, how to compromise, how to lead, how to live with difficult people. We learn how to be adults and live on our own, take care of ourselves.

Cece mulls this over. Natalie crosses to a huge photo display. We see dozens of shots of happy girls hugging each other.

NATALIE (CONT'D): We're sisters. We're there for each other. These girls are my family, not just today but forever.

Cece presses her palms to her temple, thinking hard. She's invested now.

CECE: You're the house treasurer, right? How much do we owe everyone?

NATALIE: Like, almost thirty grand. We're screwed. Alpha's over.

CECE: Thirty grand? That's it?

NATALIE: May as well be fifty million because we don't have it.

Cece presses her lips together. Very slowly, she turns

her head to look at her car through the open door. She knows what she has to do.

EXT. GREEK ROW / ALPHA HOUSE - DAY

A MAN IN COVERALLS attaches a winch to Cece's Mercedes, hooking it to the back of a tow truck. He hands her A CHECK. We see it's -- made out to Cece Bondurant Barclay for $30,000. Cece passes it to Natalie, who jumps up and down.

A vehicle with a Whitney logo on the doors cruises by slowly before stopping. A carload of CHINESE MEN get out, each snapping photos of the various Greek houses.

Mean Helene sits up, places a cap on her binoculars. She retreats inside the ZOO house.

INT. DEAN GRACE'S OFFICE - DAY

Dean Grace enters her darkened office holding a cup of coffee. Mean Helene is on the couch, in the shadows.

MEAN HELENE: Hello, Dean Grace.

Mean Helene flips on a light. She's swapped out her military gear for a sweatshirt with kittens on it. Somehow, this outfit is even more menacing.

The Dean jumps, spilling coffee all over her white blouse.

DEAN GRACE: How'd you get in here?

The Dean shouts into the hallway.

DEAN GRACE (CONT'D): Kaylee? How'd she get in here?

Kaylee enters.

KAYLEE: That's a really good question.

FLASHBACK TO:

INT. RECEPTION AREA OF DEAN GRACE'S OFFICE - DAY

Kaylee sits at her desk in front of Dean Grace's door, squealing with laughter as she spins in fast circles on her swivel chair. Mean Helene simply shuffles past her.

END FLASHBACK

INT. DEAN GRACE'S OFFICE - DAY

Kaylee narrows her eyes at Mean Helene, trying to figure out the secret to her black magic.

KAYLEE: Are you a ninja?

MEAN HELENE: Army training. War.

KAYLEE: Which war?

Mean Helene ignores her, addressing the Dean.

MEAN HELENE: You're up to something. The Chinamen are in on it, too.

The Dean stammers.

DEAN GRACE: I... I... have no idea what you're talking about. And that's an offensive term.

KAYLEE: Were you in the Vietnam War?

MEAN HELENE: Don't act innocent with me, missy. I see your handprints all over the recent chaos on Greek Row. What's your play?

KAYLEE: Was it Korea?

DEAN GRACE: I won't have you sneaking in here to level baseless accusations.

MEAN HELENE: I don't make baseless accusations. You're planning something. Fact.

KAYLEE: Kuwait? Panama? Kosovo? Grenada?

The Dean starts to sweat.

DEAN GRACE: Well, I have no plans. And you can't prove anything.

The Dean winces as soon as the words leave her mouth. Mean Helene glances at the Dean's desk blotter, SPOTTING THE -- Provost Grace doodles. She shoots the Dean a look that might just turn her into a pillar of salt.

MEAN HELENE: This ain't over, this is just beginning. This is you dropping a bomb on Pearl Harbor, Provost Grace.

Mean Helene spins on the sole of her orthopedic shoes and marches out.

KAYLEE: The Spanish-American War?

INT. ALPHA HOUSE/ENTRY HALL - DAY

A dozen SORORITY SISTERS are hard at work, some assisting a COUPLE OF WORKMEN, some painting the entry hall, some moving furniture. All the girls wear matching t-shirts.

SORORITY SISTERS (singing): Drink a beer, drink a beer, drink a beer, god damn it, drink a beer. I won't drink beer with any old man unless he is an Alpha fan.

Cece enters with Natalie.

CECE: What else is on your list?

Natalie consults her phone.

NATALIE : A ton. We're not gonna make it. We lost too much time before the contractors came back.

CECE: But we're almost done putting the house back together.

NATALIE: We still have to prep for the actual events. We've got songs, flowers, decorations, skits -- ugh. It's too much. We're out of time and we don't have enough bodies to help.

CECE: Let me handle this.

EXT. GREEK ROW / PI MU HOUSE - DAY

Cece knocks and a PI MU SISTER answers. The Pi Mu points to the side of the house. Cece dashes through the grass in heels, which keep getting stuck, so she kicks them off and runs barefoot.

Rain is placing tomatoes in a basket as Cece approaches, breathless.

CECE: Rain, hi, I know we got off on the wrong foot and I'm sorry. I'm not great with other women and that's my fault. I own that.

Rain listens, offering no response.

CECE (CONT'D): My girls are in trouble and they need help and I'm not asking for me, I'm asking for them. Please, please, can you find it in your heart to --

Rain holds up a dirty hand.

RAIN: Lemme stop you right there --

Cece nods.

CECE: I deserve that, okay. I get it. I have no right to ask for favors when you've been so nice and I've been so rude. It's just that one of these kids got to me and she made me wish I'd done a lot of things differently in my life and --

RAIN: Cece, shhh. I stopped you because we're wasting time. Let's go.

Cece is astounded.

CECE: Just like that? Oh, my God, thank you, thank you.

Rain nods. She walks towards Alpha and Cece trots along behind her.

RAIN: I don't know what your life was like before,

Cece. But around here? Our girls aren't the only ones who have sisters.

INT. ALPHA HOUSE/ENTRY HALL - DAY

Cece enters with Rain, Marilee, Janelle, and a HOST OF OTHER SORORITY GIRLS, including Ashley. Each carries an armload of supplies.

CECE: You're the best, all of you. I mean it.

Natalie comes running up to them with a plunger.

NATALIE: There's something wrong with the toilet in the first floor powder room and I can't get a plumber here until tomorrow!

JANELLE: What's wrong with it?

NATALIE: Burrito night.

Cece rolls up her sleeves, a look of grim determination on her face.

CECE: Step aside, I've got this.

JANELLE: Do you have the first clue how to fix a clogged toilet?

CECE: Flush until it's all better?

Janelle takes the plunger.

JANELLE: I can't let you go in there alone.

INT. ALPHA HOUSE/ENTRY HALL - DAY

Janelle and Cece emerge from the powder room, disheveled and damp but victorious. They high five each other and then look at their hands, which are also wet.

JANELLE: We should go boil these.

CECE: Or burn them. Either way.

INT. ALPHA HOUSE / KITCHEN - NIGHT

Rain arranges magnificent daisy bouquets while Loretta puts together hundreds of finger sandwiches.

INT. ALPHA HOUSE / MAID'S QUARTERS - NIGHT

Marilee and Edyta competitively fold napkins into origami swans.

INT. ALPHA HOUSE / LIVING ROOM - NIGHT

Janelle sits at a piano, playing the chorus to I Will Always Love You, surrounded by a group of Alpha sisters. Natalie and Cece watch in the background.

JANELLE: Let's try it like this. (singing) And I will always love you, A-l-l-pha. (talking again) Makes sense, yeah? Extending it like that?

The Alpha sisters nod.

JANELLE (CONT'D): Then let's take it from the top.

Cece and Natalie look utterly exhausted, yet calm.

CECE: We did it. We're ready.

NATALIE: Our parties are going to be amazing. We couldn't have done it without you.

CECE: Without me, you wouldn't have had to.

NATALIE: That's a gray area.

Natalie nudges Cece with her shoulder.

NATALIE (CONT'D): I almost forgot. These came for you and the other moms.

Natalie takes four envelopes out of her pocket and hands them to Cece. ON THE CARD we read -- Something stinks on Greek Row. Meet me at Eli's House of Beans on Monday at 1400 hours. H.S.

EXT. GREEK ROW / ALPHA HOUSE - DAY

FIFTY POTENTIAL NEW MEMBERS line up on the sidewalk, giddy, psyched to start the party. Cece opens the front door, then turns to the sisters behind her.

CECE: Ladies? Showtime.

INT. ELI'S HOUSE OF BEANS - DAY

Hayden is making a coffee for Cece, who stands at the counter. The rest of the group -- Marilee, Janelle, Rain, and Mean Helene are already seated. Hayden hands Cece a cup.

HAYDEN: On the house.

CECE: You said I had to learn to pay my own way.

HAYDEN: Consider this an exception.

CECE: Thanks, sweetie.

Cece joins the others at the table.

CECE (CONT'D): I almost didn't make it. I had no idea what time fourteen o'clock was.

Mean Helene scowls.

MEAN HELENE: I was just starting to think nice things about you, blondie. Don't blow it.

RAIN: What's going on, Helene? We never get together. Seriously, never.

MARILEE: Is this about taking out Mama Shirley at Lambda? 'Cause I could be down.

Janelle's phone beeps. ON THE SCREEN we see -- a text from Trevor.

TREVOR (TEXT): Dying to hang out - come over now?

Her phone beeps again. ON THE SCREEN we see -- another text from Trevor.

TREVOR (TEXT) (CONT'D): Please??

Janelle's phone beeps a third time. Mean Helene gives

Janelle a look and we see her quickly silence her phone, before placing it in her handbag.

JANELLE: Sorry. I put it on vibrate. Won't happen again.

MEAN HELENE: Something's going on with Dean Grace. She's angling for a promotion, at our expense. Looking to clear out Greek Row.

RAIN: How do you know? Have you been spying on everyone again?

MEAN HELENE: It's called reconnaissance.

MARILEE: It's called stalking.

MEAN HELENE: You won't call it stalking when we're all out of a job.

RAIN: Why now? Dean Grace hasn't been the Greek system's biggest cheerleader, but she never got in our way before.

MEAN HELENE: Because she never needed to. Now she's so blinded by ambition that she'll screw over anyone in her path.

CECE: Been there before.

MEAN HELENE: We need a preemptive strike. Like my friend Dougie Mac used to say, preparedness is the key to success and victory.

MARILEE: Dougie Mac? Do you mean General Douglas MacArthur? What the hell war were you in, anyway?

Mean Helene looks over both shoulders and motions for them to come closer. She begins to whisper.

Hayden watches the table as all the ladies lean in. She's no longer able to hear what's being said.

HAYDEN (to herself): My mother has girlfriends. Who knew?

There's a soccer game playing ON THE TV behind

Hayden. The picture cuts in and out. Hayden grabs the remote.

HAYDEN (CONT'D): Stupid satellite feed.

She flips to the news and then greets a NEW CUSTOMER at the counter. ON THE TV we see -- the newscaster and then a shot of Luis Guzman.

NEWSCASTER (O.S.): This just in, suspected Cartagena Cartel kingpin Luis Guzman is one of the inmates who escaped during the New Jersey State Prison riot last night. Guzman is --

We DRIFT from the television down to Janelle's purse. Her phone is vibrating all over the place.

ON THE SCREEN we read -- a text from Uncle Pat.

O'BRIEN (TEXT): 911, CALL ME.

END OF SHOW

CPSIA information can be obtained
at www.ICGtesting.com
Printed in the USA
LVHW081916050120
642568LV00008B/195/P